FORESHOCKS OF
ANTICHRIST

WILLIAM T. JAMES
GENERAL EDITOR

HARVEST HOUSE PUBLISHERS
Eugene, Oregon 97402

FORESHOCKS OF ANTICHRIST

Copyright © 1997 by Harvest House Publishers
Eugene, Oregon 97402

Foreshocks of Antichrist / William T. James, general editor.
     p. cm.
   ISBN 1-56507-585-4
   1. End of the world. 2. Antichrist. I. James, William T., 1942-
BT876.F67 1997
236–dc21
                                        96-45428
                                           CIP

97   98   99   00   01   02   / BF /   10   9   8   7   6   5   4   3

Acknowledgments

Without Jesus Christ, life itself is not possible. To Him alone, therefore, belong all honor, glory, praise, and worship. I know I speak accurately when I say that each and every author who contributed to *Foreshocks of Antichrist* humbly and thankfully considers it a privilege to serve our Lord as He graciously allows.

To these wonderful friends of mine who have herein shared their prayerfully considered insights into these critical times, having sifted those issues and events through the filter of God's prophetic Word, I give my profound thanks. Their devotion to Christ through generosity of spirit and dedication of their considerable gifts and talents truly inspires me.

Special thanks to Dave Breese for his many kindnesses in helping bring this book to publication with Harvest House. He and his associates at Christian Destiny were, as always, a welcome source of encouragement.

A special thanks to Bob Hawkins Jr. and all of his exceptionally proficient associates, who did so much to hone and polish this work into a book we prayerfully believe will bless its readers. Having worked with them in this effort, I now understand why Harvest House enjoys its excellent reputation.

To Dennis Byrd, my good friend and journalist/newspaper executive par excellence, and to my friend Frank Bolton, both of whom provided much needed assistance in resolving a technical matter involving computers and word processing, my sincere thanks. My thanks as well to Kathy Brown, who continues to be a source of encouragement and help in the difficult task of trying to bring me into the computer age.

To Margaret, the love of my life and my best friend, and to our sons, Terry Jr. and Nathan, my thanks for putting up with me, especially when I become so engrossed in these projects that I seem oblivious to everyone and everything except the work before me.

Angie Peters is indispensable. God gifted her with great talent from which enthusiastically springs marvelous writing, editing, and research skills, for which I am most thankful. More than this, she is first and foremost a wonderful Christian wife, mother, and daughter-close friend whose dynamic energy and task-accomplishment abilities amaze us all. My love and thanks to Angie and to her husband, Kurt, and to my two favorite little folks, Lindsey and Nick, for sharing her time with me in these projects.

Finally, to you the reader of *Foreshocks of Antichrist*, my deep gratitude for your interest and my prayerful hope that this book will help you make the all-important decision to put Jesus Christ first in your life.

–William T. James

Contents

PART THREE
At the Brink of Apocalypse

Foreshock After Foreshock

William T. James

God's prophetic clock ticks in time-bomb fashion, counting down to that apocalypse-initiating moment when earth's final and most terrible tyrant will give the world the peace that destroys.

Israel, and Jerusalem in particular, which God's prophet foretold will become a "cup of trembling" (Zechariah 12:2) for the whole world during the last seven years of this earth age, already command the attention of top-level politicians, military planners, economists, sociologists, and religionists of our time. Media eyes and ears are inevitably snapped abruptly back to this most troubling spot on the planet, no matter in which direction the cameras and microphones temporarily turn to capture other news around the globe.

Benjamin Netanyahu's May 29, 1996, election to be Israel's Prime Minister adds even greater volatility to the simmering Middle Eastern mix. His avowed refusal to acquiesce to Syrian President Hafez al-Assad's demand to give up the Golan Heights and accept many other ludicrous land-for-peace conditions (such as that of surrendering East

Jerusalem to the Palestinians) raises fears of renewed hostilities in the region. Netanyahu passionately proclaimed in his speech before the U.S. Congress:

> There have been efforts to redivide this city [Jerusalem] by those who claim that peace can come through division, that it can be secured through multiple sovereignties, multiple laws, multiple police forces. . . . This is a groundless and dangerous assumption, and it impels me to declare today: There will never be such a redivision of Jerusalem. Never.

> We shall not allow a Berlin Wall to be erected inside Jerusalem. We will not drive out anyone. But neither shall we be driven out of any quarter, any neighborhood, any street of our eternal city.[1]

The new Prime Minister's declarations stirred anger in the Arab world and considerable apprehensions in the international diplomatic community. Hence the growing outcry that the tiny nation submit to the deadly pseudopeace process.

God's Word warns "When they shall say, Peace and safety, then sudden destruction cometh upon them, as travail upon a woman with child, and they shall not escape" (1 Thessalonians 5:3).

One day, perhaps quite soon, a leader will step from the ranks of his contemporaries, and through guile, persuasion, and diplomatic acumen unparalleled in the world's long, war-torn history, he will convince even the most skeptical Israeli hard-liner to trust him to ensure Israel's security. It will be the *covenant made with death and hell* foretold by the prophet Daniel, which Isaiah the prophet said God Himself will annul (Isaiah 28:18).

Zola Levitt gives crucial insights into present-day Israel's tension-fraught relationships with her immediate neighbors and the world community at large (read Chapter 6, "Israel: Earth's Lightning Rod").

These Shocking Times

Electrifying events bombard today's world with shock after shock that would have paralyzed previous generations with astonishment and fear. Yet we go about our daily lives tuning out all but the most shattering reports. The planet quakes both literally and figuratively while we rush toward what looks like an intensely stormy future. Our hurried, harried lives impel us to move forward with restrictive nearsightedness, unable and/or unwilling to look beyond our own immediate circumstances.

The myopia grows worse daily, our self-sufficient attitudes and actions focusing more and more upon inward-turning entertainments that feed our lust for instant gratification. Phenomenal developing technologies continue to abduct our generation, holding our minds captive for hours—sometimes for days—in the dark, nether regions of cyberspace. Predicted quantum breakthroughs in virtual reality now promise—no, *threaten*—to take men, women, and children even farther into selfism and away from God, the One by and for whom they were created.

But Antichrist cannot appear on the scene as ruler of his end-time kingdom until certain events occur and certain conditions prevail. Daniel told about the specific event that will produce the world's last dictator (Daniel 9:27). Paul the apostle wrote of general conditions that will be present as history winds down, conditions that will precede the Antichrist's rise to power, paving the way for him to take control. "Let no man deceive you by any means; for that day shall not come except there come [the] falling away first, and that man of sin be revealed, the son of perdition" (2 Thessalonians 2:3).

Apostasia is the Greek word used to describe the societal, moral, and ethical breakdown which will already have occurred *before* Antichrist is recognized as the son of perdition. The English translation is *apostasy*, a major foreshock of Antichrist that we must examine to find where our generation fits into God's omniscient, prophetic outline of human history.

Apostasy means literally a *falling away*. Antichrist is defined in Scripture this way: "Every spirit that confesseth not that Jesus Christ is come in the flesh is not of God; and this is that spirit of antichrist, of which ye have heard that it should come, and even now already is it in the world" (1 John 4:3).

The terms *apostasy* and *Antichrist* really mean the same thing: a denial that Jesus Christ has come in the flesh to redeem fallen mankind through His shed blood on the old rugged cross at Calvary. Each term represents people's anti-God determination to do what seems right in their own eyes, to march to their own drumbeat in diametrical opposition to God's way.

The *spirit of Antichrist* is linked to the *mystery of iniquity* (2 Thessalonians 2:7) in a satanic chain that binds the unredeemed to original sin. Jesus Christ, who is the Way, the Truth, and the Life, came into the world to break that chain, "to seek and to save that which was lost" (Luke 19:10). That includes every human being who has ever lived on planet Earth with the exception of Jesus Christ himself: "For all have sinned, and come short of the glory of God" (Romans 3:23).

Daniel the prophet wrote that at the end of the age there will be tremendous growth in knowledge (Daniel 12:4). Computers have made our generation one in which knowledge has exploded with impact that would have dazzled the people of Daniel's day. As a matter of fact, the late twentieth century has brought changes in the gathering and dissemination of knowledge that continue to flabbergast most of us who were born before 1950. And now comes the *Age of Cyberspace!*

Internet now links together all but the most remote areas of planet Earth with instant communication capability. People are rapidly networking to become one world, just as Utopian planners have long dreamed. Just like the Babel builders of Genesis 11, the people are again moving to create a world of their own design. Like the Babel builders, they now have one language. That language is called generically *computerese.* This is a generation determined to deny reality as laid out in the Word of God; rather, it chooses to do what seems right in its own eyes—to create its own version of reality.

Virtual Reality

No development at this late date more profoundly reflects a falling away than does man's cyberspace venture into *virtual reality.* Technology is inflaming humanity's lust which began in the Garden of Eden when the serpent convinced the first man and woman that they would be as God when they disobeyed their Creator by eating from the forbidden tree. Isn't it interesting that the tree that was forbidden was the tree of knowledge of good and evil?

The chief product of our *information age* is, of course, information—knowledge in its rawest form. Humanity once again delves into a quest for knowledge that can bring only deadly consequences because mankind lost the ability to know the mind of God at the fall in Eden. When we process information today, the knowledge it formulates all too often produces destruction—e.g., the horrific weapons in today's war arsenals. The computer makes possible the growth of knowledge in geometrical progression. That is, knowledge is doubling, tripling, and quadrupling at a pace beyond which it is possible for the finite mind to grasp.

Man has reached godlike capability in knowledge but lacks God's wisdom, influence, and discipline. The New Age dream of evolution to godhood is in actuality a nightmare beyond comprehension. We stagger forward as a generation drunken on the heady promises offered by the Luciferian schemers of our time. Virtual reality is the latest promise given us in soothing assurances that we ourselves are the only deity needed while we go about creating worlds of our own choosing because we alone have the right to determine the parameters of our own existence. *Truth* is whatever we want it to be.

Virtual reality is born out of *relativism.* Relativism means, in the final analysis, choosing to do what is right in our own eyes.

The technology itself is still in its infancy. The fantastic electronic gadgets and gismos which will one day be available to home users for indulging in whatever perverse sensual pleasure the mind can conjure are not quite yet at hand. We will look at the troubling concept that lies behind virtual reality, but let us leave the physical descriptions of the gadgets and gismos of this technology for another time.

Virtual reality, born out of relativism (there are no absolutes), is ultimately meant to be a plane of existence where the individual is God. This attitude that says "I am my own god" is often reflected in the words of politicians who are being accused of or indicted for dalliances into immorality or illegal activities at public expense. We most often hear their defense made in television or radio sound bytes. The politician says, "I've done nothing wrong." Rarely does he say, "I didn't do it." He invariably says, "I've done nothing wrong."

In this age of moral and ethical relativism, those who make this defense do so apparently with a clear conscience because truth is whatever they want it to be. In their view, they've done nothing wrong. Their reality is whatever they choose it to be!

But such opposition to God creates a tormenting void in the human heart. The vacuum sucks the mind, body, and spirit of the rebel into its lonely emptiness. Arts & Entertainment (A & E) recently broadcast a segment of its ongoing *Investigative Report* program titled "Wired for Sex." The presentation examined cyberspace technologies and what they portend for the immediate future and for people of the next century. Near the end of the program, narrator Bill Kurtis summed up the human condition in relationship to man's inner-self search for love and companionship.

"In the future, no one will ever have to be lonely anymore," he said. "Maybe there will be no tears in the boudoirs of the 21st century. Maybe those who can't find real love will find synthetic love. Every man, every woman, a Pygmalion ... but probably not.

"When all the engineering is over, the lonely of the future will no doubt ask the same question as the lonely of today. Who's out there for me?"

A tremendous love-void exists in the heart of man who needs God. Apostasy, the foreshock of the coming Antichrist and his reign of control and terror, will ultimately lead mankind as far from the love of God as God can allow before He must judge this rebellious world. Man today perverts what love—that is, God's view of love—is all about. Kurtis, at the outset of the program, described how far this generation has strayed from God's prescription for human love relationships: "It usually happens in the privacy of one's home.

A computer is turned on. The modem is used to log on. The right icons are clicked and within seconds, sexually explicit pictures come into view. It's the new world of *cybersex....*"

One man gave a sound byte: "... computers and sex are a perfect marriage." Another man said, "There is something very subversive about taking a big, expensive computer system and just putting a naked person on it."

The narration continued: "For years, there was magazine sex. Then phone sex. Now there is cd-rom sex and now the latest interactive virtual reality sex. A new university study reveals there are now nearly 500,000 pornographic images ... and files available in cyberspace. And the number of people downloading them into their computers is now in the millions.... And pundits predict, 'You ain't seen nothin' yet....'"

The program presented a dark-haired, blue-eyed, 40-year-old single mom who told us she is turned on by funk, jazz, and Southeast Asia. She is "... one of hundreds of thousands of people who have turned to technology to find a date or a mate," Kurtis said. "Her voice is going out to prospective suitors as a kind of classified electronic ad. Welcome to love, sex, and romance in the interactive era...."

The woman seeking a date then talked about her feelings regarding the service. "... immediately I felt a connectedness to a network. There were people on the other end just like me, or maybe different from me, sitting in their homes, and it almost felt like a lab, that we were all sort of connected through these wires...."

Bill Kurtis then continued, "Computers have already changed the way we work and communicate with each other. Now they are electrifying our love lives with images of romance, fantasies of love, connections to the unconnected. A dance with invisible dancers in separate rooms...."

Then the mother of an 11-year-old daughter spoke excitedly about finding a site on the Web that put her in touch with an organization catering to the kind of sex she likes. It is a club for people who incur and inflict pain for pleasure. The operator of the organization said, ". . . I have a very strong interest in bondage and discipline and sado-masochism things. . . . There was really very little out there. [What] was out there was sleazy and people looked down at it. . . . I never looked at it as being something down and dirty . . . I was looking for a place where I could . . . meet and talk with other people about it, and couldn't find any. . . . "

The operator is now full-time emcee of the biggest, most successful bondage-and-discipline databank in the world.

The mother of the 11-year-old daughter has spent as much as 80 hours per week logged onto the organization's Website, and she claimed that she is proud to be so open about her sexual proclivities.

". . . And in the end," the narrator told us, "she thinks this honesty will be best for her and for her daughter. . . . "

The woman herself said of her daughter, ". . . she is at an age where . . . being normal is very important. And I really want to be an example for her. That no matter what you are, you don't have to hide it from the world. And don't let people make you ashamed of yourself for what you think, for what you do, for who you are. . . . "

The narrator introduced a man who covers and reports the ongoing evolution of erotic technology and its impact on North American culture for a number of media outlets. The writer he introduced said, ". . . The Internet is incredibly sexually open right now. You can pretty much do and say anything at the moment and take your fantasies as far as you want. That bothers the powers that be. They like control. . . . "[2]

God is the great *I Am*. He *is* the ultimate power. And He *does* want absolute control over His creation called man. But obedience must flow from the heart that loves Him because He created man a free moral agent. People are choosing to do what seems right in their own eyes by denying God control when they choose to create and then live within a synthetic reality. This is apostasy in its essence, a great falling away from God and His precepts. It is a major foreshock of Antichrist.

Foreshock After Foreshock

God's prophetic Word tells us plainly that the generation alive at the time of the coming of the Son of Man (Jesus Christ) will be indulging in precisely the same debasing activities as were the people alive just before the flood struck during Noah's day (read Genesis 6 and 7).

The end-time generation will likewise be immersed in sinful, debauched interaction of the same sort found in Sodom and Gomorrah at the time God rained fire and brimstone judgment upon that region (read Genesis 19).

Neither of those doomed societies were without forewarning that judgment was on its way. Noah preached for 120 years to the antediluvians. Lot, though vexed on all sides by the heathen of Sodom, was looked upon by Almighty God as being a *just* man—meaning he represented God's way to the perverse culture in which he lived. Lot was undoubtedly used of God to warn the people of that generation.

The people of this generation have been the recipients of God's patience and longsuffering that He has bestowed. His mercy is great. It is *not,* however, without its limits. Has our generation pushed God to the limit of His patience? Our world today parallels the ancient world of Noah and of Lot with striking similarity.

Apostasy, a major foreshock of the future Antichrist world system, seems already solidly in place as a characteristic of our day. The *falling away*, which we have already considered in some detail, will be a general societal condition which God's Word prophesies will mark the generation alive at the time of Christ's return. The people of Noah's day and Lot's day were thoroughly into apostasy—a total turning away from God. Consider these facts, along with the following Scriptures: "As the days of Noah were, so shall also the coming of the Son of man be" (Matthew 24:37); "As it was in the days of Lot; they did eat, they drank, they bought, they sold, they planted, they built; but the same day that Lot went out of Sodom it rained fire and brimstone from heaven and destroyed them all" (Luke 17:28,29). Is it not therefore wise to consider whether ours is the generation about which God's Word says, ". . . so shall it be in the days of the coming of the Son of Man"?

Foreshocks of Antichrist and of the apocalypse will cause earth to shudder and shake with increased vigor the closer we move to the end of the age. Are the convulsions which continue to rock the planet on an almost hourly basis significant in light of Jesus' words about the time He called the *great tribulation*?

Wars and conflicts rage in many regions of the world. Ethnic hatreds fuel and fan those conflagrations just as Jesus prophesied: "For nation shall rise against nation, and kingdom against kingdom; and there shall be famines and pestilences and earthquakes in various places" (Matthew 24:7).

Foreshocks of Looming Judgment?

Apostasy, the falling away, frames the solidly entrenched mindset of this generation. And Israel stands at center stage, the sticking point for the peace of the Middle East—and for that matter the peace of the whole world. This tiny sliver of land often causes the whole world to tremble.

Russia reels, dangerously unsettled and restless. Her people are hungry for food and material goods and her generals are even more voracious for respect, prestige, and expansive power. Many of her leaders approve a thrust southward into the Middle East for spoils of war that will relieve painful food shortages, provide consumer goods, and secure warmwater ports. Alliances formed with Iran and other Islamic militarists portend troubling times ahead. The Magog force appears to be in the making.

China, the great dragon to the East, glares lustfully at Western wealth, desiring to build a power base from which to launch a drive for world conquest. The *kings of the East* bide their time while surreptitiously courting the U.S. and others who will fall for their deception.

The *European Union* awaits the *prince that shall come*, who will take the new Roman Empire of prophecy to world domination.

Builders of the New World Order call for all peoples of the world to join hands as one as they march together into a New Age. The New Age movement itself proposes religious amalgamation through ecumenism. It preaches the Luciferian lie that there are many ways to God and salvation, of which Jesus Christ is but one way. Earth worship and other pagan practices flourish and grow, nourished by reborn interests in matters involving psychic and occultic powers. Sorceries are part of this nation's daily diet, the drug culture opening particularly the young to every sort of demonic influence.

Unborn babies are murdered by the millions through abortion practices unthinkable just a few decades ago. Homosexuality is flaunted as a "gay lifestyle" rather than the abomination that God's Word says it is. Today even the United States Congress seriously debates whether to allow married "gay couples" the same rights and privileges under the Constitution as heterosexual married people. Ours is a generation exhibiting the characteristic "without natural affection" (2 Timothy 3:3).

Knowledge increases exponentially while we run to and fro in a mad dash toward oblivion (Daniel 12:4). Evil men and seducers grow worse and worse by the day, deceiving and being deceived (2 Timothy 3:13). Our headlines report rape, murder, and every other category of crime imaginable, testifying that the love of many has grown cold. Both the United States and Russia possess enough nuclear firepower to destroy the planet many times over. China, England, France, Israel, South Africa, and other nations are not far behind in the inglorious distinction of being able to destroy the world. And now nuclear weapons are reported to be in the hands of Mafia-like turf bosses who rule areas of the republics which used to comprise the USSR. These small-time dictators are feared to have sold weapons-grade nuclear material to radical Islamic fanatics and terrorists all over the world.

AIDS, a plague of catastrophic proportions, threatens to wipe out entire national populations in some African regions. Strange, grotesque diseases such as those spawned by ecoli bacteria and ebola viral strains menace everyone everywhere. Such pestilence has been termed "the apocalypse bug" by some scientists.

Astronomers and other observers of the astrophysical increasingly express concern that asteroids and other heavenly debris are approaching our planet in dimensions and numbers that present ever-greater dangers to life on earth.

Is it any wonder God's Word prophesies that there will come a time when conditions will be so frightful that men's hearts will fail them for fear of things they see coming upon the earth (Luke 21:26)?

Launching Pad to Heaven

We find ourselves in truly momentous times. This generation regularly witnesses occurrences remarkably similar to those prophesied for the end of this earth age. If that is so, we stand on the launching pad poised to take part in a stupendous event: *the rapture*—that lightning-quick moment when Jesus Christ shouts to those saved during this church age, "*COME UP HERE!*" (Revelation 4:1).

The rapture will occur, we believe Scripture teaches, at least seven years before the second advent, that climactic event when Christ will return with the armies of heaven to put an end to mankind's last and bloodiest war, called *Armageddon.*

Therefore, since we are already seeing upheavals and rearrangements taking place that are starkly similar to those which God's Word foretells will mark the seven-year-period when Antichrist is on the world scene, what should be our exciting expectation? The signals are dramatic and clear: Jesus Christ must even now be standing at the doors of heaven ready to shout, as He did to the apostle John, who faithfully recorded the Revelation vision, "*COME UP HERE!*"

All true believers in Christ will vanish from the planet's surface in the twinkling of an eye and split the heavens to be eternally with their Lord and their God. It will be the great escape from a time of God's wrath which He must, in His righteous indignation, pour out upon the rebellious ones who remain on earth. We who have contributed to this volume have done so with the fervent, prayerful hope that you too will be among that great company of God's children who are deemed worthy to escape judgment through Christ the Redeemer. While you read *Foreshocks of Antichrist*, which covers most relevant topics of significance surrounding end-time matters, listen intently to God's Holy Spirit while He whispers softly and tenderly to your soul, "For God so loved the world that he gave his only begotten Son, that whosoever believeth in him should not perish but have everlasting life. For God sent not his Son into the world to condemn the world, but that the world through him might be saved" (John 3:16,17).

Accept Christ today, for "now is the day of salvation" (2 Corinthians 6:2). Repent of your sin of disbelief, and believe in Christ as your Savior, "for with the heart man believeth unto righteousness, and with the mouth confession is made unto salvation" (Romans 10:10).

You are a child of God when you truly believe. You need never fear coming judgment. Rather, your future is one of brilliance beyond the finite mind's ability to grasp, for "eye hath not seen, nor ear heard, neither have entered into the heart of man, the things which God hath prepared for them that love him" (1 Corinthians 2:9).

As God's child, you'll look not for Antichrist, but for Jesus Christ, who is the Author and Finisher of your faith.

PART ONE

Brainwashing for the Antichrist's Reign

❖ ❖ ❖

1

Globalism's Siren Song

William T. James

❖ ❖ ❖

Come, young citizens of the world, we are one,
we are one.
Come, young citizens of the world, we are one,
we are one.
We have one hope, we have one dream, and
with one voice we sing:
Peace, prosperity, and love for all mankind.[1]

The lyrics are set to an enchanting, rhythmic melody and are sung by a chorus of sweet-voiced children. Soon you are humming, then singing along. What could possibly be wrong with those sentiments so innocently expressed? *Peace, prosperity, and love for all mankind*–are these not among the most noble of objectives?

Powerful humanistic allurements beckon seductively, promising a golden future if all of earth's people will come together as one. Such a glorious world order, long dreamed about and even fervently pursued, seems at last achievable. Those who hold the worldview that national boundaries must fall and sovereignties must diminish because we are all citizens of planet Earth passionately embrace the earth-shrinking technologies that science continues to produce. For example, the Internet. Yes, the Utopian dream at last seems achievable. However, while the sirens of globalism—like the twin sisters who lured unwary sailors to their deaths in Homer's *The Odyssey*—sing their lovely, mesmerizing songs of New World Order, the words pronounced by the Ancient of Days reverberate through the corridors of antiquity and leap at this generation from the pages of God's Holy Word:

> Behold, the people are one and they have all one language, and this they begin to do; and now nothing will be restrained from them which they have imagined to do (Genesis 11:6).

The Creator of all things was not expressing His pride in His creation called man. God was concerned and saddened because all peoples of that time were united in their determination to build a world to their own specifications. And why was this very first globalist effort displeasing to the One who built into man the marvelous ability to do whatever man could imagine? Did not God himself create man in His own image, infusing the creature with phenomenal creative drive?

The Cradle of Globalism

It seems at first glance a supreme paradox: The Creator made the creature called man in His own image, gifting him with powerful conceptual abilities, and thus with the ingenuity to build a tower that could ultimately reach into the heavens. Then, just as man began to fulfill his potential, the infallible Creator-God manifested His displeasure in the people of that day as recorded in this biblical account:

The whole earth was of one language and of one speech. And it came to pass as they journeyed from the east that they found a plain in the land of Shinar, and they dwelt there. And they said to one another, Come, let us make bricks and burn them thoroughly. And they had brick for stone, and slime had they for mortar. And they said, Go to, let us build a city and a tower whose top may reach unto heaven; and let us make us a name, lest we be scattered abroad upon the face of the whole earth. And the Lord came down to see the city and the tower, which the children of men built. And the Lord said, Behold, the people are one and they have all one language, and this they begin to do; and now nothing will be restrained from them which they have imagined to do. Come, let us go down and there confound their language, that they may not understand one another's speech. So the Lord scattered them abroad from there upon the face of all the earth, and they left off building the city. Therefore is the name of it called Babel, because the Lord did there confound the language of all the earth; and from there did the Lord scatter them abroad upon the face of all the earth (Genesis 11:1-9).

God Almighty gave the human race a touch of His own genius, but when those people used it in this rebellious way, He confused that genius by disrupting their ability to communicate. Thereby He put an end to the globalist project. God's dealings with His creation seemed incongruous: Did He change His mind about having made man in His own image? Did He resent competition in matters involving the creativity which this building project might have represented? Why did He break up the one-world building effort at Babel?

Image of God, Imagination of Man

God puts His mighty finger upon the answer to the question *Why did He break up the one-world building effort at Babel?* His answer at the same time pierces to the heart of the reason He had to destroy by flood the entire antediluvian world, with the exception of Noah and his family and select animal life.

The root cause of why God scattered the Babel builders, thereby ending their venture in globalism, is found even farther back in human history than the era of the flood. God's Word records about those ancient times and His divine judgment: "The Lord smelled a sweet savor; and the Lord said in his heart, I will not again curse the ground anymore for man's sake; for the imagination of man's heart is evil from his youth; neither will I again smite anymore every thing living, as I have done" (Genesis 8:21).

The key thought from the mind of God for our purposes here is *"The imagination of man's heart is evil from his youth."* Let us examine this indictment in the framework of its context.

God declared that He would never again curse the ground as He did following man's rebellion in the Garden of Eden. Neither, He said, would He ever again smite all living things as He did with the worldwide flood of Noah's day. God placed between these two promises the statement of truth about *the fallen state of man,* a fact absolutely rejected by today's humanistic social architects. *Their denial of this reality is at the core of globalism.* So too is the demented assertion that man is evolving toward a higher order of being that will ultimately produce heaven on earth: *peace, prosperity, and love for all mankind.*

Adam's and Eve's God-attuned senses must have changed from perfection to imperfection in one cataclysmic moment. What a heart-wrenching scene it must have been when they willfully disobeyed God, choosing instead to yield to the tempter, who told them they would be as God when they ate from the tree of knowledge of good and evil. How devastating must have been that eternity-rending moment when those magnificently beautiful humans discarded the effulgence of God that had shrouded their nakedness. The image of God emanating from within their beings must have begun to dissipate, to change into frightening, darkened countenances. So, too, their minds no doubt convoluted within their sin-infected thought processes. Both image and imagination altered in that moment into a perpetual state of opposition to the Creator with whom they had previously walked in perfect trust and love along the Garden's lush pathways.

Mankind's course has been spiraling downward since that willful decision by the first man to do what was right in his own eyes rather than obey God. The fall brought a curse upon planet Earth and death to man. Every generation of people since Adam and Eve were evicted from Eden contributes ample proof that "the heart is deceitful above all things, and desperately wicked" (Jeremiah 17:9).

From the first murder, when Cain slew his brother Abel, to the slaughter during the more than 15,000 wars of recorded history, to the most recent terrorist atrocity or one-on-one killing, fallen man continues through his vile actions to testify to the truth of God's indictment: *"The imagination of man's heart is evil from his youth"* (Genesis 8:21).

Babel Revisited

We make the mystery of the paradox more understandable when we reconsider these fascinating facts. God, who is perfect in all His ways, created humankind perfectly, actually making man in His own image. Once again we realize that He gifted man with a powerful imagination so that whatever man could imagine, he could eventually do. However, when man began to use that imagination in building a tower that would reach into heaven, God was displeased and stopped the project by confounding the language of the builders, then scattering them abroad. We again consider the question: *If a perfect God created a perfect man, why did God act in such a seemingly harsh manner when the creature used his God-given talent as recounted in the story of Babel?*

The answer, of course, is that God also created man with free moral will, or *volition*. The creature was not made a robot, but was made with brilliant conceptual abilities and was given freedom of choice—which includes discernment for choosing wisely. But Adam chose to disobey God and so sin entered into the world. The human bloodstream became instantly contaminated by the infection. The minds of men, including their imaginations, became darkened in the mystery of iniquity that engulfed them.

The paradox understood, the question is now answerable: *What is wrong with people coming together in a united effort to construct a one-world order with the objectives of achieving peace, prosperity, and love for all mankind?* The answer is that *man is spiritually separated from the Creator because of original sin.* His thinking is therefore fatally flawed. Nothing good can come from thinking and planning that excludes God.

Had God allowed the globalists of Nimrod's day to continue their tower project, He would have had to ultimately curse the earth again as He did when Adam disobeyed, or He would have had to destroy all living things upon the earth as He did because of the corruption that required cleansing by the great flood of Noah's day. God was not acting harshly at Babel, nor was He acting contrary to His perfect character.

Rather, He was displaying unfathomable love by keeping His promises to the tiny fallen creature who was deserving of judgment and for whom He would one day sacrifice His only begotten Son in order to redeem them.

The World Order Schemers

Children of the tower of Babel builders today carry on the globalist agenda despite the differences in language and geographical separation. They circumvent the barriers through use of technologies designed to serve their one-world purposes. The siren song grows louder: *We have one hope, we have one dream, and with one voice we sing: Peace, prosperity, and love for all mankind.*[2]

The obsessive drive toward bringing all men, women, and children into one-world configuration arose shortly after the time Jesus Christ walked the earth. It is perhaps indicative of our sordid day that since the time Jesus walked the earth in the flesh, this era has been called A.D., but now we are to acknowledge that we live in the period of human history called the *Common Era,* or *C.E.* The revisionists, you see, demand that all vestiges of Jesus Christ be erased from even our lexicon. There must be *many* ways for the people of the coming New World Order to come to God, if indeed there is a God.

Jesus Christ, who said He is the Way, the Truth, and the Life, and that no one can come to the Father but by Him, simply does not fit the globalist mold.

Thinkers who formed that mold wanted there to be no doubt that man, through his intellect, can do whatever he imagines. He can build a perfect world without input from any deity who might or might not be out there somewhere. This arrogant attitude of self-sufficiency is summed up in the document titled "The Declaration of Interdependence," released by the United Nations' World Affairs Council on January 30, 1976. It reads in part:

> Two centuries ago, our forefathers brought forth a new nation; now we must join with others to bring forth a new world order. To establish a new world order . . . it is essential that mankind free itself from limitations of national prejudice. . . . We affirm that the economy of all nations is a seamless web, and that no nation can any longer effectively maintain its processes for production and monetary systems without recognizing the necessity of collaborative regulation by international authorities. We call upon all nations to strengthen the United Nations and other institutions of world order.[3]

The zeal for stampeding everyone into a totally controlled global village has not subsided. Elitist power brokers continue to fuel the humanist engine that drives the globalist machinery with grandiose declarations and promises of heaven on earth.

The Secretary General of Habitat II, the most recent U.N. forum aimed at laying groundwork for the New World Order, predicted that there will be " . . . a new beginning of the requests to implement the actions called for at this unprecedented continuum of global conferences that have marked the closing decade of this century."

He then made this ominous statement: "A new global social contract for building sustainable human settlements must be forged for the new global urban world order. . . ." He made his statement in Istanbul, Turkey.[4]

For superbly documented analyses on these U.N. planners and what their plans portend, read carefully Chapters 2 and 8 of this book. Berit Kjos and Chris Corbett portray in stunning fashion the humanity-convulsing realities that confront America and all other nations while we approach the year 2000.

J.R. Church gave the following astute observations about the extremely troubling U.N. agenda. His report predates the June 1996 Istanbul conference, thus providing excellent background for helping us understand the developments we continue to see.

> The United Nations released a report January 1, 1994, setting the agenda for upcoming conferences designed to establish world government in the near future. . . . Many are beginning to ask how long it will take the U.N. to implement plans to accomplish their New World Order. . . .[5]

Certainly God remains in control. Those who are His children through belief in His Son, Jesus Christ, should not look with trepidation upon these foreboding harbingers of the coming tribulation period described by Jesus in the Olivet discourse. However, it is abundantly obvious that developments we have seen in wave after wave of U.N. intrusions into the lives of Americans should make all of us know that real agendas and activities lie behind our concerns.

All the World As One

Neo-Babel builders construct even their music in a way that clearly demonstrates the Luciferian desire to usurp God's throne. John Lennon's universally popular song could easily be mistaken as portraying the biblically prophesied millennial reign of Jesus Christ. But Lennon, like Lenin, preached manmade heaven on earth—an imitative mockery of the true Messiah's coming kingdom. The words and melody are infectious.

Imagine there's no heaven
It's easy if you try
No hell below us
Above us only sky
Imagine all the people
Living for today . . .

Imagine there's no countries
It isn't hard to do
Nothing to kill or die for
And no religion too
Imagine all the people
Living life in peace . . .

You may say I'm a dreamer
But I'm not the only one
I hope someday you'll join us
And the world will be as one . . .

Imagine no possessions
I wonder if you can
No need for greed or hunger
A brotherhood of man
Imagine all the people
Sharing all the world . . .

You may say I'm a dreamer
But I'm not the only one
I hope someday you'll join us
And the world will live as one.[6]

Globalism's siren song is a one-world anthem that the true child of God cannot follow to its murderous, destructive end. The Holy Spirit within us is the tether who binds us to the masthead of truth. With Jesus Christ as the Captain of our salvation, we navigate through the treacherous seas of our time. Still, we must be alert and heed the wake-up call.

Globalist Storm Warning

There seemed to come a calming, refreshing breeze that restored common sense in America with the election of November 8, 1994. The vicious, destructive winds of socialistic madness had begun to stir early in the twentieth century. They grew to full hurricane strength while being channeled through increasingly liberal legislative and judicial bodies, with powerful assistance from equally liberal media.

The storm raged throughout the nation's culture by the time the 1990s arrived. Occasional executive-branch resistance slowed it only momentarily while it roared against the country's rapidly weakening moral barriers.

Suddenly, just as the great storm seemed to reach its full fury, American voters arose almost as one entity and the howling leftist assault was brought to a dead calm.

Many reasons have been suggested for the loud repudiation of liberal ideology and its influence upon America's governmental policies. Certainly, the electorate's majority voice unmistakably demanded that politicians begin serving the people in a way that benefits the nation rather than continue serving their own parochial interests at taxpayers' expense, as had been the case for decades.

But a sudden pulse of wind disrupted the calm only days after the people's actions in the voting booths brought the tempest to a standstill. The gust seemed to burst from nowhere, although the clouds of its origin had been seething for many years in the financial stratosphere of the European Common Market.

GATT (General Agreement on Tariffs and Trade) swept down on the U.S. ship of state while the nation sat in the calm eye of the storm. NAFTA (North American Free Trade Agreement) joined in the sovereignty-assaulting blow.

The new storm front is even now whipping up monstrous economic waves which might very well swamp the nation in their wake. What the socialist engineers of the first part of the hurricane could not accomplish with their internal assault, the socialist world economic powers that comprise the backside of the sovereignty-killing storm managed to achieve with little more than a tropical front. When the American voters swept the one-nation-under-Godlessness liberal Utopian schemers out the front door, the ejected ones quickly ran around the side of the house, where they joined with the globalist New World Order builders, who were being welcomed in the back door with eager smiles and open arms by a lame-duck Congress which was composed in part by rational-thinking patriots who should have detected the ruse.

But there are none so blind as those who will not see. Under the guise of free trade, the one-world parasitic apparatus has now apparently been contrived and has begun siphoning strength and resolve from this nation and others. The globalist elitists now channel America's wealth, along with funds from other geopolitical and economic spheres, into Third-World countries at a rate greater than ever before. They constantly strive to solidify their one-world power base through material goods giveaways. They continue to create and consolidate an ever-increasing constituency dependent on the New World Order hierarchy for absolutely everything as those poorest of earth's people move through their miserable lives from cradle to grave.

The one-world schemers would have us believe that all this *noblesse oblige* is being undertaken on behalf of humanity for humanity's own good: egalitarianism at its most glorious peak of achievement!

Mankind in general and Americans in particular fell prey to the sedative effects of globalism's siren song while the eye of the storm passed calmly overhead. GATT certainly was not perceived to be a storm warning by most; it was rather proclaimed to be salvation for the economic stability of the world. God, however, is never fooled and cannot be sedated. He put out the storm warning long ago that just such a time in human history will arrive when an elitist ruling class will combine its power and authority to create a mechanism of control through which it will attempt to enslave every human being on the planet.

God's warning foretold that the world's authority and power will ultimately be given to one man, the world's last and most terrible despot (read Daniel 9:27, Revelation 13, and Revelation 17:12,13).

What Is America's Role?

Those who analyze prophetic matters have long puzzled over why the United States of America is not mentioned specifically in God's prophetic Word. Certainly there has never been a nation more blessed or more active in the spread of the gospel of Jesus Christ. Small and seemingly insignificant nations and regions like Libya and Ethiopia are recorded in passages of prophecy yet to be fulfilled, but not America. Could we with the superhurried movement of America into the World Trade Organization (WTO) be witnessing at least a partial answer to the question of what will happen to the United States, since it is not mentioned by name in biblical prophecy?

John Gizzy, editor of *Human Events*, in commenting on the highly questionable way the U.S. was speedily ushered into the GATT arrangement and membership in the WTO, said:

> I don't think anyone will argue that we have to play in an international market. The world *is* a smaller place

and the relaxed tariffs of agreement on the part of the U.S. will help us get into a world market and sell our products with ease overseas. . . . Nonetheless, the problems persist. Some thoughts: If you accept that free trade is good and necessary, why on earth do we need a 22,000-plus page agreement that only one senator who voted on it bothered to read? I might add that after actually reading through the document, Sen. Hank Brown of Colorado voted "no." And could we not simply have bilateral agreements with individual countries we want to trade with? For that matter, why didn't we have a trade agreement in one simple sentence: "All tariffs will decrease 20 percent per year over the next five years"? We didn't do it the simple way. We needed a new, superpowerful, secret World Trade Organization, one with 350 employees and a $7 million annual budget, a fourth of which Uncle Sam will pay for to implement GATT. There was great concern that the WTO, which represents 123 countries, permits the United States only one vote and no veto. And to be sure, small countries, such as Castro's Cuba—or any of them—could vote to sock it to the U.S. with million-dollar-plus fines if local regulations violated world environmental rules. . . . Finally, the avenue of passage for GATT that was utilized by our men and women in Washington makes us a bit suspicious. If this is such a significant agreement, with such a far-reaching impact, why were only 20 hours of debate permitted, with no amendments, and why on earth did a lame-duck Congress, a huge number of whose members were defeated last month, make a decision that will impact you and me well into the twenty-first century? What would have been the matter with the next Congress taking office in January dealing with this lofty agreement? What were Bill Clinton and other GATT supporters afraid of? . . . But as it becomes law and as the vote was taken, I could not help but think of the warnings issued by one of the greatest Constitutional scholars in the U.S. Senate, the late Sen. Sam J. Ervin of North Carolina. One of his greatest apprehensions was that [of] the danger [which] international agreements posed to our national sovereignty. In Ervin's words, "The United States has never lost a war nor won a treaty."[7]

A Reprieve for America?

To repeat the opening thought expressed at the beginning of this section: With the election of November 8, 1994, there seemed to come a calming, refreshing breeze that promised a return to government that serves the people rather than seeks to rule with mastery over them. America seemed to have been given a reprieve from the death sentence which the woolly-minded had pronounced upon religious and a growing number of other liberties. But how deep a commitment to return to those earlier, saner principles (and thus how realistic the reprieve) remains to be seen.

To those who have truly studied the Word of God, it is clear that man-made government that refuses to be guided by God's principles of morality will inevitably degenerate and fall to tyranny within its own borders or without. Political parties cannot muster the fortitude to either restrain or constrain the oppression and tyranny that incessantly seek to enslave. Government of, by, and for a moral people can ensure those inalienable rights which our forefathers fought, bled, and died to secure for us. It is we the people, under God, who must determine to govern wisely. President George Washington said in his farewell address, "Reason and experience both forbid us that national morality can prevail in exclusion of religious principle." John Adams, America's second President, said, "The United States Constitution was made only for a moral and religious people. It is wholly inadequate for the government of any other."

We must begin by governing our own lives in a way that is pleasing to the Creator. There is only one way to please Him, and that is to put ourselves under the lordship of His blessed Son, Jesus Christ, who shed His blood on the cross of Calvary for the remission of our sins. How wonderful it would be if not just the majority of American people but a majority of people throughout the entire world turned to Jesus Christ in humble repentance!

But, tragically, we can be certain that this will not happen. God in His omniscience tells us through His Holy Word that in the last days perilous times shall come and that evil men and seducers will become worse and worse, deceiving and being deceived. The man who will be the world's last and most vicious tyrant is perhaps even now waiting in the shadows just beyond the spotlight's circle. He will take the crown given to him by his New World Order sycophants and use the platform of globalism they have erected to build a monolithic throne upon which he will ultimately sit, claiming to be deity while demanding worship.

Paving the Way for Antichrist

Today, movers and shakers in the world of global politics are paving the way for the world's last dictator, called in God's Word the Antichrist. They do so most likely oblivious to biblical prophecy. But whether wittingly or unwittingly, they rush headlong into that dark night of apocalypse.

David Allen Lewis, one of the most reliable observers of eschatology that I know, reported the following about the latest developments on the globalist's agenda.

What went on in San Francisco, September 1995, was nothing less than extraordinary. Mikhail Gorbachev and a bevy of politicians, futurologists, and New Agers took the world a giant step closer to global dictatorship. From September 20 to October 1, 1995, a landmark meeting, headed by Marxist Mikhail Gorbachev, former head of the Soviet Union, was conducted at the Fairmont Hotel and a nearby Masonic Auditorium in San Francisco. Billed as the State of the World Forum–Toward a New Civilization, it was one of the most significant steps forward in implementing the coming world government, which President Clinton recently referred to as the "global village." It was previously hailed as the New World Order by former President George Bush in many speeches made while he was president of the USA.

Jim Garrison, executive director of the Gorbachev Foundation, made a very revealing statement in the May 31 issue of *SF Weekly,* a far left San Francisco newspaper: "Over the next 20 to 30 years we are going to end up with the world government . . . it's inevitable." Garrison writes of the problems of violence in the USA and the rest of the world, proclaiming that ". . . in and through this turbulence is the recognition that we have to empower the United Nations and that we have to govern and regulate human interaction." Garrison is from the New Age Esalen Institute and Soviet American Exchange Program, San Francisco.

Yes, the Cold War is over, but looming before us is the ideological Hot War of hegemony (domination) and oppression. The globalists know that the human race must be blinded to the real intentions of these elitist one-worlders if they are to succeed. They must endeavor to use the media to brainwash you into thinking that they have your best interests at heart.

> I have no doubt that history will record The World Forum as a momentous occasion in the annals of the coming Antichrist.
>
> And the world lies in darkness, ignorant, blindly stumbling along, vaguely uneasy but nonetheless pathetic. . . . [8]

Lewis quoted from the document titled "State of the World Forum—Toward a New Civilization," September 20–October 1, 1995, San Francisco. He writes:

> . . . On page three of the document, the mission of the conference is clearly stated. "The State of the World Forum is the launching of a multiyear global initiative to focus on the fundamental challenges and opportunities confronting humanity as we enter the next phase of human development. It is being held in the belief that at this momentous juncture in history—between the ending of the Cold War and the dawn of the new century—we are experiencing the birth of the first global civilization. . . . The goal of the Forum is to articulate a clearer vision of new international priorities. Its product will be an ongoing process to generate innovative approaches to the challenges facing human society. This historic gathering will 1) Analyze the current state of the world, and 2) Launch a multiyear process, culminating in the year 2000, to articulate the fundamental priorities, values, and actions necessary to constructively shape our common future.
>
> "Ultimately, the State of the World Forum is an invitation. It is a call to individuals throughout the world to join in this dialogue and to work directly with the convening of committed individuals as

an active member of an historic and timely global initiative...." [9]

Lewis writes further:

> ... On the last page of the Document we read, "The State of the World Forum is a project of the Gorbachev Foundation/USA, an international nonpartisan, nonprofit educational foundation created in 1992 to address the immediate challenges of the post-Cold-War world and assist in the process of building global consensus for our common future." [10]

Lewis goes on to report a long list of attendees. Many of the high-profile names are familiar to most Americans. For further information about those meetings, write your request to David Lewis Ministries, P.O. Box 11115, Springfield, MO 65808-1115.

The Lull Before the Storm

Thankfully, even though God's judgment upon sin is sure, He is also slow to anger and His mercy is great. It is my opinion that we are currently in a lull that God has graciously granted just before the prophesied end-of-time storm that will devastate a wrath-deserving generation. Even so, a brisk wind is already snapping the flag of warning that apocalypse approaches.

God the Holy Spirit earnestly and tenderly beckons all who will heed His call to take shelter within the only harbor where protection from the deadly whirlwind to come can be found. That safe harbor is Jesus Christ. Those who refuse to accept the haven or safety offered by Christ will perish beneath the raging, crashing surge as surely as did the antediluvians during the judgment of Noah's day.

Revelation 22:18,19 warns, "I testify unto every man that heareth the words of the prophecy of this book, If any man shall add unto these things, God shall add unto him the plagues that are written in this book; and if any man shall take away from the words of the book of this prophecy, God shall take away his part out of the [tree] of life, and out of the holy city, and from the things which are written in this book."

God cannot tell a lie. He *is* truth. Everything within His Word points toward the revelation of Jesus Christ and His return to planet Earth to put an end to man's disastrous attempts to govern himself.

Globalism's siren song is the anthem to which one-world builders march. It is made up of many beautiful, hypnotic words and emotion-packed promises that desensitize and delude its hearers. Powerful human forces are moving and shaking in the world today to bring planet Earth under one humanistic banner.

2

Classroom Earth: Educating for One World Order

Berit Kjos

❖ ❖ ❖

God is going to change. We women ... will change the world so much that He won't fit anymore.[1]

–Naomi Goldenberg, *Changing of the Gods: Feminism and the End of Traditional Religions*

The spiritual sense of our place in nature ... can be traced to the origins of human civilization ... [when] the prevailing ideology of belief ... was based on the worship of a single earth goddess, who was assumed to be the fount of all life and who radiated harmony among all living things. ... It seems obvious that a better understanding of a religious heritage preceding our own by so

45

many thousands of years could offer us new insights. . . .[2]

The fifth strategic goal should be the establishment of a cooperative plan for educating the world's citizens about our global environment . . .[3]

—Al Gore, *Earth in the Balance: Ecology and the Human Spirit*

Nations that stick to stale old notions and ideologies will falter and fail. So I'm here today to say, America will move forward. . . . New schools for a new world.

—George Bush, Introduction to America 2000, which became Goals 2000

Be still, and know that I am God; I will be exalted among the nations, I will be exalted in the earth.

–Psalm 46:10 NKJV

"Diving. Diving deep. Diving deep inside the earth . . . " intoned Diana, a workshop leader at the 1996 United Nations Conference on Habitat held in Istanbul. Draped in flowing orange garb, she moved in and out among the women gathered in a circle to celebrate "The Spirit of Place"– the new spirituality that would guide the next century community and reconnect its people to Mother Earth. Bending down to whisper into a listener's ear, she continued:

Diving. Diving. Diving deep inside me . . .
Diving deep. Deep inside the earth. Diving. . . .

With eyes closed, the women followed the imaginary journey to an inner self mysteriously linked to the heart of the universe. Diana's voice faded to a hypnotic whisper, then rose to a shout with her answer:

Who are you? Diving deep, deep. Who am I?
Power? Light? Energy? A particle of light from the sun?
Power! Light! Energy!
Diving deep, deep inside. . . .

A Turkish woman passed a bowl of dried henna—a reddish Egyptian plant symbolizing a woman's "life-giving blood"—around the circle. The participants dipped their hands into the crushed leaves. "It has a long tradition associated with witchcraft," she explained. "Women who used henna [to color their skin or nails] were arrested. Anything which connects us to earth is never liked in patriarchal cultures."

"We need to remember the old ways and reinvent new ways," suggested a pagan from New Mexico. "Rituals help us to remember our connection to the earth."

"Every morning I do Tai Chi to get my *chi* going," said a Chinese teacher from Germany. "When I miss it, my days are in disarray."

"O, oooooo," chanted Diana.

"Ai, ai, ai, ooooo," echoed the group. "Lalalalala . . . Ahaaaa . . . Oioioioi . . . Hohohohoooo . . . Rororoo-roooo . . . " Their voices blended into eerie harmonies that became louder, bolder, deeper. . . .

"How about a scream?" asked Diana. The group agreed and the room erupted into an earsplitting cacophony of menacing growls, animal howls, and piercing screams. Chilled by these personal expressions of untamed wildness, I covered my ears, turned off my tape recorder, and prayed. *How could these women be so captivated with rage, pain, and evil—the very opposite of the peace and freedom they sought?*

Outside the building, among the rows of NGO (Non-Governmental Organization) tents, hung a large banner warning "YOUR MOTHER IS WATCHING YOU!" Nearby, a group of teenage actors was preparing for a skit. A girl dressed as a mystical mother in a long white gown cradled a "baby" globe in her arms. "We haven't taken care of the earth as we should," she explained.

Transforming the World

Caring for the earth was a major theme at the U.N. conference in Istanbul, but it meant far more than finding solutions to environmental abuses. Ever since the 60s, when radical feminists joined "peaceniks," Marxists, and religious rebels to form the "green" movement, environmentalism has included a broad socialist agenda. Now packaged as "sustainable development," this agenda weds the 3 Es of the U.N. vision: *Environment, Economy,* and *Equity.* Its nice-sounding promises mask unthinkable restrictions on the use of *natural* resources, worldwide redistribution of *economic* resources, and global surveillance to ensure socialist *equality* everywhere.

But this totalitarian plan couldn't touch America, could it? After all, we have our Constitution!

Yes, it could. The environmental, economic, and socialistic ideology behind "sustainable development" already colors every aspect of Goals 2000, the Clinton Administration's education plan. Together with the new global spirituality, it forms the basic tenets of training in global citizenship. In fact, Vice President Al Gore tells us that "we must make the rescue of the environment the central organizing principle for civilization." This means that "trivial sacrifices" won't do. Instead–

> ... it means embarking on an all-out effort to use every policy and program, every law and institution, every treaty and alliance ... to halt the destruction of the environment.... Moderate improvements in laws and regulation [and] rhetoric offered in lieu of genuine change–these are all forms of appeasement, designed to satisfy the public's desire to believe that sacrifice, struggle and a wrenching transformation of society will not be necessary.[4]

The local framework for the U.N. plan is already being established through the community "partnerships" touted in Hillary Clinton's book, *It Takes a Village*, and mandated through Goals 2000.[5] A team of educators, school psychologists, labor leaders, social workers, and other "stakeholders" in your child's socialization are usurping the right of parents to guide their children to Christian maturity. Yes, even home-schooled students are targeted for transformation. Meanwhile, a new "civil government" praised as "local control" is linking global-minded community leaders and their supporters directly to the U.N., bypassing representative government at every level.

But you are not supposed to know this yet. Both U.N. and U.S. plans suggest hiding the intended outcome from the general public until the needed groups of loyal stakeholders and supporters have been established at the local level. These groups will be trained to communicate the *right* "facts" in the right way to the *right* people at the *right* time. Honesty matters little. As North Carolina school superintendent Dr. Jim Causby told educators at an international Model School Conference in Atlanta:

> We have actually been given a course in how not
> to tell the truth. How many of you are adminis-
> trators? You've had that course in public relations
> where you learn to put the best spin on things.[6]

Their goal? To involve the whole community in "lifelong learning"–an international strategy designed to persuade the people of the world to embrace the new earth-centered values "needed" to unify the world and build sustainable next-century communities.

Worldwide Solidarity

To define these values, the U.N. conference in Istanbul held a daylong Dialogue on Solidarity. "I have gathered leaders with tremendous wisdom and prestige," began Dr. Wally N'Dow, Secretary-General of the U.N. conference. "They are bringing the spiritual dimension, the only ingredient that can bind societies together." To add credibility, he had chosen Robert MacNeil (of MacNeil-Lehrer)–"one of the spiritual lights of the media industry today"–to moderate the dialogue.

"How would you define solidarity?" I asked MacNeil during a break.

"In our culture, it was probably exemplified most often by the union movement," he answered. "Industrial unions often used the phrase 'solidarity'–'solidarity forever.' And in the socialist movement, of course, solidarity was a very strong word–the solidarity of the workers *against* the employers, their oppressors, capitalists, running dogs of capitalism, whatever it was. So solidarity means people of like interests, needs, and responsibilities coming together to pursue their common goals."

The handpicked panel left little doubt that solidarity also meant a worldwide shift to common beliefs and values.

"What's needed is an interfaith center in every city of the globe," said James Morton, dean of the Episcopal Cathedral of St. John the Divine, who organized the panel. "The new interfaith centers will honor the rituals of every . . . faith tradition: Islam, Hinduism, Jain, Christian [a universalist version that ignores the cross and instead blends with other beliefs] . . . and provide opportunity for sacred expressions needed to bind the people of the planet into a viable, meaningful, and sustainable solidarity."

"We should stop bemoaning the growth of cities," added Dr. Ismail Serageldin, Vice President of The World Bank. "It's going to happen and it's a good thing, because cities are the vectors of social change and transformation. Let's just make sure that social change and transformation are going in the right direction."

To guide the masses in "the right direction," communities around the world must reeducate their "human capital" for the global workforce through "lifelong learning." This UNESCO concept become a legal mandate in the U.S. through Goals 2000. It will ensure that the same multicultural blend of the world's earth-centered religions now taught in our nation's classrooms will reach parents and everyone else.

"Citizenship for the next century is learning to live together," said Federico Mayor, Director General of UNESCO. "The 21st Century city will be a city of social solidarity. . . . We have to redefine the words . . . [and write a new] social contract."

This "contract" would make it illegal to resist the new solidarity. To make sure that people understand the need to seek "consensus" and find "common ground," UNESCO brought its official Declaration of Principles on Tolerance. Not only does tolerance mean "appreciation" for the world's religions and lifestyles–a violation of God's command to shun idolatry—but it also means "the rejection of dogmatism and absolutism." In other words, faith in the *absolute* truth of God's Word would be *in*tolerable. Worse yet, this politically correct tolerance is "not only a moral duty, it is also a political and legal requirement."[7]

Tolerance also "means that one's views are not to be imposed on others"—at least not the old views. Yet the panel called for a *paradigm shift*—a total change in the way people think and view reality. "Change your whole way of thinking, because the new order of the spirit is confronting and challenging you," said Millard Fuller, president of Habitat for Humanity, who shared the globalist perspective and the U.N. platform with James Morton and Dr. Ladner. Everything must be seen through a new globalist lens or filter.

Like the popular Native American fetish called a dream-catcher, this new paradigm would filter out all the wrong thoughts and permit only the right beliefs to settle in one's mind. It would be based on these basic assumptions:

- Everything is connected to the same pantheistic or universal god, though the names may differ: Goddess, Great Spirit, Universal Energy, Cosmic Mind, etc.;

- Therefore everything is naturally sacred and good;

- Therefore there is no need for the cross;

- Therefore biblical Christianity is too extremist and exclusive to fit.

CHRISTIANITY (Biblical Absolutes) *Old Religion*	HUMANISM (Relative Values) *Killed Religion*	GLOBALISM (Global Absolutes) *"New" Religion* ©1994 Kjos
The Bible reveals reality	Science explains reality	Feelings and experience define reality
God is transcendent and personal	God is a nonexistent crutch	A pantheistic god(dess) or force is present in all
God created the earth	The earth evolved by random chance	The earth evolved by its own (or cosmic) power
Trusting God is key to success	Trusting self is key to success	Trusting one's inner god-self is key to success
Good and evil are incompatible	Good and evil are relative	Joining good and evil brings wholeness

Strategies for Change

To establish this global paradigm, the old biblical lens or worldview must be abolished. Tolerance must become a greater virtue than obedience. The public must be so immersed in earth-centered suggestions that paganism will seem good rather than evil. Young and old must learn to mix (synthesize) truth with myths until Christianity loses its uniqueness. The end product may *sound* Christian but would actually be pagan.

While the cross is *out,* guilt is not. Today's self-proclaimed "change agents" know that pain, blame, guilt, and especially anger are essential steps to social transformation. People don't change their beliefs without plausible reasons—and

*ridicule
promise
keepers*

*Black
Farra
marsh*

angry *feelings* fuel social revolutions far more effectively than mere facts or logic.

To arouse the needed rage, feminists, educators, environmentalists, and globalists have identified the *victims* of oppression that can best serve their purpose: women, minority groups, indigenous people, and the earth itself. They point accusing fingers at the *oppressors*: Western patriarchal institutions such as the church, the traditional family, capitalist economics, and traditional male leadership.

The influential Club of Rome, a globalist society not known for feminist leanings, chose the earth as its most useful victim:

> In searching for a new enemy to unite us, we came up with the idea that pollution, the threat of global warming, water shortages, famine and the like would fit the bill.... All these dangers are caused by human intervention.... The real enemy, then, is humanity itself.[8]

On the other hand, the powerful WEDO (Women's Environmental and Development Organization) links its visions of a mutilated earth to abused women. Guiding the global sisterhood under the spirited leadership of former congresswoman Bella Abzug, it summarizes this victimhood well:

> We have survived femicide. We have rebelled.... We are whale-song and rainforest... the lost and despised.... The exercise of imagining is an act of creation. The act of creation is an exercise of will. All this is political.... We are the women who will transform the world.[9]

Feminists and male globalists may not agree on the details—or even like each other—but their partnership is speeding the transformation. Joined by environmentalists, educators, media leaders, bankers, business leaders and others, they have become a formidable movement indeed. The fact that the whole world is under the control of Satan[10]– who despises God and aims to destroy His people–multiplies their power and potential for evil. Only God can block their progress!

But where are His people? What's happening to the church?

Unholy Worship in Holy Places

When Rachel Holm walked into her son's Sunday school classroom, she found a new poster on the wall. It announced the Sunday school theme for the coming months: "Gathering into the Sacred Circle." Surprised, she stopped to look at the symbol under the words. It showed a cross inside a circle, but it didn't quite look like the Christian cross. Could it be the medicine wheel–an occult symbol used by Native Americans in many of their rituals? Her heart began to pound. Why would a Lutheran Sunday school curriculum use this symbol?

Moments later she saw her pastor, so she asked him. He seemed reluctant to answer her directly, but indicated that in today's pluralistic culture, Christians must be open to new ideas. What did he mean? Rachel felt confused.

Curious, she ordered the manual describing the curriculum, called "The Whole People of God," from a distributor for Augsburg Publishing House. She learned that it was being used by more than a thousand congregations from coast to coast, including most mainstream denominations: Presbyterian, Methodist, Lutheran, United Church of Christ, etc. "Sales are booming," said the telephone representative.

When she received the manual, Rachel noticed that matching lessons were prepared for each age group from young children to adults. It also explained the poster she first saw in her son's Sunday school class:

> The logo for Unit I is a circle symbolizing God and the interconnection of the whole creation.... The center that keeps the circle together may be called Creator or Great Spirit, or God. The circle in our logo is made with braided sweetgrass which is used by many people of the First Nations to purify or cleanse the body and soul.... [11]

Did it imply that cleansing came through the Native American sweetgrass ritual and not through Jesus Christ? What about confession and repentance? Rachel turned the page and found an unexpected answer to her question: an "apology to Native Congregations" submitted by the United Church of Canada in 1986. She read the words to the strange confession:

> In our zeal to tell you of the good news of Jesus Christ we were closed to the value of your spirituality.... We tried to make you be like us and in so doing we helped to destroy the vision that made you what you were. As a result you, and we, are poorer and the image of the Creator in us is twisted, blurred.... We ask you to forgive us.... [12]

"This is a politically correct Sunday school curriculum," Rachel told me later. "It tells our children that it's *wrong* to be missionaries, but *right* to blend Christianity with Native American spirituality. Our children learn that they are guilty simply because they are part of a culture that taught others to trust Jesus Christ."

Rachel knew the Bible well enough to see the gulf between God's truth and today's new standards, but others prefer not to look. A few years ago I visited a Presbyterian church which had invited the public to share in an Earth Day celebration. Watching the ceremony, I wondered if the Creator Himself would have been welcome. At one point the members of the youth group stepped forward to present their offerings at the altar:

"I bring to our Mother, the Earth, the gift of a new beginning. . . ."

"I bring to our Mother, the Earth, the birth of a new consciousness."

"I bring to our Mother, the Earth, the gift of immortality that you may live forever cherished by your beloved children."

The congregation responded to this strange ritual with a standing ovation.

An Old Testament verse that fits our times flowed through my mind:

> Woe unto them that call evil good and good evil, that put darkness for light and light for darkness. . . . Woe unto them that are wise in their own eyes and prudent in their own sight! (Isaiah 5:20,21).

Birth of a New Consciousness

Back in the 50s, most people still viewed our nation as Christian. While many people rejected Christ's personal message, our laws, values, and worldview were based largely on biblical teachings. But the rapid rise of the counterculture in the 60s changed everything. On campuses from coast to coast, students explored ancient myths, Eastern spirituality, Marxist economics, and alternative lifestyles. By the 80s, these young activists were established in positions that would influence politics, education, entertainment, publishing, the media . . . even Christian seminaries and churches.

You may remember the Re-Imagining Conference in 1993. Over 2000 women from mainline churches in 49 states and 27 countries came together in Minneapolis to reimagine God, themselves, their sexuality, and the world. Funded in part by their Presbyterian, Methodist, Baptist, and Lutheran denominations, the four-day gathering sent shock waves through the church.

Like many neopagan celebrations, the conference began by creating a sacred space—here they called it "Making Holy Space"—to the beat of Native American drums. "The drum is feminine," explained the printed program, "and the drumbeat is the heartbeat of the earth . . . The heart of Mother Earth indeed beats with our own as one."[13]

"As one we sing to her our sacred song," sang the women over and over, affirming their oneness with the world's earth-centered religions. "As one we touch her, as one we heal her, her heart beats with our own as one."

Seated in intimate Native American "talking circles" around the tables, the assembly imagined the faces of their god. "What does your god sound like, taste like, look like?" they asked each other, while the sounds of a water drum throbbed in the air. "Tell each other. . . . Re-imagine your God. Name! Tell! Imagine!"[14]

To help each woman visualize her own goddess, the leaders suggested a medley of exotic images. Sophia might be her "Christian" name, but the options were boundless: Mystery, Lover, Earth Mother, Spirit Woman, She Who Is, Cosmic Maxim, Transforming Laughter, Womb of Creation, Yin Yang, Unknown God. . . .

Each speaker brought new images that fed the imagination. "If we cannot imagine Jesus as a tree, as a river, as wind, and as rain, we are doomed together,"[15] warned Kwok Pui-Lan, a Chinese theologian.

"The three goddesses I want to share with you are Kali [Hindu], Kwan-in [Buddhist], and Enna [Philippines] ... my new trinity,"[16] said Chung Hyun Kyung, a Korean theologian educated at Union Theological Seminary. She explained why:

> I came from ... a Shamanist, Buddhist and Confucian and Taoist and Christian tradition.... When I look at our history of religion, we have more than 5000 years of Shamanism, more than 2000 years of Taoism, and almost 2000 years of Buddhism, and 700 years of Confucianism and only 100 years of Protestantism in Korea. Therefore, whenever I go to temples ... and look at Buddha, I feel so young ... Buddha died in his 80s and Jesus died when he was 33. Maybe ... Jesus should be called "Too young to understand."[17]

Her mockery sent ripples of laughter through the room. "I feel like my bowel is Shamanist, my heart is Buddhist, my right brain is Confucianist, and my left brain is Christian," Kyung continued. "I call it a family of gods and ... they are together."[18]

Yet such spiritual synthesis is not new. Back in Old Testament days, God's people would burn incense to their idols in "sacred groves" one week, then worship God the next. Shortly before God allowed the Babylonian armies to destroy Jerusalem and carry His precious people into exile, His rebellious children had built altars to "the host of heaven" inside His holy temple (2 Kings 21:5). He often warned them to shun "other gods," for He knew that violence and oppression would follow occult worship. But, then as now, people refused to listen.

To speed the shift from the biblical God to pagan images, the Re-Imagining Conference taught rituals that would clash with Christianity and support neopaganism. The women prayed Native American prayers, blessed ritual "rainsticks," and joined in Hawaiian chants and Zulu songs. They anointed themselves with red dots on the forehead to celebrate "the divine in each other"[19] and to protest the oppression brought to India by Christian missionaries.

Any spiritual expression was welcomed–except biblical Christianity. "In a global context where violence and the use of force have become the norm," said Indian feminist Aruna Gnanadason, "the violence that the cross symbolizes and the patriarchal image of an almighty invincible Father God needs to be challenged and reconstructed."[20]

Out of the ashes of the old patriarchal ways would spring the new global consciousness. As lesbian theologian Virginia Mollenkott said, "Women would worship 'god herself,' give 'honor to every world religion,' and agree that 'everything that lives is holy.' "[21] Together they would change their world.

Spreading the Message

Like other revolutions, the current transformation feeds on publicity and propaganda. "The media must act as part of the education process," said Ismail Serageldin, Vice President of the World Bank, during the Dialogue on Solidarity in Istanbul. Mass media leaders know that well! From newspapers to movies, they show the world from an earth-centered perspective.

Do you remember Disney's Pocahontas? Brave, assertive, and free-spirited, the Indian maiden scales mountains, climbs trees, and steers a canoe better than a man.

Like *Women Who Run with Wolves*,[22] she does what *she* wants and submits to no one.

"What is my path?" she asks the wise old spirit of Grandmother Willow, a magical tree in the forest. "How am I ever going to find it?"

"Listen. . . . " says her enchanted counselor. "All around you are spirits, child. They live in the earth, the water, the sky. If you listen, they will guide you."

The Indian maiden believes. Why shouldn't she? It offers answers that appeal to human nature. It feels good! Not only does the tree spirit's advice fit the context of Disney's fictionalized history, but it also fits the trends of our times and the envisioned global spirituality.

The villains in the story are the greedy, arrogant white males who have come to exploit the land and steal its gold. Even handsome John Smith looks foolish compared to the nature-wise woman he loves. Their exchange of wisdom flows one way only: from Indian to European. So when Smith unwittingly offers to build English cities on Indian lands, Pocahontas shows her disgust, then sings him a lesson on pagan oneness: Everything is filled with spiritual life and linked in a never-ending circle. Nature worship is good, and Judeo/Christian values are bad.

It all makes sense when you watch the movie. With subtle mastery, its makers highlight the anti-Western message and stir predictable indignation: How can the crude Christian sailors, so ignorant of spiritual things, call the natives "heathen"? Those arrogant intruders are the *real* savages who batter the earth and rob its friends.

In contrast, the natives seem flawless. They care for the land. They commune with its spirits. They love each other. Their shaman protects and guides.

In line with the feminist quest for gender equity, the deep spiritual insights come from women. The new multicultural and gender lessons tell us that patriarchy brings war and oppression, while matriarchy brings love and wisdom. So when chief Powhatan feels the spirit of Pocahontas' dead mother guiding him, he heeds her lofty wisdom: "There will be no more killing. Let us be guided instead to a place of peace."

Fact or Feeling?

Those who love God's Word know that paganism can never bring peace. The Disney film turns biblical truth and history upside down, but it fits the trends of our times. People believe the story, not because it's true, but because it *feels* right. The fact that Pocahontas became a Christian would have clashed with today's earth-centered illusions. So would the fact that the not-so-peaceful Iroquois Indians "hated the Huron [Indians] intensely" and "massacred . . . more than 10,000 Huron."[23]

But do the facts really matter? After all, this is only a Disney movie!

The facts really don't matter, at least not to those who see themselves as contemporary "change agents" creating a better world. But the message does matter. Pocahontas continues to bring ecofeminist ideology—a blend of environmental myths and feminist activism—to people everywhere. Few notice the lies cloaked in feel-good propaganda.

Radical feminists and environmentalists "know they are in a cultural war, as those on the other side often do not," warns columnist and author Thomas Sowell. What's worse, "only one side is battling. That is why they are winning."[24] He asks an insightful question: Was the feminist movement discredited when its claim that Superbowl Sunday was the day when the most wives were battered could not be supported by any evidence? Has Paul Ehrlich or the Worldwatch

Institute been discredited by the repeated failures of their hysterical predictions?

> ... Being factual does not matter to those who are politically correct. Some of the bolder members of the anointed have openly expressed the view that various radical charges which turned out to be hoaxes do not bother them because these charges serve to raise consciousness. Similarly, some of the brassier feminists declare that they are untroubled by false charges against some men because men in general are guilty of the things charged.[25]

Sowell suggests that today's cultural battle will be won in the arena of consciousness, where propaganda means more than facts, anger wields more influence than science, and the ends justify the means. If he is right, history could teach us some sobering lessons about totalitarian rulers who promised to serve "the people" but despised the individual.

Global Controls

Few people would deny that Communism has spread terror and environmental devastation throughout the world, yet no one received a more jubilant welcome at the Istanbul conference than Fidel Castro.

"Why are you so enthusiastic?" I asked some of Castro's cheering fans after his plenary speech.

"Because he stood up to America," someone answered.

"Because he is a living myth," explained another. "He was a simple guerrilla, fighting for the oppressed against the rich and powerful."

"Fighting for the oppressed." The U.N. claims that mission, but Third World women who have faced its abusive birth-control practices tell a different story. Like the Communist Manifesto, the growing body of U.N. declarations is full of alluring promises designed to win worldwide support. Viewed as international laws by many, they cloak an agenda that would show little compassion once power has been won.

In fact, Communist ideology permeated major NGO (Non-Governmental Organization) workshops, official U.N. literature, and the organizational guidelines for local communities. Entering the huge "Best Practices" exhibition of model cities, visitors immediately faced wall-sized pictures and elaborate models of Chinese housing projects and community plans. Displays from the rest of the world merely shared the strips along the outer perimeter of the cavernous hall.

The guiding force behind the new universal education system is the social, economic, and spiritual ideology of *sustainable development.* We must "meet the needs of the present without compromising the ability of future generations to meet their own needs,"[26] say U.N. leaders, but they agree that the real meaning of sustainability signals the end of Western culture. No longer can the world allow rich nations to continue to consume the world's scarce resources. People everywhere must be taught "scientific facts" about "environmental risks" that are sensational enough to scare them into compliance. They must be persuaded to accept a global welfare system so that all will be equal. And they must embrace an earth-centered spirituality that will unify the world's diverse cultures. Then peace will reign on our planet at last!

History has shown the emptiness of these promises. Long ago the Communist Manifesto announced a proletarian revolution that would empower the poor by redistributing wealth. Everyone would be equal. Men and women alike would join the socialist workforce, and children would be trained by the state.

It happened! In Communist nations, all but the leaders became equally poor, and all the children were indoctrinated with an anti-Christian socialist philosophy. Morally and economically, the masses sank to the level of the lowest common denominator.

If people knew real history—not just the selected stories and events emphasized in politically correct curricula and movies—they would resist this horrendous movement toward a totalitarian world without God. But globalist change agents fear such resistance. That's one reason why our national-international education system feeds our children biased, dumbed-down lessons that strip them of the needed factual foundation, distorts their historical perspective, and undermines their ability to think for themselves.

The similarities between the Communist Manifesto and the U.N. agenda (outlined in the Beijing Declaration and incorporated into the Habitat Agenda) would have been a call to action—if people only knew. Both revolutions:

- use psychology and sociology to establish the victimhood, blame, and anger needed to fuel the revolution;

- use education to conform minds to the new ideology;

- use synthesis (blending opposing views into compromise beliefs that match new goals) to produce group consensus;

- promise economic equality to seduce the masses;

- spread hatred toward "extremists" who refuse to compromise. As Andrei Vishinsky wrote in *The Law of the Soviet State,* "Naturally, there can be

no place for freedom of speech, press, and so on
for the foes of socialism."[27]

The Communist Manifesto led to religious, moral, economic, and environmental bankruptcy. Yet U.N.-led activists and their U.S. partners are determined to fulfill their Utopian visions. What will happen to those who oppose the revolution?

No Tolerance for Christians

You may remember that the U.N. dubbed 1995 the Year of Tolerance. Yet the tolerance shown in Beijing that year excluded all who opposed the feminist agenda. Women could speak freely as long as they fit the planned "consensus," and U.N. organizers would block pro-life groups that tried to "unbalance the proceedings."[28]

Small wonder, considering the spiritual forces behind WEDO, the leading feminist NGO (Non-Governmental Organization). Led by the indomitable Bella Abzug, it sponsored a series of workshops in Beijing called "Daughters of the Earth." Each session was dedicated to a different goddess–Athena, Ishtar, Nu Kwa, Tara. Opening the first meeting, a Brazilian woman presented a thank offering of fruit to Mother Earth. Then she lifted a Christian cross, saying, "The people from my community used to believe in the crucifixion, but we have decided 'No more crucifixion.' We believe in life!" She began chanting, "We are power ... No one empowers anyone, we do this ourselves."

The indomitable Abzug arose and the rest followed. Clasping each other's hands, they raised their arms and chanted, "I am power! I am power!"

And so they are! Wielding its political muscle, WEDO "advocates 50/50 quotas of men and women in all government and policy-making bodies; prefers socialist economic models over free market options; argues against 'traditional family values' and 'fundamentalism' . . . supports 'abortion as a basic method of fertility regulation' and an essential reproductive right; and seeks to indoctrinate children and youth on its understanding of 'women's rights,' "[29] reported Diane Knippers, President of the Institute on Religion and Democracy. Most of these demands were included in the final Beijing Platform for Action. The officials from the U.N., the World Bank, and the International Monetary Fund who joined the last WEDO meeting added their unspoken authority to its revolutionary demands.[30]

"We want to change things," declared Abzug nine months later in Istanbul. "We'll be on executive boards. We want the participation of NGOs on the security council."

She serves the globalist purpose well. By mobilizing worldwide rebellion against Christian values, pushing birth control and gender-role equality for every family, demanding sex education for every student, and requiring international surveillance to monitor compliance, her followers are speeding the paradigm shift. Like countless other U.N. partners, they are winning by propaganda, intimidation, and growing popular consent. But few people realize that their angry idealism can be used by hard-core globalists to reach a more ominous goal. As economist Thomas Sowell wrote in his review of *Road to Serfdom:*[31]

> Idealist socialists create systems in which idealists are almost certain to lose and be superseded by those whose drive for power, and ruthlessness in achieving it, make them the "fittest" to survive under a system where government power is the ultimate prize. . . . The issue is not what anyone intends but what consequences are in fact likely to follow.[32]

In other words, idealists can persuade, but they seldom rule. Utopian idealism can awaken the masses and inspire a revolution, but it seldom governs. During the first part of the Russian revolution, ideology raised awareness and paved the way to change. But the ruthless, manipulative forces of Communism soon seized the victory and captured the throne.

Like the radical feminists at the Beijing Conference, former U.N. Under-Secretary General Robert Muller and his fellow U.N. leaders have little tolerance for noncon-formists. When speaking at a 1995 event celebrating the fiftieth anniversary of the United Nations, Muller shared his vision for the future: a united world where all would live in harmony sharing a common set of values. People were free to believe anything–as long as it was pantheistic and inclu-sive and fit the U.N. vision of global spirituality. Cross-less Christianity would fit. Biblical faith would not.

Muller, who authored the controversial, earth-centered World-Core Curriculum for schools around the world, told us how to reach this lofty goal: The world would be taught "a global ethic," a universal code of beliefs and behavior. It would be universally enforced–yes, in the U.S.A as well as the rest of the world–by a new World Court with power and authority to condemn "wrong behavior" and prosecute "vio-lators."

What kinds of legal standards would guide humans in their pursuit of peace? Muller listed some of them. The new laws would deal with the problems of overpopulation, overconsumption, garbage, business, and religious differ-ences. "The next millennium must heal what is wrong," he concluded. Those "wrongs" included free enterprise, bib-lical Christianity, large families, and freedom to dissent.

When the moderator invited questions from the audi-ence, a man stood up. What happened next left a chilling awareness of an intolerance that is incomprehensible to most Americans. He simply asked two questions:

> In a pluralistic world, would a centralized institution tend to become insensitive to ideas other than its own? And if the U.N. becomes involved in spirituality, could it cause church-state violations?

His questions seemed thoughtful and legitimate, but they proved strangely offensive. An angry woman in the audience stood up and shouted, "In Oklahoma we saw the result of men who hate our central government." She stormed out of the auditorium.

Sounding just as angry, Muller leaned into the microphone to denounce dissenters, nationalism, and U.S. reluctance to fully support U.N. policies. Then he swore and left the podium.

Despising the Truth

Muller's hatred for dissenters permeates the movement toward global spirituality and oneness. It doesn't matter whether the pantheistic bond is called witchcraft, Mother Earth, New Age, or Native American shamanism. Like Diana, most contemporary pagans and New Agers try to "dive deep" into a mystical inner self where they supposedly connect with some kind of a universal force. Carl Jung called it the "collective unconscious." Popular "Christian theologian" John Bradshaw called it "unity consciousness." Wiccans call it the Goddess. But all of these draw insight from the same satanic mastermind, and all of these despise biblical truth and the God we love.

Jesus said that the world hates Him " . . . because I testify of it that its works are evil."[33] The world hates us as Christians for the same reason. Yet, ironically, some of the most cruel assaults against us come from those who also call themselves Christians. Indeed, "the time cometh that whosoever killeth you will think that he doeth God service" (John 16:2).

"Then shall they deliver you up to be afflicted, and shall kill you," said Jesus, "and ye shall be hated of all nations for my name's sake" (Matthew 24:9). Remove the phrase "all nations" and He could have been referring to almost any time during the last 2000 years. Long ago, persecuted Christians in the Roman Empire fought lions and faced tortures that defy the imagination of our cushioned culture. They would rather die at the hands of their tormentors than deny the God they loved more than their own life. In more recent years, missionaries to Asia, Africa, and South America have joyfully followed the early martyrs through doorways of horrendous torture, fire, and deprivation. Untold millions were tormented and killed by Communists and Nazi tyrants inspired by occult powers to hate God and His people. Uncompromising Christians faced torture, slashing, guns, and gas chambers (along with millions of Jews as well).

During the last few centuries, when the spreading influence of Christianity calmed the seething madness of occultism in other parts of the world, many of God's people found a momentary haven. But the shelter that Americans have taken for granted may soon be ravaged by the coming spiritual storms, leaving us no place to hide but in Jesus.

"And then shall many be offended, and shall betray one another, and shall hate one another," warned Jesus. "And many false prophets shall rise, and shall deceive many. And because iniquity shall abound, the love of many shall grow cold. But he that shall endure unto the end, the same shall be saved" (Matthew 24:10-13).

Endurance is crucial to the battles ahead. The biblical and historical pattern shows us that when God's people or nations ignored truth, returned to paganism, and worshiped other gods, everyone suffered. With a heart that ached over the pain of His people,[34] God pulled back His hand of protection[35] and allowed His people to face the terrors of life without Him—droughts, famines, wars, and plagues as well as tyranny, violence, injustice, and fear.

At times the people would see what life was like without the Shepherd. The priests would roll out the dusty old Scriptures, rediscover God's holy standard, tear their clothes in despair over their own failure, repent of their rebellion, and pray for healing. And God always forgave and restored, for then as now He wants nothing more than to bless His precious people.

Yet our times are different. The acceleration of satanically inspired activity, the vast communication network for occult indoctrination, the proliferation of seductive spiritual counterfeits, and our ignorance of occult dangers have set the stage for a demonstration of evil that knows no precedent.

One day, maybe soon, our King will come and gather us to Himself. It could happen this year, before Americans face the persecution that His saints through the ages have endured. But if He delays, we had better prepare for spiritual battles as intense as God's people have ever fought. Paul's words could have been written for our times:

> ... be strong in the Lord and in the power of His might. Put on the whole armor of God, that ye may be able to stand against the wiles of the devil. For we wrestle not against flesh and blood, but against principalities, against powers, against the rulers of the darkness of this world, against spiritual wickedness in high places.
>
> Wherefore take unto you the whole armor of God, that ye may be able to withstand in the evil

day, and having done all, to stand. Stand therefore, having your loins girded about with truth,
and having on the breastplate of righteousness;
and your feet shod with the preparation of the
gospel of peace; above all, taking the shield of
faith, wherewith ye shall be able to quench all the
fiery darts of the wicked.

And take the helmet of salvation, and the sword
of the Spirit, which is the word of God; praying
always with all prayer and supplication in the
Spirit, and watching thereunto with all persever-
ance and supplication for all the saints (Ephesians
6:10-18).

Hidden in Christ

God's "armor" outlines the truths needed to expose and
counter all the main pagan deceptions that have seduced
people through the ages. But it's more than that. When we
choose to believe the truth about God and accept His provision for our sin, Christ our King not only fills us with His
holy life, but also "clothes" us with Himself (Galatians 3:27).
He not only covers us with Himself, but also makes us one
with Himself. We "abide" with Him and are hidden in Him.
While the neopagan's "sacred space" invites the forces of
evil, God's *holy place* shuts out the darkness, fills us with His
light, and surrounds us with His life.

"The night is far spent, the day is at hand," wrote Paul;
"let us therefore cast off the works of darkness and let us put
on the armor of light.... Put ye on the Lord Jesus Christ, and
make not provision for the flesh ... " (Romans 13:12,14).

I put on Christ not by rote recitation of the parts of the
armor but by affirming wonderful truths that first brought
me into an eternal love-relationship with the living God. For

my sovereign King who reigns over all—including the counterfeit powers of Satan—is not only the whole armor but also each individual part. He is:

- The *truth,* the filter and reference point for all I see and hear (John 14:6).

- My *righteousness,* who has cleansed me and continues to renew me daily as I confess my sins, so that I may stand spotless and without shame before my King (1 Corinthians 1:30).

- My *peace,* who assures me of His sovereignty, wisdom, and love (Ephesians 2:14).

- My *faith,* or trust, who shields me from doubt and despair (Acts 3:16; Psalm 71:5).

- My present and future *salvation,* who saves me today from every trial and will one day exchange this decaying, earthly body for a fresh, new, beautiful body (Psalm 62:2).

- The victorious *Word,* with power to win every battle (John 1:1,14).

Having revealed Himself to me, God seeks a response from me. He longs to give me all that He is and has, but He can only fill and clothe me when I come to Him in love, trust, humility, and surrender—the attitude of true worship. To live each day in His strength and confidence, I thank Him for the truths outlined in the armor. The first and primary truth— God's own revelation of Himself—is basic to all the rest, for the most dangerous deceptions are today's counterfeit gods and unholy distortions of His holy character. Remember, the Ten Commandments began with: "You shall have no other gods. . . ."

Next in importance is the truth about God's righteousness. In today's permissive climate, it's easy to trade God's view of sin for the world's view of goodness, then forget our need for the cross. Years ago I would remind my youngest son that the armor is not like a magic shield he can casually slip on in order to be safe anywhere he wanted to go. One day he asked if he could see a popular movie with some friends.

"No, I'd rather you didn't," I told him.

"Why not?" he asked.

"Because it makes occultism seem both fun and right," I answered.

"But I'll put on the armor."

"It won't help. When you go somewhere that you shouldn't, you disobey God and lose the breastplate of righteousness. You're never safe if you go somewhere Jesus wouldn't want you to go."

David got the message and stayed home. He knew that by himself he was no match for occult forces. But with God he was on the winning side.

The chart below shows the main truths of the armor. Notice how they counter today's most popular religious lies. Let them remind you that our God reigns, that our righteousness comes from Him and not from ourselves, that He is our peace in a troubled world, and that we can count on Him to save us no matter what storms we face. Hide those truths in your heart[36] and pray them back to Him in all your spiritual battles. Then trust Him to provide the wisdom and strength needed to persevere until He brings the victory.

An Eternal Perspective

Keep in mind that our Shepherd doesn't promise to rescue us *out of* trouble, but He will give us winning strength

The Armor of God

EACH PIECE	OLD (CHRISTIAN) PARADIGM	NEW (PAGAN) PARADIGM
Put On:	*Know and Affirm:*	*Recognize and Resist:*
Belt of TRUTH	His sovereignty, love, wisdom, and holiness. (Deut. 4:39; Psa. 18:1-3)	Pantheistic, monistic, polytheistic gods and goddesses.
Breastplate of RIGHTEOUSNESS	Jesus Christ and His blood, which cleanses us from sin. The cross which frees us from bondage to selfish nature. (Rom. 3:23,24, 6:23; Gal. 2:20,21; 1 John 1:9)	The natural goodness, connectedness, and sacredness of all life.
Sandals of PEACE	Our peace through our union and ongoing relationship with Jesus Christ. (Eph. 2:14; John 14:27, 16:33)	Peace through occult practices and union with a cosmic force of nature spirits.
Shield of FAITH	Our continual trust in God, His Word, and His promises. (Rom. 4:18-21; Heb. 11:1; 1 Pet. 1:6,7)	Trust in Self, inner wisdom, dreams, visions, gods, goddess, cosmic forces, coincidence, etc.
Helmet of SALVATION	God's promises of daily and eternal salvation in Jesus Christ. (Psa. 16; 23; 2 Peter 1:3,4; 1 John 3:1-3)	Evolving spiritually by growing in consciousness and staying tuned to the cosmic mind.
Sword of the Spirit, His WORD	The power of God's Word to counter deception and triumph over spiritual foes. (Heb. 4:12; 2 Cor. 10:3-5; 1 Pet. 3:15)	The power of thoughts, words, and affirmations to change reality and direct spiritual forces.

in the midst of trouble. He doesn't promise to insulate us against the storms of the world,[37] but His armor will protect us against the cruel and blinding deceptions of Satan, whose arrows use the circumstances of the world to crush and destroy us far more than any storm ever could.

If I refuse to suffer with Jesus, I cannot be His friend and disciple. Since I'm one with Him, I must go where He goes. Since He hides me in Himself, I become part of His life. I share His heart, thoughts, and concerns. I feel the winds that beat on Him. Together we bear the stab of rejection. The very circumstances I would avoid He will use to make me a living proof of His triumph over Satan's powers and the world's pressures.[38]

"If any man will come after me," says Jesus, "let him deny himself, and take up his cross daily, and follow me. For whosoever will save his life shall lose it, but whosoever will lose his life for my sake, the same shall save it" (Luke 9:23,24).

Dietrich Bonhoeffer understood the meaning of self-denial. During Hitler's reign he saw what happens in churches that compromise truth and exploit God's grace. He knew the inhuman cruelties of tyrants who despise God and trust occult forces. Yet he stood "unbroken before his tormentors," and "died with admirable calmness and dignity."[39]

Bonhoeffer's treasured classic, *The Cost of Discipleship*, shows the way of the disciple, the Christian who wears the armor and follows the King. In it the beloved martyr wrote:

> To deny oneself is to be aware only of Christ and no more of self, to see only Him who goes before and no more the road which is too hard for us. . . . All that self-denial can say is: "He leads the way, keep close to Him. . . . "

If our Christianity has ceased to be serious about discipleship, if we have watered down the gospel into emotional uplift which makes no costly demands and which fails to distinguish between natural and Christian existence, then we cannot help regarding the cross as an ordinary everyday calamity.... We have then forgotten that the cross means rejection and shame as well as suffering....

When Christ calls a man, He bids him come and die.... The wounds and scars he receives in the fray are living tokens of this participation in the cross of his Lord....

Christ transfigures for His own ... the hour of their mortal agony by granting them the unspeakable assurance of His presence. In the hour of the cruelest torture they bear for His sake, they are made partakers in the perfect joy and bliss of fellowship with Him. To bear the cross proves to be the only way of triumphing over suffering.[40]

Long ago Jesus told His friends, "If they persecute me, they will persecute you." This promise makes no sense to Christians who love the world more than our King. Nor does it touch churches that conform to changing cultures rather than to God's changeless truth. But to those who love Him, it brings a comforting reassurance of intimacy with Him. "I count all things but loss for the excellency of the knowledge of Christ Jesus my Lord," exulted Paul, "... that I may know him, and the power of his resurrection, and the fellowship of his sufferings ... " (Philippians 3:8,10).

Today as always, God reminds us that discipleship means separation unto Him[41]—an intolerant notion to those who seek global oneness based on earth-centered spirituality. We can expect "reproaches, persecutions, distresses for Christ's sake," but God shows us how to overcome. His gentle voice still whispers to those who will hear, "My grace is sufficient for thee, for my strength is made perfect in weakness" (2 Corinthians 12:10,9).

Blessing us far beyond human understanding, our Lord opens our eyes to see Him. Now we can "run with patience the race that is set before us, looking unto Jesus, the author and finisher of our faith, who for the joy that was set before him endured the cross ... " (Hebrews 12:1,2).

Polycarp's Confidence

A story I heard years ago deepened my understanding of this eternal joy. I don't remember the exact words, but I'll never forget the message. Back in the second century A.D., Roman authorities told the beloved bishop Polycarp to stop telling people the truth about Jesus Christ and His warnings about pagan gods and goddesses. Polycarp refused.

"Then we'll take all your possessions," they told him.

"Go ahead," he said. "My God has promised to supply all I need according to His riches in glory. He will take care of me."[42]

"If you don't stop preaching, we'll take your wife and children from you," they threatened.

"They belong to God and He will take care of them," he answered, "and I will spend all eternity in heaven with them."

"Then we'll kill you."

"That would be best of all, for I would go immediately into the presence of my Lord. Nothing could be more wonderful!"

The officials did kill Polycarp, but his martyrdom only magnified the peace and joy of his eternal perspective. His faith lives on as a rich reminder to us that when we are joined to Christ, we have an eternal and imperishable treasure in heaven. This assurance doesn't diminish our present life; it only makes it richer and fuller. "For to me, to live is Christ and to die is gain," said Paul. Living or dying, he enjoyed heavenly citizenship. Either way he would serve the God he loved. Death would have been the easier option, for while he lived, he was stoned, imprisoned, chained, tortured, starved, and beaten for his faith. Yet he radiated hope:

> For which cause we faint not; but though our outward man perish, yet the inward man is renewed day by day. For our light affliction, which is but for a moment, worketh for us a far more exceeding and eternal weight of glory, while we look not at the things which are seen, but at the things which are not seen; for the things which are seen are temporal, but the things which are not seen are eternal (2 Corinthians 4:16-18).

3

The Psychic Guide Dogs

Bob Anderson

When thou art come into the land which the Lord thy God giveth thee, thou shalt not learn to do after the abominations of those nations. There shall not be found among you anyone that maketh his son or his daughter pass to through the fire, or that useth divination, or an observer of times, or an enchanter, or a witch, or a charmer, or a consulter of mediums, or a wizard, or a necromancer. For all that do these things are an abomination unto the Lord; and because of these abominations the Lord thy God doth drive them out from before thee. Thou shalt be perfect with the Lord thy God.

–Deuteronomy 18:9-13

Today's world confronts a strange and growing paradox that could well mark a pivotal point in human history. Even as the scientific and technological advancement which ushered in the space age accelerates at an exponential rate, we are witnessing far and away the greatest occult explosion of all time. The evidence seems to indicate that something of unusual historic significance is in process.[1]

Rise in Occultism

The Bible absolutely condemns occult practices of any kind. The word "occult" comes from the Latin word *occultus*, which means "dark, secret, hidden, or mysterious." It expressly alludes to the intrusion of a spirit realm—a fourth dimension—into our three-dimensional world. Throughout the Old Testament, God repeatedly warned His people about participating in such activity. In much the same way, the New Testament forbids such actions (Galatians 5:20). Today, however, occultism besieges America, once considered a Chrisian nation.

I am not the first to point out that the New Age movement, so prevalent today, is anything but new. Historians trace New Age roots back thousands of years to the occult religions of the Babylonians and India's pantheistic (all-is-God) beliefs of the Hindus. Hinduism claims to be the world's oldest religion. However, New Age beliefs ultimately go back to the beginning of time. It was in the Garden of Eden that Satan beguiled Eve through his subtlety, convincing her that she and Adam could become as gods, knowing good and evil.

The serpent was more crafty than any of the wild animals the Lord God had made. The Bible tells us in Genesis 3:1-6 that the serpent said to the woman, "Did God really say, 'You must not eat from any tree in the garden'?"

The woman replied to the serpent, "We may eat from the trees in the garden, but God did say, 'You must not eat fruit from the tree that is in the middle of the garden, and you must not touch it or you will die.'"

"You will not surely die," the serpent said to the woman, "for God knows that when you eat of it your eyes will be opened, and you will be like God, knowing good and evil." When the woman saw that the fruit of the tree was good for food and pleasing to the eye, and also desirable for gaining wisdom, she took some and ate it. She also gave some to her husband, who was with her, and he ate it.

New Agers teach the same lies that Satan dispensed at Eden:

1. God's Word cannot be trusted (verses 1,4,5).

2. Man does not have to die (verse 4).

3. Man can become a god (verse 5).

4. Man can evolve through hidden knowledge (verse 6).

Satan is the author of this so called "movement," and all of the thousands of other cults in the world today as well. His goal is to deceive the world through his emissaries of darkness who appear as angels of light (2 Corinthians 11:13-15).

Encompassing thousands of autonomous (and sometimes contradictory) beliefs, organizations, and procedures, "New Age movement" is simply an umbrella term that masks its devious teachings and practices that have greatly influenced our society as a whole. Packaged as the latest advance in science, medicine, psychology and physical fitness (thus making it more palatable to the American mind), the New Age movement has made large gains in our technologically oriented society.

Christian apologists and cult experts have been warning us for years about the perils of occult activity. The warnings have gone largely unheeded, however, and New Age and other occult practices have become commonplace in America today. The Pledge of Allegiance still proclaims that we are "one nation under God"–but which god? New Age beliefs and practices have blitzed America, ranging from goddess and nature worship to reincarnation, psychics, UFOs, and Astral Projection (out-of-body experiences). Furthermore, New Agers and other enemies of the biblical gospel have tried in our schools, on television, and in other public arenas to lump Christianity with Santa Claus, the Easter bunny, and other childhood fantasies. At the same time they deem shamanism, witchcraft, Native American superstitions, and other occult beliefs worthy of our respect and admiration.

Purveyors of Delusion

Pluralism has led to great confusion in our society. Challenging the validity of someone's spiritual or religious belief is no longer politically correct, no matter how absurd that belief or doctrine might be. The social engineers now ask that we accept all religions as equally valid. But if, as they maintain, all religions are equal and all ultimately lead to God, why do we need so many new ones? And why don't these new religions at all resemble the old ones? It has been hard enough for many people to distinguish between Baptists, Lutherans, Pentecostals, and Catholics. But now they are being offered everything from the Aquarian Gospel to Zen Buddhism to examine. As a society we are cajoled, deluded, beguiled, and seduced into believing and accepting occultism under the cloak of tolerance and religious pluralism.

The problem with the growth of pluralism is that it reduces the authenticity of any one religious practice. Christianity becomes merely one of many alternatives. This explains in part why we now have more than 5000 cults in

America, with tens of millions of followers. It also accounts for the fact that about one out of every four Americans has now embraced a belief in reincarnation. Another revealing statistic comes from a poll conducted by George Barna in 1993:

> About four out of every ten adults strongly concur that when Christians, Jews, Buddhists, and others pray to their god, all of those individuals are actually praying to the same god, but simply use different names for that deity.[2]

Presidential candidate and author/broadcast journalist Pat Buchanan writes, "Americans of left and right no longer share the same religion, the same values, the same codes of morality; we only inhabit the same piece of land."[3]

The psychic guide dogs, who lead the way through the metaphysical realm, are found at virtually every level of culture—the spiritually blind leading the spiritually blind. Statistics show a marked increase in psychic interest. Some 70 percent of baby boomers believe in psychic powers. Some 67 percent of American adults claim to have had a psychic experience such as extrasensory perception.[4] Hollywood actors and entertainers, such as Dionne Warwick and Billy Dee Williams, star in television programs urging people to call "America's top professional psychics." A popular New Age magazine, *Body, Mind & Spirit*, recently proclaimed, "Now with a single phone call, you can choose for yourself from among the country's leading Master Psychics including: ASTROLOGERS ... NUMEROLOGISTS ... DREAM INTERPRETERS ... TAROT CARD READERS ... CHANNELERS ... PAST LIFE THERAPISTS ... CLAIRVOYANTS ... AURA READERS ... and HEALERS."[5]

All of this is available for a mere $3.95 per minute on a convenient 900 number.[6] Today's psychic hotlines and mystic infomercials, as well as movies, documentaries, and television programs that frequently promote occult phenomena, attest to the fact that we live in a time that must be very close to the end of the age.

God has spoken clearly in His Word about occult workings. The Old Testament book of Deuteronomy deals with the detestable practices and idolatrous customs of the Canaanites. Through the prophet Moses, God warned His people not to participate in the evil practices of those nations they were about to possess. However, many of those same practices, or modified versions thereof, are now commonplace in America.

Let us examine some of the things that God labeled detestable in Deuteronomy 18:9-13 in light of what is happening in America today.

Abortion

First, the Lord cautions His people *not to sacrifice our sons or daughters in the fire.* The Canaanites and Ammonites reverenced many pagan gods. Among them was Molech (Leviticus 18:21, Jeremiah 32:35), whose worship was accompanied by the burning of children offered as a sacrifice by their own parents.[7] All life is precious to God, particularly children: "Suffer the little children to come unto me, and forbid them not, for of such is the kingdom of God" (Mark 10:14).

Although here in America we do not legally throw living babies into the fire, we do kill 4000 of them every day in an equally repugnant ceremony called abortion. This highly profitable industry uses many methods of destruction. Most of them are much more hideous than death by fire. Partial birth abortion, for example, employs an instrument that sucks the brains out of the partially born baby before crushing its skull. Remains of abortions are disposed of in a variety of ways that may at times include burning. Based on current figures, by the year 2000 we will be approaching 50 million abortions in the United States alone. In a short 27 years (1973-2000), we will have aborted 30 *times* the number of Americans lost in all U.S. wars.[8] The same spirit that led the Ammonites to sacrifice their children to a pagan god now leads Americans to sacrifice more than 1.5 million babies each year through abortion.

Astrology

In the same verse of Deuteronomy, God warns against *divination* or *sorcery*. Divination was the act of foretelling future events, an imitation of prophecy. Today divination and sorcery are found in many New Age activities. One of the most prevalent of New Age divination practices is astrology. Astrology, or observing times, is a contemporary myth that America widely accepts. In 1975 a Gallup poll showed that more than 32 million Americans believed "that the stars influence people's lives" and that many of them consult their daily or weekly horoscopes. Estimates of the number of astrologers reached as high as 10,000 who practice it full-time and 175,000 who engage in it part-time. Nine years later, in 1984, a Gallup poll revealed that among teenagers (ages 13-18), 55 percent believed in astrology. This figure was up from 40 percent in 1978. A 1988 Gallup poll showed that 10 percent of evangelicals believe in astrology.[9]

Just as many people once believed that the stars were gods, many today believe that the positions of the stars and planets at the time of one's birth determine one's character, abilities, and destiny. These people identify the document that aspires to accomplish this as the horoscope, which also serves as the doorway through which many people enter pagan religions.

Many of today's astrologers frankly admit that ancient Babylonians developed their craft, just as they invented about every other type of divination known to man. More than 80 percent of all newspapers in America now carry horoscope columns. According to a past White House source, former President Ronald Reagan and his wife, Nancy (both of whom are considered by many to be godly people), are very superstitious. Nancy is reported to have consulted horoscopes and a California astrologer before making major decisions affecting both the Reagans' private and political lives.[10]

Necromancy in the White House

This was not the first time that occultism had occurred in the White House. A TV network reported that Mary Todd Lincoln held seances in an upstairs room—a practice which President Lincoln apparently tolerated with amusement. It certainly is not amusing to God, who labels the practice of contacting spirits of the dead (necromancy) detestable.

More recently, first lady Hillary Rodham Clinton used New Age psychic Jean Houston, Codirector of the Foundation for Mind Research, to talk to the spirit of Eleanor Roosevelt. Reports say that Mrs. Clinton had talks with Roosevelt and Mohandas Gandhi.

Mrs. Clinton said, "Now I'm sure that there will be a talk show host somewhere who will point out with great glee that I have gone over the edge and am talking to myself and to Mrs. Roosevelt on a regular basis, but I believe the world, and particularly our country, would be better off if we all spent a little time talking with Mrs. Roosevelt...."[11]

Interestingly, when Houston suggested that Mrs. Clinton next have a conversation with Jesus Christ, the first lady declined, saying that it would be "too personal."[12] Incredibly, the United Methodist Bishop of Arkansas, Richard

Wilke, endorsed Mrs. Clinton's involvement with necromancy, saying, "I think it's marvelous that she's having experiences like this," adding that Mrs. Clinton was "one of the most profound lay theologians in the United Methodist Church."[13] This is simply further evidence of how deficient we are in biblical discernment and godly wisdom among our mainline denominations.

Spiritual Frauds

What position should Christians take when discussions of astrology and other forms of divination arise? Do the stars shape our destiny? Are there unseen influences in the unconscious mind related to the position of the planets in their orbits? Again, we must go to the Bible. God branded these practices as detestable. In other words, they were particularly offensive to Him. When Israel wanted to know God's divine will, they were commanded to avoid the magic and superstitious practices of the Canaanites. Instead, they were to wait upon the Lord, who would raise up a prophet from among them. God's prophets were not primarily to tell the future, but to instruct and reprove people in the Lord's name. God intended prophecies and miracles primarily as a sign to establish the prophet's credentials, and God's prophets were accurate 100 percent of the time when they prophesied (Deuteronomy 18:20-22). Anything less than total accuracy resulted in death by stoning for the false prophet.

Check the record of any modern-day astrologer or psychic, even the famous Jeane Dixon, and you will discover that, unlike God's prophets, they are extremely inaccurate. Yet many people believe Dixon to be a good Christian. In her book *Yesterday, Today and Forever* Dixon asserts that the Holy Spirit guided her in uniting Christianity with astrology. "As I understand it ... the Catholic Church and many other religious bodies as well have never condemned the study of

Astrology...." Dixon says. "I have never experienced any conflict between my faith and the guidance I receive from my church on the one hand and the knowledge I find in the stars on the other ... Actually, much of what I know I learned from a Jesuit priest, who was one of the best-informed scholars I ever met."[14]

Deuteronomy 13:1-5 informs us that even a prophet who prophesies correctly, but leads a person to worship other gods, is a deceiver and a betrayer of God. We are not to follow that prophet. Most prophecies of modern-day psychics do not come to pass. Deuteronomy 18:22 states:

> When a prophet speaketh in the name of the
> Lord, if the thing follow not nor come to pass,
> that is the thing which the Lord hath not spoken,
> but the prophet hath spoken it presumptuously;
> thou shalt not be afraid of him.

Ruth Montgomery, Dixon's biographer and close personal friend, is the first to admit that Dixon has made false prophecies, but (in spite of evidence to the contrary) she says those errors are infrequent: "Jeane made a few forecasts that failed to occur.... She predicted that Red China would plunge the world into war over Quemoy and Matsu in October of 1958; she thought that labor leader Walter Reuther would actively seek the presidency in 1964."[15] According to the Word of God, the sign of a false prophet is false prophecy. Jeane Dixon qualifies as a false prophet.

There is also an occult connection to Dixon. For example, she uses a crystal ball and telepathy plus astrology in her activities, all of which Scripture condemns. Furthermore, her call to become a prophet was dispensed by a fortune-telling gypsy.

Does any scientific evidence support astrology? Do the sun-signs really influence our lives? In test after test, the answer to both questions is no. One experiment involving nearly 3000 married couples and 500 divorced couples tested compatibility based on astrological signs. The results showed that astrological signs did not significantly alter the outcome of either group. Those born under the "compatible" signs married and divorced as often as those born under the "incompatible" signs.[16]

Astrologers have also claimed that certain professions, such as politicians and scientists, tend to be born under one certain sun-sign or another. In other words, they link a person's sign to his or her chances of succeeding in a particular field of endeavor. Yet research involving more than 16,600 scientists and nearly 6500 politicians detected no relationship between the sun-signs and the particular vocation in which a person worked. Sun-signs among the two occupations mentioned were as arbitrary as for society at large.[17] Robert A. Morey declares in his book *Horoscopes and the Christian,* " . . . it is idolatry to ascribe to the stars that which belongs *only* to the God who created them."

Witchcraft

In America, witchcraft has received a great revival of interest and participation. Occult book stores, which now proliferate in this land, are busily trying to satisfy the immense interest for books and other information on witchcraft and black magic. Browse through any mall bookstore and you will find an entire section of occult books that children of any age can acquire. These occult sections are typically much larger than the Christian sections. Public libraries also have great demand from people with an ardent curiosity in books dealing with witchcraft, demonology, and the occult.

However, the Bible calls sorcery witchcraft, and strictly forbids the practice (Deuteronomy 18:10; Exodus 22:18).

Witchcraft was a means for extracting information or guidance from a pagan god. The word describes the activity of Balaam the soothsayer, or professional prophet, who was hired to curse Israel. It also describes the woman at Endor who brought up the spirit of Samuel. All the major prophets condemned witchcraft.

Yet, here again, some witches and sorcerers have tried to sanitize their practice by calling it "white" witchcraft or "white" magic as opposed to "black" witchcraft and "black" magic. Those who use such terminology are merely trying to conceal their works of darkness with religious or spiritual words and symbols. White magicians teach that there is only one source of universal power. Black magicians, on the other hand, believe in a good source and a bad source of power. White magic is nothing more than Satan transforming himself into an angel of light (2 Corinthians 11:14).

Anton LeVey, author of the *Satanic Bible* and Pope of the first Church of Satan in San Francisco, California, has said explicitly that to believe that there is any such thing as white magic is mythology. There is no such thing as white magic, according to LeVey. All of it has its source in occult psychic power and has nothing to do with God.[18]

Satanism

Some who practice black magic have made a pact with the devil. Some occult churches right here in America require submission to Satan as a requirement for membership. Maury Terry, an investigative reporter, writes in his book *The Ultimate Evil*:

> There is compelling evidence of the existence of a nationwide network of satanic cults, some aligned more closely than others. Some are purveying narcotics; others have branched into child pornography and violent sadomasochistic crime,

including murder. I am concerned that the toll of innocent victims will steadily mount unless law enforcement officials recognize the threat and face it.[19]

The Bible teaches of a literal being called Satan who is out to deceive the world:

The great dragon was cast out, that serpent of old, called the Devil and Satan, who deceives the whole world; he was cast to the earth, and his angels were cast out with him (Revelation 12:9 NKJV).

The devil is not only real, but his ultimate goal is our destruction (John 10:10). He will use any deception at his disposal, but generally uses the most subtle deceit (2 Corinthians 11:3,4).

Spirit Guides

A *wizard* is a person who has a familiar spirit. In the Old Testament, a familiar spirit was a spirit that had frequent communication with the wizard. New Agers call this practice "channeling." This is a term for spirit possession. A familiar spirit, called a "spirit guide," speaks through the channeler (automatic speaking) or writes through him (automatic writing). According to reliable sources, there are thousands of channelers in America today. Some, like J. Z. Knight (who channels a 35,000-year-old spirit called Ramtha), have made enormous amounts of money. Knight owns a 50-acre ranch in Yelma, Washington and earned at one time a reported 4 million dollars a year from her various Ramtha enterprises. The estate in Yelma evolved into a New Age mecca, with a 2-million-dollar, 10,000-square-foot house and a giant maze where Ramtha initiates develop their relationship with the tutelary spirit.[20] Like wizards and channelers, many psychics and occultists also acknowledge that their powers come from spirits they have contacted, whether they initially realized it or not. Channelers, however, knowingly and willingly allow spirits to control them.

Devil Music

Rock music has become an occult religion to many people. At some of their concerts, the heavy-metal group Black Sabbath has given altar calls for Satan, inviting young people to come forward to make Satan their lord. Lyrics in their song "Master of Reality" call Satan the "Lord of this world" and "your confessor now." Ozzy Osbourne, son of a Christian minister and former lead singer for Black Sabbath, has also given an altar call for Satan at one of his concerts.[21]

Some members of the group Iron Maiden openly admit that they are dabbling in the occult, including witchcraft.[22] One Iron Maiden concert in Portland, Oregon, opened with the words "Welcome to Satan's sanctuary." Glenn Tipton of the group Judas Priest confessed that when he goes on stage, he goes crazy: "It's like someone else takes my body."[23] Rock music has become a purveyor of occultic and satanic activities. Some of the most common themes found in this style of music are illegal drugs, illicit sex, violence, incest, rebellion against authority, and rebellion against God. There is little question as to who energies this activity.

Occultism and the Movie Industry

Not only has Satanism affected rock music, but its presence has been heavily felt in the American motion picture industry. Movies such as *The Exorcist, Rosemary's Baby, The Amityville Horror,* and *Poltergeist* exalt and glorify Satan. Jesus Christ, meanwhile, has been degraded. For example, Martin Scorsese's film *The Last Temptation of Christ* depicts Jesus in a highly offensive manner. The film portrays the Son of God as a sinner, a coward, and a homosexual who stumbles through life, having an affair with Mary Magdalene along the way before being executed for his troubles.

Perhaps the most dangerous movies, however, are not the blatant ones just mentioned. Most people recognize those movies as flagrant attacks on Christianity. The more subtle films that plant seeds of occultism in the minds of our unwary youth are much more dangerous, in the opinion of many critics. Most of the films of George Lucas and Steven Spielberg would fall into this category. Enormously successful movies such as the *Stars Wars* trilogy, *Close Encounters, Poltergeist, Raiders of the Lost Ark, Indiana Jones, Ghost,* and *Cocoon,* to name just a few, are rooted in Eastern occult religion. We are raising an entire generation of young people who are unaware that their minds are being filled with Eastern religious thought.

God's Final Warning?

The spiritual roots upon which this nation was built have eroded from every vestige of society. The Bible has been removed from public life and replaced by occultic and pagan ideas of the past, even though America achieved greatness because it was founded upon Christian principles and values. But God is not mocked; if He brought judgment upon nations in the past that turned to occultism, how can He ignore a land where 30 percent of our children are born out of wedlock, where 1.5 million unborn babies are murdered in their mother's womb each year, where an estimated 30 million people belong to cults, and another 60 million believe in or practice some form of occultism?

We desperately need to heed the words of Scripture:

> If thou do at all forget the Lord thy God, and walk after other gods and serve them and worship

them, I testify against you this day that ye shall surely perish. As the nations which the Lord destroyeth before your face, so shall ye perish, because ye would not be obedient unto the voice of the Lord your God (Deuteronomy 8:19,20).

4

Tidal Wave of Apostasy

Grant Jeffrey

"He carried me away in the Spirit into the wilderness. And I saw a woman sitting on a scarlet beast which was full of names of blasphemy, having seven heads and ten horns. The woman was arrayed in purple and scarlet, and adorned with gold and precious stones and pearls, having in her hand a golden cup full of abominations and the filthiness of her fornication. And on her forehead a name was written: Mystery, Babylon the Great, the mother of harlots and of the abominations of the earth"

—Revelation 17:3-5 NKJV*

These verses in John's Revelation warn about the pagan apostate church that will rise after the true followers of Christ

---

* All Scripture quotations in this chapter are taken from the New King James Version. Used by permission. See credit line on copyright page.

are taken to heaven by Jesus Christ. During the rapture, hundreds of millions of true Christians from Protestant, Catholic, and Orthodox churches will be instantaneously translated to heaven. However, among these churches are hundreds of millions of people who will remain on earth during the tribulation period because they had never truly repented of their sins and trusted completely in Jesus Christ as their Lord and Savior. Jesus warned, "Not everyone who says to Me, 'Lord, Lord,' shall enter the kingdom of heaven, but he who does the will of My Father in heaven" (Matthew 7:21).

In the book of Revelation, one of the angels spoke to the prophet John as follows: "Come, I will show you the judgment of the great harlot who sits on many waters, with whom the kings of the earth committed fornication, and the inhabitants of the earth were made drunk with the wine of her fornication" (Revelation 17:1,2). This key verse indicates the universal, worldwide nature of the pagan apostate church that will be allied to the rising power of the Antichrist during the first 3 1/2 years of the tribulation period. The ecumenical church will provide propaganda support for the consolidation of the Antichrist's New World Order. During her period of great power this church will ruthlessly persecute anyone who refuses to join in her pagan worship rituals.

John described his vision of this coming inquisition by Mystery Babylon against those new Jewish and Gentile tribulation believers who will become martyrs for their faith in Christ during this terrible tribulation period: "I saw the woman, drunk with the blood of the saints and with the blood of the martyrs of Jesus" (Revelation 17:6). Obviously, Mystery Babylon, the apostate pagan church of the last days, will not develop overnight. Such an ecumenical organization, involving many diverse religious groups, will be created by negotiation and conferences over a number of years leading up to the beginning of the seven-year tribulation period. It is therefore quite probable that we will witness the initial steps toward this one-world church of the last days before the rapture takes the Christians home to heaven.

Mystery Babylon and Rome

I realize that there are many born-again Catholics who are grieved in their spirit when a Bible teacher comments on the prophecies that reveal Rome as the headquarters of the Mystery Babylon religion of the last days. The only thing I can say is that I do not feel any animosity toward Catholics as individuals. However, I do feel strongly about the unbiblical heresies that have led hundreds of millions of people over the last 1500 years to endanger their eternal souls. While it is true that there are many born-again Catholics, we cannot ignore the profound gulf that exists between the teaching of the Roman Catholic Church and the teaching of Jesus Christ as found in the Bible. The most fundamental difference is the ultimate source of spiritual truth. As the Roman Catholic Council of Trent declared in 1564 (it has never been rescinded), Rome believes that the truth concerning salvation, etc., is determined solely by the popes and church councils, not by the Bible as the Word of God.

In contrast, as a Protestant Christian, I recognize that the only authoritative source of divine knowledge about salvation, etc., is the inspired Word of God. In addition, while Rome declares that people cannot be saved apart from membership in the Roman Catholic Church, the sacraments, the confessional, and the last rites, the Bible assures us that we are saved solely based on our faith and trust in Jesus Christ's completed atonement for our sins that He paid for us on the cross 2000 years ago. The Roman Catholic Cardinal D'Allen stated that the Protestant focus on the Bible's authority was an obstacle to the ecumenical union together of all churches of the world. Cardinal D'Allen declared, "The Reformation was a Protestant revolt disrupting the unity of the church. Union will take place when the rebels accept the authority of the Pope and abandon the authority of Scripture. Rome can accept nothing short of this."

What is the proper identification of this mysterious symbol of religious persecution, Babylon the Great, the Mother of Harlots? In Revelation 17:7,9 the angel tells the prophet John, "I will tell you the mystery of the woman and of the beast that carries her, which has the seven heads and the ten horns.... Here is the mind which has wisdom: The seven heads are seven mountains on which the woman sits." This inspired statement that the woman sits on seven mountains or hills is the clearest possible declaration that the final apostate church will be based in Rome. While the apostate Babylonian church of the tribulation period will involve all religions joined together, the Revelation prophecy indicates clearly that this worldwide church organization will have its headquarters in Rome.

Coins issued by the Roman government during the first century of the Christian era carried the motto "the city on seven hills" as the well-known designation of the capital of the Roman Empire. Virtually every one of the classical Roman writers and poets, including Virgil, Horace, and Ovid, referred to Rome as the "city of seven hills." Interestingly, some of these classical writers referred to Rome as *Septiceps*, the seven-headed city, which is virtually identical with the phrase used by the prophet John. It is also fascinating to note that the angel described the apostate harlot church as wearing her name on her forehead: "On her forehead a name was written: MYSTERY, BABYLON THE GREAT" (Revelation 17:5). According to the Roman writer Marcus Seneca in *Controversia* (chapter V.i), the harlots of that ancient city used to identify themselves to their customers by wearing their names on a label on their foreheads.

A Roman Catholic commentary on the prophecies of Revelation published in 1956 by Bernard F. Leonard called *The Book of Destiny* also identified this city as Rome. Although there are few Catholic commentaries on Revelation, it is fascinating to note that *The Book of Destiny* was approved by the Roman Catholic censor with the words *Nihil Obstat* and contained the imprimatur of the bishop of Sioux City, Iowa. Leonard writes: "This great harlot is a city whose apostasy from the true faith is a monstrous thing. This may point to Rome. Rome is the Holy City of Christ, the center of His eternal kingdom.... And the apostasy of this city, and her becoming the head of an empire that would lead all possible nations and peoples into Antichrist-worship, would indeed merit for her the title of THE GREAT HARLOT. The apostles called ancient Rome 'Babylon' (1 Peter 5:13). So the conclusion is near that the great harlot of the future shall be Rome." It is interesting that this book is still sold in many Roman Catholic bookstores.

Pope John Paul II and the Last Days

Karol Wojtyla of Poland was elected pope in October 1978. While he is a strong supporter of world government, he is not the first pope to promote this idea. His predecessor pope, Paul VI, wrote a Papal Encyclical that called on the nations to abandon sovereignty to form a world government. Pope John Paul II is constantly calling for the nations to abandon their opposition to world government. Malachi Martin, a Jesuit writer who is very close to the pope and has excellent sources in the Vatican, wrote in his book *The Keys of This Blood* about the pope's plans for a one-world government. Martin says that the pope "has plans and is working for a genuinely geopolitical structure: a One World Government that is both viable and humanly acceptable." John Paul II believes that "the establishment of an order based on justice and peace is vitally needed today as a moral imperative valid for all peoples and regimes . . . this is the only path possible."

The Fatima Vision

A curious bit of information was recently revealed about the thinking and motivation of Pope John Paul II. Several books, including Malachi Martin's *The Keys of This Blood*, revealed that the political and religious agenda of the pope is strongly influenced by various predictions regarding the future of the papacy. One of these is the so-called "vision of Fatima." When he became pope, in 1978, John Paul II was given access to the secret message of Fatima, which Catholics believe was entrusted to the Church through a series of visions granted to several children in Fatima, Portugal, beginning on May 13, 1917. Supposedly, a vision of Mary appeared to three peasant children in six different visions over a five-month period in 1917, and they claimed she gave them three secret messages.

Let me explain that I do not believe that the Fatima vision is a genuine prophecy from God. Regardless of the apparent sincerity of the witnesses, the vision's message is absolutely in opposition to the Bible. Fundamentally, this vision elevates Mary and demands that the world, and Russia especially, "must be consecrated to Mary." There is not a single passage in the Bible that supports such a demand. On the contrary, we are commanded to worship God alone. Isaiah warned, "I am the Lord, that is My name; and My glory I will not give to another" (Isaiah 42:8). The significance of the Fatima vision (and the Malachi vision, discussed later) is that they give us an insight into the thinking and motivation of John Paul II as one of the key individuals moving our world toward the one-world government prophesied in the Scriptures.

The first two of these secret messages of Fatima were revealed during the decades following 1917. The first vision supposedly warned that mankind as a whole was proceeding down a path of sinful rebellion that would lead millions to an eternity in hell. Then, during the 1930s, the second message was gradually released to the public, warning about the beginning of World War II and the growing physical and spiritual danger to the West from the godless Communist state of Russia. The third vision was held in total secrecy until 1944.

At that time the sole survivor of the children who witnessed the apparition was still living. She was commanded by her bishop to write the secret message on a piece of paper, seal it in an envelope, and deliver it to the Vatican. The child witness, now an adult named Lucia, claimed that Mary demanded that the third message remain secret until 1960, when the pope at that time should open it and act on its instructions. This third vision, known as the Third Secret of Fatima, is believed to concern the military and political dangers that would afflict the West in the closing years of this millennium. While the actual wording of the Third Secret remains known to a very few people, the general outline of its message emerged during the papacy of John Paul II.

This last vision of Fatima is apparently in three parts. First, if the Vatican neglects to take the actions demanded, physical catastrophes—wars, earthquakes, floods, et cetera—will supposedly destroy the nations and peoples as a punishment for rejecting God's laws. Second, a refusal to comply with the message's demands would trigger a growth of atheism and massive worldwide apostasy from the Catholic

Church. In addition, Russia's godless ideology would sweep throughout the world, causing millions to lose their faith. This will conclude with a devastating world war that will bring mankind to the very edge of extinction. However, a remnant will survive the holocaust and gradually revive in the next millennium. The third part of the Fatima message supposedly promises that this devastating war, followed by spiritual catastrophe, could be averted if, first, the pope and his bishops will publish the warnings of Fatima in 1960, and second, the pope and cardinals will "consecrate" Russia to the Virgin Mary. This continuing focus on Mary rather than the Bible's command to focus on Jesus Christ convinces me that the Fatima vision is not sent by God but is simply one more deception launched by Satan.

The pope in 1960, John XXIII, allegedly read the Fatima message but rejected its authority and refused to carry out its instructions. According to Malachi Martin, Pope John XXIII explained his refusal to his papal successors in these words: "These [predictions] do not concern our times." The next pope, Paul VI, also refused to comply with the demands of the vision. In a fascinating comment on their actions, Pope John Paul II told one interviewer, "Given the seriousness of its contents, my predecessors in the Petrine Office diplomatically preferred to postpone publication [of the vision] so as not to encourage the world power of Communism to make certain moves."

It is fascinating to note that these popes believed the West was so vulnerable at the time that Russia's dictators would have accelerated their plans to launch their attack on Western nations if they had known the precise words of the Fatima warning. In 1957, Cardinal Ottaviani, a very politically astute churchman, told Malachi Martin that the dangerous "Secret" must be buried "in the most hidden, the deepest, the most obscure and inaccessible place on earth."

Pope John Paul II and the Fatima Message

During his painful convalescence following the assassination attempt, John Paul II spent hours studying the secret Fatima message. He tried to obey the command of the Fatima vision by holding a special service in Fatima, Portugal, on May 13, 1982, one year to the day after the assassination attempt. In the ceremony he "consecrated" the world to Mary with "a special mention of Russia" in his attempt to fulfill the dictates of this strange vision. Pope John Paul II is unusual among the popes of this century in his earnest devotion to Mary. His personal motto is "Totus Tuus" (Entirely Yours). He consciously and publicly attributes his motivation and the direction of his life to Mary. John Paul II has stated that he consecrated and dedicated himself as "priest, as bishop, and as cardinal to Mary."

The Bible tells us that Mary was truly blessed by God as she was granted the privilege of becoming the birth mother of Jesus Christ. All Christians of all denominations rightly consider Mary as one of the most blessed persons in the Bible and in history. Her admirable character and spiritual life stimulate sincere admiration among all those who love Jesus Christ as their personal Savior and Lord.

However, the Bible, which is the only infallible source of God's commands to Christians, has never commanded or permitted the worship of anyone other than God Himself. The Bible tells us, through the words of the apostle Paul, that "there is one God and one Mediator between God and men, the Man Christ Jesus, who gave Himself a ransom for all, to be testified in due time" (1 Timothy 2:5,6). None of the apostles mentioned Mary during the decades following Christ's ministry. Through God's grace, every Christian can approach God's throne directly because Christ shed His blood for us on Calvary. We do not need anyone to intercede on our behalf. Jesus Christ, as Almighty God, loves each of us so much that He came to this earth to die on the cross, bearing the punishment for the sins and guilt of each of us so that, once we repent and turn from our sinful path to follow Him as our Lord, we might enter into a complete and joyful relationship with Him forever.

During a papal audience in Saint Peter's Square on May 13, 1981, the pope noticed a little girl wearing a picture of Mary at Fatima. At that exact moment the Turkish assassin Mehmet Ali Agca fired two bullets at John Paul's head. He missed his target by several inches because the pope bent his head to greet the child. The next two bullets hit John Paul's body, disabling him for many months. Apparently, while he recovered, the pope began to seriously consider the Fatima vision and its meaning for his mission and the Roman Catholic Church. John Paul II believes his personal destiny is to rule over the Catholic Church during the crisis described in the Third Secret of Fatima.

According to Malachi Martin, John Paul II is waiting for a miraculous intervention from heaven that will stun the world with its display of supernatural power. In the book *The Keys of This Blood,* Martin wrote about the pope's belief, based on the Fatima visions, in a miraculous appearance of Mary in the future in connection with a spectacular astronomical event involving the sun.

> He is waiting, rather, for an event that will fission human history, splitting the immediate past from the oncoming future. It will be an event on public view in the skies, in the oceans, and on the continental land masses of this planet. It will particularly involve our human sun, which every day lights up and shines upon the valleys, the mountains and the plains of this earth for our eyes. But on the day of this event, it will not appear merely

as the master star of our so-called solar system.
Rather, it will be seen as the circumambient glory
of the Woman whom the apostle describes as
"clothed with the sun" and giving birth to "a child
who will rule the nations with a scepter of iron."
Fissioning it will be as an event, in John Paul's
conviction of faith, for it will immediately nullify
all the grand designs the nations are now forming
and will introduce the Grand Design of man's
Maker. John Paul's waiting and watching time
will then be over. His ministry as the Servant of
the Grand Design will then begin. His strength
of will to hold on and continue, and then, when
the fissioning event occurs, to assume that ministry, derives directly from the Petrine authority
entrusted solely to him the day he became Pope,
in October of 1978. That authority, that strength,
is symbolized in the Keys of Peter, washed in the
human blood of the God-Man, Jesus Christ, John
Paul is and will be the sole possessor of the Keys
of this Blood on that day.

Apparently John Paul believes this global apparition will
astonish the population of earth. It is alleged by Malachi
Martin that the pope thinks this phenomenon will give him
the religious authority to create a new religious renaissance
and rule over a new church/state world government. Various catholic organizations such as Opus Dei, the Catholic
Campaign, and others are now working behind the scenes
to abolish the separation of church and state. *Time* magazine
in December 9, 1991, carried an article questioning the historic separation of church and state.

The Saint Malachi Predictions

Apparently another series of curious predictions from
A.D. 1148, the prophecies of an archbishop of Armaugh,

Ireland (known as Saint Malachi), also convinced Pope John Paul II that he is presiding over the last days of his church. On several occasions the present pope has indicated that he believes he is the last pope who will follow the teachings of Christ and truly believe in Jesus Christ as the Lord God Almighty. It is an open secret in Italy and Europe that many of the present priests, cardinals, and bishops are no longer true believers in the inspiration of the Scriptures and the historical credibility of the gospel of Christ. Just as in the growing apostasy in the Protestant denominations, many of these modern Catholic leaders have rejected the fundamentals of New Testament faith, such as the virgin birth and the resurrection of Jesus Christ. Pope John Paul II fears that, following his death, the conclave of cardinals who will choose the next pope will elect someone who will not uphold historic Christianity. Apparently one of the reasons for this is his belief in an 800-year-old prediction from Saint Malachi.

Maol-Maodhog O'Morgair, later known as Saint Malachi, was born in Armaugh, Ireland, in A.D. 1094. After a life of faithful service he was appointed Metropolitan Bishop of Ireland in 1133. Following a lifetime of devotion to Jesus Christ as his Lord, he died in A.D. 1148. Many people in the Irish Church and some in the Vatican today believe he authored an unusual prophecy that foretold the future of the Roman Catholic Church for the next 850 years. The prophecy supposedly described all of the popes from Pope Celestine II (who ruled in A.D. 1143) until the last pope who would rule during the final destruction of the Catholic Church, almost a thousand years later, during the Battle of Armageddon.

This curious prophecy of Saint Malachi consists of a series of prophetic poetic stanzas in Latin that purports to describe 111 future Roman popes who would rule the Vatican.

According to Saint Malachi's prediction, there would be
only 111 popes in the Catholic Church following Pope Celestine, who died in A.D. 1146. Some researchers have suggested that these descriptions of the future popes were quite
accurate, but it is very hard to verify this. Let me reaffirm
that I do not place any faith or confidence in any prophecy
or prediction except those found in the inspired pages of
Holy Scripture. All other predictions are simply human spec-
ulations. However, since Pope John Paul II apparently believes in the Fatima vision and the poetic vision of Saint
Malachi and looks to them for guidance, it is vital that we
explore these visions to understand the motivations and
thinking of those who will play major roles in the events of
the last days.

Saint Malachi's list of the last few popes to rule the
Roman Catholic Church:

Number	Poetic Description	Name	Years of Rule
106	Pastor Angelus	Pope Pius XII	1939–1958
107	Pastor et nauta	Pope John XXIII	1958–1963
108	Flos Florum	Pope Paul VI	1963–1978
109	De Medietate Lunoe	Pope John Paul I	1978–1978
110	De labore soils	Pope John Paul II	1978–present

The papal leadership still to come is described as:

Number	Poetic Description	Name	Years of Rule
111	Glorioe Olivoe	Pope Peter	The Final Years of This Age

The ancient Irish prophecy of Saint Malachi concluded
with a prediction that the last pope of the Roman Catholic
Church will rule following the death of the present pontiff,
Pope John Paul II, pope number 110. Furthermore, this

curious ancient prediction suggests that the last pope will be the first pontiff in 2000 years who will dare to assume the name of Peter, choosing the name of Peter II of Rome. Following the poetic style, the ancient prophecy purports to describe the details of the destiny of the final pope of the Roman Catholic Church.

After detailing his visions to be fulfilled, Saint Malachi wrote the following words to describe his vision of the last pope. Malachi's prophecy, written in Latin, reads as follows: "*In persecutione Extrema Sanctae Romanae Ecclesiae sedebit Petrus Romanus qui pascet oves in multis tribulationibus, quibus transactis, certus septi collis dirurtur et pie ex tremendis predicabit populum suum.*" Translated into English, this curious ancient prediction reads as follows: "In the last persecution of the Roman Church, Peter the Roman will rule. He will have great tribulation which will end with the destruction of the city on seven hills." According to Malachi's vision the final pope of the Roman Catholic Church will be from Italy. The prediction suggests he will take the name Peter II and will come to power in the Vatican in the final days of this century, during the tribulation when the world is overcome by military and political catastrophes as described in the book of Revelation. The important point is that Malachi believed his prophecy would conclude the final days of this millennium. Apparently Pope John Paul II believes that he is following an agenda based on these extrabiblical predictions, and that he will lead the world during the political, religious, and military crisis that will lead to the appearance of the Antichrist.

The Emerging Worldwide Church

Pope John Paul II has an agenda to create a universal church involving all of the world's religions. Following ecumenical discussions between the Archbishop of Canterbury (representing the Church of England), and John Paul II (as reported in *Time* magazine in October 1989), the archbishop commented on a beautiful ring the pope had given him. The archbishop stated that it was not a wedding ring, but it could be considered an engagement ring symbolizing the coming reunion between their two churches.

The pope also met with the Dalai Lama, the head of Tibetan Buddhism, and other false religionists at Assisi, Italy, in 1986. Incredibly, in this historic meeting the pope joined in a circle to pray and meditate with snake handlers from Togo, shamans and witch doctors from Africa, Hindu gurus from India, Buddhist monks from Thailand, and liberal protestant clergymen from Great Britain! Many Catholics were stunned to hear the pope declare, at this interreligious meeting in Assisi, that there are many paths to God. Incredibly, during his February 1993 visit to Africa, the pope preached his message of unification with false satanic religion. He held meetings with a number of voodoo practitioners and sorcerers.

The *Associated Press* gave an account of the pope's visit to the African country of Benin with the following headline: "Pope Meets With Voodoo Believers." The newspaper reported, "Pope John Paul II on Thursday sought common ground with the believers in voodoo, suggesting they would not betray their traditional faith by converting to Christianity." In other words, they could retain their voodoo while joining the Catholic church! Voodoo worshipers believe in many deities and use snake rituals. Incredibly, Pope John Paul explained to the voodoo witch doctors that as they worship their ancestors, Christians also revere their "ancestors in the faith, from the Apostles to the missionaries." According to the Associated Press account, voodoo priests warmly welcomed the pope. "'I have never seen God, but today when

I have seen the pope, I recognize that I have seen the good God, who prays for all the voduns,' said Sossa Guedehoungue, head of Benin's vodun community."

Catholic Apostasy

Pope John Paul II has noted with alarm that during the last few decades the Roman Catholic Church has experienced massive defections from the faith by bishops, priests, nuns, and laymen. Many churches in Western Europe and North America have abandoned traditional Catholic doctrines and now minister to only a few attendees. Many parishes have no priest because so few young men join the priesthood. Some parishes are forced to hire priests from South America because none are available from North America. John Paul II confided to associates that his attempts to reform the moral atmosphere in the Vatican were thwarted by a large network of actively homosexual priests and higher church leaders who resist every attempt at moral reform. Malachi Martin reported that a number of wicked and immoral priests and bishops had infiltrated the highest levels of the Vatican during the reign of Pope Paul VI in 1963.

Ominously, Pope Paul VI warned about "the smoke of Satan which has entered the Sanctuary," referring to incidents of satanic ceremonies and pagan initiation rituals in the Vatican that defiled the holy name of Jesus Christ. European newspapers have reported numerous cases of satanic pedophilia involving priests, nuns, and bishops in Turin, Italy, and various cities in America. These diabolically evil rituals involve the sexual defilement of innocent children by satanic priests as part of a Luciferian initiation ceremony that involves open worship of Satan.

Researchers who explored the sudden mysterious death of Pope John Paul I in 1978 revealed that this genuine and humble Christian leader, who preceded the present Pope John Paul II, was appalled at his discovery of the lack of spirituality and true faith among those who rule the Vatican. During the 30 days in which he ruled the papacy, John Paul I discovered that more than a hundred members of the secret occult group the Freemasons had infiltrated high positions within the Vatican, including its powerful financial institutions. According to Roman Catholic law it is illegal for a priest or bishop to belong to the Freemasons or any other secret occult group. It is significant to note that the list of secret Masons within the Vatican, selected by John Paul I for immediate dismissal, was found in his papal apartment when his body was discovered by his servants. Although the evidence strongly indicated that he had been poisoned, there was no serious investigation and his body was immediately cremated to prevent an autopsy being performed, though required by Italian law.

Subsequently, Italian government investigations revealed that a large and powerful Fascist and Freemason intelligence organization called Propaganda Due (P2) existed within the highest levels of Italian society and the government. Propaganda Due is an anticommunist, Fascist organization founded in the early 1960s with Licio Gelli as its Grand Master. P2 has its headquarters in Rome and branches in France, Switzerland, U.S.A., and South America. It is a private intelligence organization created by the Masonic Lodge that receives funds from the CIA and the Vatican. P2 was used to secretly transfer over 100 million dollars to the Solidarity labor organization in Poland. The Italian Parliamentary Commission that investigated P2 concluded that it was controlled by secret sources "beyond the frontiers of Italy." Two months before he was murdered, Mino Percorelli defected from P2 in 1979 and claimed that the CIA was behind it.

Members of P2 included Michelle Sindona and Bishop Paul Marcinkus, high officials of the Vatican Bank, who were later charged with massive bank fraud. Other key P2 members included the former prime minister of Italy, Biulio Andreotti, the Vatican Secretary of State Cardinal Villot, and Agostino Casoroli, the Vatican foreign minister. Investigators found thousands of secret members of P2 in the judiciary, the police, and the military. The judicial investigation determined that the Fascist P2 group had plans to overthrow the existing democratic government of Italy. Unfortunately, after the election of John Paul II, the individuals implicated in Freemasonry and illegal financial dealings of the Vatican Bank still remain in their powerful positions.

Opus Dei, which means "God's Work," was created as a secret organization under the direct control of the pope by a Catholic priest named Jose Maria Escriva de Balaguery in Spain in 1928. Escriva was succeeded in 1975 by Alvaro del Portillio. Pope John Paul II made Alvaro del Portillio a bishop. The membership of Opus Dei includes 1500 priests and 75,000 lay members. This organization has a goal to achieve "a practical union of church and state." Another secret Vatican organization, Pro Deo, meaning "For God," is in reality the Vatican's secret intelligence agency. It was created during World War II in Lisbon, Portugal, but was moved to the Vatican after the war. Opus Dei was funded by William Donovan, the World War II director of the Office of Strategic Services, which later became the Central Intelligence Agency.

Protestant Apostasy

"The Spirit expressly says that in latter times some will depart from the faith, giving heed to deceiving spirits and doctrines of demons" (1 Timothy 4:1,2). The Bible warns that growing worldwide apostasy will characterize the church during the last generation leading to the return of Christ. "For the time will come when they will not endure sound doctrine, but according to their own desires, because they have itching ears, they will heap up for themselves teachers; and they will turn their ears away from the truth, and be turned aside to fables" (2 Timothy 4:3,4). While we should not be surprised at the progressive abandonment of the authority of Scripture among the churches because the prophets warned that this would happen, it is tragic to realize that many new believers are in great spiritual danger due to the lack of teaching of doctrine in our churches today.

A 1982 confidential survey by sociologist Jeffrey Hadden on the private religious convictions of 10,000 Protestant pastors found that a majority of these mainline ministers have lost their faith. Anyone considering these horrifying results will realize why the mainline churches have lost their moral and spiritual influence in society. When asked if they still believed that Jesus Christ was God, over 45 percent of the ministers said no. An astonishing 80 percent of the ministers rejected both the claim that the Bible is the inspired Word of God and the claim that Jesus is the Son of God. Thirty-six per cent of these pastors do not believe that Jesus Christ actually rose from the dead.

Ministers who have abandoned the fundamentals of the Christian faith should be honest enough to leave the church and admit they no longer hold the historic faith of the fathers. This rejection of the fundamental doctrines of the Christian faith by a majority of these Protestant ministers explains why these religious leaders are willing to abandon the theological differences that have separated the Protestant and Catholic churches over the years and instead join in the powerful ecumenical one-world church of the last days. The apostate church of the end times will be a church with a lowest-common-denominator faith, one that holds almost no fundamental doctrines other than secular humanism and a pagan, idolatrous worship of "the god within."

God's command to those who will repent of their sin and follow Him is that we must base our life, our teaching, and our eternal hope solely on the truth revealed by the unchanging Word of God. "But as for you, continue in the things which you have learned and been assured of, knowing from whom you have learned them, and that from childhood you have known the Holy Scriptures, which are able to make you wise for salvation through faith which is in Christ Jesus. All Scripture is given by inspiration of God, and is profitable for doctrine, for reproof, for correction, for instruction in righteousness, that the man of God may be complete, thoroughly equipped for every good work" (2 Timothy 3:14-17).

Catholic-Protestant Ecumenical Unity

Throughout South America and many other countries, Catholics are abandoning the Mass in record numbers to accept Jesus Christ as their only Savior and to worship with fellow Christians in both Pentecostal and evangelical churches. Those who are working behind the scenes to produce an ecumenical world church recognize that these evangelistic efforts are proving very effective in leading Catholics and mainline Protestants to a personal faith in Jesus Christ as their Savior and Lord.

In response to this problem for the Catholic Church, a group of 40 prominent Protestant and Catholic scholars met on March 29, 1994, to sign a historic and astonishing compromise to ban evangelism efforts directed at each other's members. Entitled *Evangelicals and Catholics Together: The Christian Mission in the Third Millennium*, this unprecedented agreement commits these leaders to reject the command of

Christ to "go into all the world and preach the gospel to every
creature." Incredibly, according to this covenant, these
Protestant leaders agreed that "Christians must stop aggressive proselytizing of one another's flocks and work together
more closely." A Catholic priest, Richard Neuhaus, stated
that this was the first time since the Protestant Reformation
that Protestants and Catholics "joined in a declaration so
clear in respect to their common faith and common responsibility."

Significantly, although the document is not an official
agreement between the denominations, Neuhaus told the
National and International Religion Report on April 4, 1994,
that he had received strong encouragement from "appropriate parties at the Holy See" in the Vatican at Rome. These
Catholic theologians would love to put an end to Protestant
evangelical missions in Catholic countries and the presentation of the Protestant teaching of the authority of Scripture
and the necessity of personal faith in Jesus as essential to our
salvation because it has been so successful. The evangelistic
efforts are entirely one way in that the Protestants are winning great numbers of Catholics to faith in Christ. Therefore
this agreement to cease proselytizing will only serve the
Catholic desire to prevent their Catholic members from
learning about faith in Jesus Christ alone to assure their salvation.

In this same ecumenical theme, the Archbishop of Canterbury, Dr. Carey, who presides over the Church of England, has severely criticized Anglican pastors who have
persevered in evangelical efforts to preach the gospel of Jesus
Christ to Hindus, Jews, Buddhists, and other non-Christian
groups. Incredibly, in a demonstration of the spiritual bankruptcy of the Church of England, Archbishop Carey has
instructed his ministers that nonbelievers in Jesus Christ are
just "fellow travelers" on the road to spiritual enlightenment,

and therefore they must not be evangelized! In addition, the archbishop declared that he plans a trip to Rome in the near future to discuss how to remove obstacles to ecumenical interfaith unification.

New Age Neopaganism

During the unprecedented Presbyterian Church's Reimagining 1993 Conference, the leaders led participants in an astonishing neopagan New Age religious service that evoked the ancient pagan religions. The speaker is reported to have said, "Sophia, Creator God, let your milk and honey flow. Sophia, Creator God, shower us with your love." A celebration of the "Lady's Supper" was reported on by a traditional conservative church magazine, the *Presbyterian Layman*, in its January/February 1994 issue. The magazine article stated, "The conference glorified lesbianism and ... some conference speakers advocated adding books to the Bible to justify feminist and homosexual activism."

In an astonishing statement given at the Presbyterian conference, another feminist speaker declared, "I don't think we need a theory of atonement at all. . . . Atonement has to do so much with death. . . . I don't think we need folks hanging on crosses and blood dripping and weird stuff. . . . We just need to listen to the god within." This infiltration of New Age philosophy continues to grow among a number of older mainline denominations, and it was apostasy was prophesied by our Lord to occur in the last days.

For those who still doubt that the religious elite in the largest denominations are planning to create an ecumenical one-world church, they should carefully consider the information in this chapter. Several years ago Archbishop Ramsey, President of the World Council of Churches, addressed a public meeting at the Roman Catholic Saint Patrick's

Cathedral in New York which was attended by Archbishop Lakovas of the Greek Orthodox Church and Cardinal Cook of the Catholic Church. Incredibly, the President of the WCC declared, "I can foresee the day when all Christians might accept the Pope as Bishop of a World Church."

The World Council of Churches (WCC) was founded in 1948 as a Christian organization dedicated to bringing about a universal cooperation among Christian churches world-wide. However, over the last 47 years liberal and socialist theologians have taken control of the WCC, until today the organization is barely Christian in any sense that would be recognized by Christians in the early church. Universalism and secular humanism have replaced biblical Christianity and its emphasis on teaching a lost humanity about the need for personal repentance. We are witnessing instead the creation of embryonic organizations that will ultimately produce the Mystery Babylon church of the last days.

An article in the April 5, 1993, edition of *Christianity Today* by Tokunboh Adeyemo indicated the direction that the World Council of Churches is now pursuing. Significantly, the WCC Life and Work Slogan is "Doctrine Divides–Service Unites," thereby indicating its rejection of biblical doctrine as divisive in the interests of achieving a common consensus on the basis of the lowest common denominator theology. The WCC Secretary for Evangelism, Raymond Fung, indicated that evangelism encompasses every effort to improve the human condition whether it is made by Christians or non-Christians. He declared that Christians have no monopoly on evangelism. Yet the Bible teaches that evangelism is the proclamation of the good news of salvation in Christ for the express purpose of spiritual conversion. The WCC teaches an implicit universalism and believes that the best of the non-Christian pagan religions are equal in value to (if not better than) the best of Christianity. As a result, the WCC believes that dialogue and cross-fertilization are their highest goals. In contrast, the historic teaching of Christianity is that all non-Christian religions are products of fallen human cultures.

David Gill, a WCC representative based in Geneva, Switzerland, announced to a radio audience during a 1974 British Broadcasting Corporation interview that the most important goal of the WCC is to "De-Protestantize the Churches" to prepare them to join the coming world church. The true biblical priority of the church is to evangelize the world and create churches everywhere for teaching, fellowship, and worship of Jesus Christ. But now the WCC has declared that cross-cultural evangelism is wrong and presumptuous! The WCC now demands that Western Christian churches declare a moratorium on evangelism so that non-Christian cultures will not be offended by the claims of the gospel of Christ. Obviously, the leaders of the WCC assume a universalism where everyone will be saved in the end whether or not they respond to the gospel of Christ.

The 1973 Conference on World Mission in Bangkok articulated a new Christian world mission. This new WCC view taught that salvation should be replaced by a dedication to social/political/economic well-being. The historic Christian focus on the need of sinners for reconciliation to God, sanctification, and the hope of heaven were replaced by a radical secular humanism that focused solely on improving the social, political, and practical conditions of life. Incredibly, the leadership of the WCC declared at the Bangkok conference that this was "the close of the era of missions and the beginning of the era of mission."

The Good News!

"This gospel of the kingdom will be preached in all the world as a witness to all the nations, and then the end will come" (Matthew 24:14). One of the final prophetic signs that Jesus Christ is about to return is His prophecy that "this gospel of the kingdom will be preached in all the world." Despite all the bad news, the gospel is truly being preached in all the world in the last days. The true growth of the church in the last days is astonishing! From only one million Christians in China in 1949 when the Communists took over, researchers estimate that over 80 million Chinese have accepted Jesus Christ as their Lord and Savior despite the terrible persecution. One estimate suggests that over 25,000 Chinese are dedicating their lives to Jesus Christ every day despite tremendous religious persecution.

In the Muslim nation of Indonesia more than 20 percent of the population has accepted Christ. Despite decades of dedicated missionary efforts, by 1900 only 3 percent of Africans had accepted Christ. However, in the last 90 years over 45 percent of the 500 million citizens in Africa have accepted Christ! In Russia, the introduction of the gospel and the availability of Russian-language Bibles has led 100 million Russians to follow Christ. In South Korea the gospel was rejected for many years despite the valiant efforts of missionaries. However, as the winds of the Holy Spirit began to move throughout Asia following World War II, 30 percent of the population of Korea found faith in Christ. Around the world more than 85,000 people accept Christ as their Savior every single day. In the 2000-year history of the church we have never seen such an astonishing move of God as we are witnessing today.

The Spectacular Growth of the True Church

A recent study by the Lausanne Statistics Task Force on the progress of evangelism concluded that the growth of the church is far greater than previously reported. In only 15 years, from 1980 until now, the number of born-again Christians is growing at a rate three times faster than the growth of the world's population. These historically verifiable records reveal this incredible growth in the number of Christians worldwide:

> In 1430 Christians amounted to one in 99 of the world's population.

> In 1790 Christians amounted to one in 49 of the world's population.

> In 1940 Christians amounted to one in 32 of the world's population.

> In 1970 Christians amounted to one in 19 of the world's population.

> In 1980 Christians amounted to one in 16 of the world's population.

> In 1983 Christians amounted to one in 13 of the world's population.

> In 1986 Christians amounted to one in 11 of the world's population.

> In 1994 Christians amounted to one in 10 of the world's population.

Consider these figures carefully. We are winning a significant remnant of the world's population during these last days! In only 60 years the number of Christians worldwide has grown by an astonishing 1300 percent, from only 40 million in 1934 to 540 million Christians today, while the world's population has grown by only 400 percent. Christian radio broadcasts are now reaching almost half of the world's 360 "mega-languages," covering 78 percent of the earth's population, according to the broadcasting group

World By 2000. Evangelical broadcasters are now providing the gospel to every language group in the world. The combination of tremendous evangelism efforts by mission organizations, hundreds of thousands of dedicated national pastors, and the work of Christian broadcasters is rapidly fulfilling the Great Commission.

The accomplishments by the Wycliffe Translators and many others translating the Bible into the languages of millions who have not yet heard the gospel is one of the little-known miracles of the last days. Despite the pessimistic analysis of many that the population of the earth is growing faster than the growth of the church, the truth is that the gospel is being preached in all the world with astonishing success during these last days. A 1991 study by the National Council of Churches concluded that church membership is growing at twice the rate of the overall population throughout the world. Their study also noted that the greatest growth is in evangelical churches.

5

Cyberspace: The Beast's Worldwide Spiderweb

David Webber

Without the world taking much notice, we are silently and steadily getting ready for high-fi in the sky. Internet, the newest form of communication that touches lives, young and old, for business or for pleasure, is just now—after more than 25 years—beginning to come of age.

Internet is invading our homes and our privacy through the seemingly innocent process of sending and receiving e-mail, paying bills, shopping, and communicating with our unknown, on-line neighbors. This fascinating process is highly addictive.

More than an earthbound entity, Internet will one day operate on star time: Already in our ambitious programs we talk of "Primestar" and "EchoStar." These new companies are developing so quickly that many investors will probably be left behind.

Reports involving the swift movement of communications technology saturate our daily news. The burgeoning industry is revolutionary on a scale as great as the Industrial Revolution of the first half of the twentieth century.

An article in *USA Today* reported some fascinating facts and figures in June of 1996:

> Cable giant Tele-Communications, Inc. said Wednesday that it is putting its satellite business on the launching pad in an effort to get the company's stock price off the ground. The company will spin off TCI Satellite Entertainment late this year, giving shares in the new company to TCI stockholders. . . . [1]

USA Today reported that the venture, estimated at a value of more than 2 billion dollars, " . . . will include TCI's 21% stake in Primestar Partners, which broadcasts to 1.25 million owners of 36-inch backyard satellite dishes. . . ."[2]

CEO John Malone reported that he expects the move will enhance the overall value of TCI by enabling the market to "more readily evaluate the operations and growth potential" of its satellite holdings. And satellite company shares are soaring, according to the report: " . . . U.S. Satellite Broadcasting (USSB) is up 24% to $33 3/8 since it went public in February. And EchoStar is up 33% in 1996 . . . "[3]

According to *USA Today*, CEO Malone apparently expects TCI president Gary Howard, a mergers-and-acquisitions specialist, " . . . to help craft a big deal that gives TCI access to the close to 2 million homes using the new generation of 18-inch direct broadcast satellite (DBS) dishes. . . ."[4]

Rush to Market

Competition is growing rapidly in the area of USSB, DirecTV, and EchoStar, according to the article, " . . . by beaming TV shows to these popular small dishes. . . ."[5]

The *USA Today* article continues:

"There's a rush to market," says Howard. "It's a 4-to-5 year race and then your market share is pretty secure."

Howard says TCI will be in the DBS business by year's end.

It's unclear how he'll get there. TCI doesn't have federal approval to launch its satellites into one of the few orbital slots available to broadcast DBS signals across the USA.

TCI is trying to secure orbital slots under the jurisdiction of the Canadian government. The company is waiting to see if the Federal Communications Commission will agree to that idea.

In addition, TCI has tried to cut a deal with News Corp. CEO Rupert Murdoch and MCI– who want to offer DBS service from the slot they bought last year for $683 million.

But Howard says, "We're not in any negotiations with Murdoch about a satellite deal."

TCI's satellite spin-off is "a good move," says Media Group Research President Mark Riely. "Other cable operators may be invited to join in."[6]

While these phenomenal technologies network and interweave into what will ultimately become Antichrist's worldwide spiderweb, it is thrilling to note that interspatial travel, communication, and all kinds of cosmic activities can be envisioned in the coming kingdom of God's choosing:

Many of those that sleep in the dust of the earth shall awake, some to everlasting life and some to shame and everlasting contempt. And they that

> be wise shall shine as the brightness of the firma-
> ment, and they that turn many to righteousness
> as the stars for ever and ever. But thou, O Daniel,
> shut up the words and seal the book, even to the
> time of the end; many shall run to and fro, and
> knowledge shall be increased (Daniel 12:2-4).

America On-Line, an offshoot of Internet, is also racing along the information superhighway to dominate the commercial industry of computers and modems. The expanding communications juggernaut, with its sinister all-seeing-eye emblem, seems to be at a crossroads:

> Vienna, VA—Steve Case is running late. The
> CEO of America On-line is expected at a Wash-
> ington hotel to give a speech in 30 minutes. It
> doesn't look like he'll make it.

> The 37-year-old Case hops into his 1992 Infinity
> J30 sedan and turns the ignition key. Nothing.
> Once, twice, three times. Still, the engine won't
> turn over.

> It's been that kind of month for Case. AOL's stock
> price is down 40% from its early May high of $70
> a share. New subscribers are becoming harder to
> find even as large numbers of customers defect.
> And the company's existing management sys-
> tems are struggling to handle its rapid growth.

> Case is unfazed—both by the balky car and the
> mounting challenges. Slinging his black canvas
> briefcase over one shoulder, he accepts a ride
> from a reporter. At the nation's largest on-line
> computer service, such on-the-fly adjustments are
> standard procedure.

For two days earlier this month, *USA Today* trailed Case and Ted Leonsis, AOL senior vice president and the company's creative guru, through critical meetings with their content providers. It was a strange juncture for AOL. The company has doubled its membership to 6 million in one year and achieved unquestioned dominance of the commercial on-line industry.[7]

Yet the industry is so dynamic and uncertain in its thrust for the future that even AOL's dominance and long-term viability are open to doubt, according to the *USA Today* article. The market potential is staggering; it is literally global in its scope. Obviously, no one commercial entity with the capability of capturing such a gargantuan market is currently on the scene.

The article continues:

"They'll be relevant for a while," says Emily Green, an analyst with Forester Research. "I don't think they'll be able to sustain a dominant role."

Today, only 11% of US households subscribe to on-line services, which offer access to news, entertainment and transactions through personal computers.

Case's battle plan involves growing AOL into a genuine mass-market business. But no matter how appealing he makes AOL, the former Procter & Gamble marketing executive can't do it alone.[8]

High-Tech Terrorism

The danger presented by terrorism and unauthorized hackers gravely threatens the activities of businesses, banks, and members of the defense industry who interact via

Internet. According to the CIA and government officials, the threat to the infrastructure of all the networking computers is very real, and we need to prepare for such alien invasions from foreign countries or individuals. A recent newspaper article addressed this subject:

> Washington (Reuter)–The United Sates faces a growing threat of cyberspace attacks against its computer networks by terrorists, CIA Director John Deutch warned Congress Tuesday.
>
> "We have evidence that a number of countries around the world are developing the doctrine, strategies and tools to conduct information attacks," Deutch told a Senate Governmental Affairs hearing.
>
> "International terrorist groups clearly have the capability to attack the information infrastructure of the United States, even if they use relatively simple means," Deutch said.
>
> "I am certainly prepared to predict some very large and uncomfortable incidents."
>
> Deutch said a large-scale attack that disrupted U.S. computer networks could cripple the nation's energy, transportation, communications, banking, business and military, which are all dependent on computers and could be vulnerable to sabotage ranging from break-ins by unauthorized "hackers" to attacks with explosives.[9]

In case we are prone to think of those frightening possibilities as undue paranoia, let us remember the summer of 1996, when much of the western U.S. lost electrical power for reasons that even the experts cannot yet fully explain. When asked to compare the threat of a computer attack to threats such as nuclear, chemical, and biological weapons, Deutch said, "I would say it was very, very close to the top. Virtually any 'bad actor' can acquire the hardware and software needed to attack some of our critical information-based infrastructures."[10]

The article continued:

> Deutch said the Central Intelligence Agency and the Defense Department plan to create a center of computer attacks at the National Security Agency. Another witness, Peter Neumann of Computer Science Laboratory, warned of "an electronic Pearl Harbor" unless government and businesses prepare.[11]

Big Government

The intrusion of big government into our private files is rapidly making privacy in business or personal life a thing of the past.

Note the following:

> U.S. Attorney General Janet Reno has proposed a plan that a computer security specialist compares to "giv[ing] copies of the keys to all your file cabinets and all your doors" to the government.

> The Associated Press reported that "Internet users would be asked to give the government the digital 'keys' to their computers in exchange for more security when doing business on-line." Those "keys" are the encryption codes used anytime a business or individual conducts a financial transaction on-line. UPI reported that Reno wants to create a new agency to oversee all digital encryption. Jim

Bidzos, president of RSA Data Security in Redwood City, Calif., says this degree of oversight is not necessary, because all companies can keep copies of their own encryption codes that could be subpoenaed for evidence.

Consider the following points:

- When Communications Decency Act was overturned, millions of computer screens worldwide flashed the words, "Free speech!" Now, bureaucrats propose a measure that clearly violates the free-speech and commerce rights of all on-line users.

- While this measure may help to curb on-line business fraud, it also allows the federal government to track all private and commercial transactions conducted on-line.[12]

Is this what business and banking want? Business of, by, and for the government? The all-seeing eye emblem of America On-Line would surely come alive under such an arrangement.

Because of the tremendous increase in the interfacing of computers and databanks, our world is a shrinking complex of nations. Since the beginning of internetworking of computers and their melding with communication systems 25 years ago, commerce and trade, business and banking have become a whole new ball game.

By means of fiber optics and digital computerization, national communications transcend borders and even entire continents. It was said almost a decade ago that the world would eventually be wired for sound by a single wire. It was so described as one wire for one world.

Much of what the scientists envisioned 25 years ago has been accomplished. I would suggest that the birth of the global computer network known as "The Internet" is the technological arm of the New World Order. Quoting from a *Newsweek* article titled, "The Birth of the Internet":

> In the summer of 1969, not everyone was at Woodstock. In laboratories on either side of the continent, a small group of computer scientists were quietly changing the future of communications. Their goal: to build a computer network that would enable researchers around the country to share ideas. That network became the foundation of the Internet, the vast international computer network that today has become one part buzzword, one part popular obsession. But its birth required a leap of the imagination. Instead of seeing computers as giant, plodding number-crunchers, they had to be viewed as nimble tools that could talk to each other. After that paradigm shift, the rest was just doing the calculations.[13]

That sounds deceptively easy today, in this time of modems that spit out whole textbooks at what seems to be the speed of light. But it took a few visionaries, along with teams of engineers and programmers, to bring the Net to life.

God's Internet

As man rapidly covers the earth with his mostly-unseen wires, so God surely has a celestial system that internetworks the universe. As evidence of this, consider God's heavenly watchers referred to in Daniel 4:13: "I saw in the visions of my head upon my bed, and, behold, a watcher and a holy one came down from heaven." Also note Revelation 4:4-8:

Round about the throne were four and twenty
seats; and upon the seats I saw four and twenty
elders sitting, clothed in white raiment; and they
had on their heads crowns of gold. And out of
the throne proceeded lightnings and thunderings
and voices; and there were seven lamps of fire
burning before the throne, which are the seven
Spirits of God. And before the throne there was
a sea of glass like unto crystal; and in the midst
of the throne, and round about the throne, were
four beasts full of eyes before and behind. And
the first beast was like a lion, and the second beast
like a calf, and the third beast had a face as a man,
and the fourth beast was like a flying eagle. And
the four beasts had each of them six wings about
him, and they were full of eyes within; and they
rest not day and night, saying, Holy, holy, holy,
Lord God Almighty, which was, and is, and is to
come.

God's Internet is stunning in its implication for mankind.
It brings all of His heavenly interactives into play in His
loving desire to interface with mankind. Consider the living
creatures of Ezekiel 1:4-18:

I looked, and, behold, a whirlwind came out of
the north, a great cloud, and fire infolding itself,
and a brightness was about it, and out of the midst
thereof as the color of amber, out of the midst of
the fire. Also out of the midst thereof came the
likeness of four living creatures. And this was their
appearance: they had the likeness of a man. And
every one had four faces, and every one had four
wings.

And their feet were straight feet, and the sole of their feet was like the sole of a calf's foot, and they sparkled like the color of burnished brass. And they had the hands of a man under their wings on their four sides; and they four had their faces and their wings. Their wings were joined one to another; they turned not when they went; they went every one straight forward. As for the likeness of their faces, they four had the face of a man, and the face of a lion, on the right side; and they four had the face of an ox on the left side; they four also had the face of an eagle. Thus were their faces; and their wings were stretched upward; two wings of every one were joined one to another, and two covered their bodies. And they went every one straight forward; whither the Spirit was to go, they went; and they turned not when they went. As for the likeness of the living creatures, their appearance was like burning coals of fire, and like the appearance of lamps: it went up and down among the living creatures; and the fire was bright, and out of the fire went forth lightning. And the living creatures ran and returned as the appearance of a flash of lightning.

Now as I beheld the living creatures, behold one wheel upon the earth by the living creatures, with his four faces. The appearance of the wheels and their work was like unto the color of a beryl, and they four had one likeness; and their appearance and their work was as it were a wheel in the middle of a wheel. When they went, they went upon their four sides, and they turned not when they went. As for their rings, they were so high that they were dreadful; and their rings were full of eyes round about them four.

We can continue with the Internet analogy while considering the wondrous omniscience of the true and living God:

> The eyes of the LORD run to and fro throughout the whole earth, to show himself strong in the behalf of them whose heart is perfect toward him. Herein thou hast done foolishly; therefore from henceforth thou shalt have wars (2 Chronicles 16:9).

Concerning the Scriptures designated–God's Internet– we have a glimpse of God's dynamo that runs the universe. God's computers never rest. They are living computers and don't have to be plugged in. They possibly are described by Ezekiel and John in apocalyptic language: "wheel in a wheel, ring upon ring"; "infolding fire and flashes of lightning" show the activities of God's "living computers."

New Agers value crystal as a source of power or energy. Notice that in Revelation 4:4-8 God has a sea of glass like crystal–a huge crystal before the throne of God.

Think about it! Daniel's bright, terrible, manlike image comes alive in Revelation 13:14-17, directs all worship to the Antichrist, and has power to put to death those who refuse to worship him. Won't this fearful image be somewhat like God's living creatures that are full of eyes? We might describe it as "power-packed full of microchips."

God is not a little old man operating a hi-powered, hi-tech board in a celestial room in heaven; but man, made in the likeness and image of God, gets all of his capacity for ideas and input from God. Therefore it ultimately all makes sense.

Read again 2 Chronicles 16:9 in light of God's living creatures or computers that keep track of every living thing as the Internet aspires to do on a global basis.

Battle for the Soul of Internet

The world's largest computer network, once the playground of scientists, hackers, and gearheads, is being overrun by lawyers, merchants, and millions of new users. Is there room for everyone?

If Internet has a soul, might I suggest a possible fulfillment for this gigantic electronic marvel: *the image of the beast.* This compelling image of the beast of Revelation 13:1 ultimately directs all attention and worship toward the devil's supreme ruler, the Antichrist. Revelation 13:15-17 says:

> He had power to give life unto the image of the beast, that the image of the beast should both speak and cause that as many as would not worship the image of the beast should be killed. And he causeth all, both small and great, rich and poor, free and bond, to receive a mark in their right hand or in their foreheads; and that no man might buy or sell save he that had the mark or the name of the beast or the number of his name.

This image could appear on our television or computer screens at the impulse of Internet. In fact, during the seven-year period of Antichrist supremacy, the image of the beast could be synonymous with the soul of the Internet. Think about it.

A lengthy article in *Time* magazine, "The Strange New World of the Internet: Battles on the Frontier of Cyberspace," presented an intriguing look at that netherworld into which this generation has been thrust. The article reads in part:

> There was nothing very special about the message that made Lawrence Canter and Martha Siegel the most hated couple in cyberspace. It

was a relatively straightforward advertisement offering the services of their husband-and-wife law firm to aliens interested in getting a green card–proof of permanent resident status in the U.S.

The computer that sent the message was a perfectly ordinary one as well: an IBM-type PC parked in the spare bedroom of their ranch-style house in Scottsdale, Arizona. But on the Internet, even a single computer can wield enormous power, and last April this one, with only a tap on the enter key, stirred up an international controversy that continues to this day....[14]

The Internet, the article reminded its readers, is the world's largest computer network, as well as, in effect, a working prototype of the *information superhighway*. Explaining that the Internet is a global system of networks that link large commercial computer communications services such as CompuServe, Prodigy, and America On-Line, as well as tens of thousands of smaller university, government, and corporate networks, the article pointed out that the Internet is "...growing faster than O.J. Simpson's legal bills...."[15]

The article continues:

...According to the Reston, Virginia-based Internet Society, a private group that tracks the growth of the Net, it reaches nearly 25 million computer users–an audience roughly the size of Roseanne's–and is doubling every year.

Now, just when it seems almost ready for prime time, the Net is being buffeted by forces that threaten to destroy the very qualities that fueled its growth. It's being pulled from all sides by commercial interests eager to make money on it, by veteran users who want to protect it, by governments that want to exploit its freedoms, by parents and teachers who want to make it a safe and useful place for kids. The Center and Siegel affair, says Net observers, was just the opening skirmish in the larger battle for the soul of the Internet.

What the Arizona lawyers did that fateful April day was to "Spam" the Net, a colorful bit of Internet jargon meant to evoke the effect of dropping a can of Spam into a fan and filling the surrounding space with meat. They wrote a program called Masspost that put the little ad into almost every active bulletin board on the Net—some 5,500 in all—thus ensuring that it would be seen by millions of Internet users, not just once but over and over again. Howard Rheingold, author of The Virtual Community, compares the experience with opening the mailbox and finding "a letter, two bills and 60,000 pieces of junk mail. . . ."[16]

According to the article, the advertisement was a provocation that evoked anger in Internet users all over the world, who instantaneously responded ". . . with angry electronic mail messages called 'flames.' . . ."

"Within minutes," continues the article—

> . . . the flames—filled with unprintable epithet— began pouring into Center and Siegel's Internet mailbox, first by the dozen, then by the hundreds, then by the thousands. A user in Australia sent in 1000 phoney requests for information every day. A 16-year-old threatened to visit the couple's "crappy law firm" and "burn it to the ground." The volume of traffic grew so heavy

that the computer delivering the E-mail crashed repeatedly under the load. After three days, Internet Direct of Phoenix, the company that provided the lawyers with access to the Net, pulled the plug on their account.

Even at that point, all might have been forgiven. For this kind of thing, believe it or not, happens all the time on the Internet—although not usually on this scale. People make mistakes. Their errors are pointed out. The underlying issues are thrashed out. And either a consensus is reached or the combatants exhaust themselves and retire from the field.

But Canter and Siegel refused to give ground. They declared the experiment "a tremendous success," claiming to have generated $100,000 in new business. They threatened to sue Internet Direct for cutting them off from even more business (although the suit never materialized). And they gave an unrepentant interview to the New York Times. "We will definitely advertise on the Internet again," they promised.... [17]

Internet: A Brief History

Internet grew out of computer technology more than 25 years old. The technology sprang from the efforts of America's defense industry to develop a system that would allow academic and military researchers to continue their crucial government work even if part of the computer network was destroyed in a nuclear attack.

The resultant computer network eventually linked military, corporate, and academic entities together in a shared cost/usage consortium which also shared responsibility for running the system. Scientists involved in the quickly expanding enterprise soon discovered that the network could be used in fascinating ways other than for official business only. Thus developed the sending of private messages (e-mail) and the posting of news and information on public electronic bulletin boards. These became known as Usenet news groups.

Scholarly types and computer hackers almost immediately became addicted to staying on-line for hours and sometimes days at a time. Their immersion in the system (which at the time they were given virtually free rein to manipulate) led to tremendous innovations and developments that continue to evolve to this day.

The *Time* magazine article continued:

> ... Until quite recently it was painfully difficult for ordinary computer users to reach the Internet. Not only did they need a PC, a modem to connect it to the phone line, and a passing familiarity with something called Unix, but they could get on only with the cooperation of a university or government research lab.

> In the past year, most of those impediments have disappeared. There are now dozens of small businesses that will sell access to the Net starting at $10 to $30 a month. And in the past few months, mainstream computer services like America On-line have started to make it possible for their subscribers to reach parts of the Internet through standard, easy-to-use menus.

> But with floods of new arrivals have come new issues and conflicts. Part of the problem is technical. To withstand a nuclear blast and keep on ticking, the Net was built without a central

command authority. That means that nobody owns it, nobody runs it, nobody has the power to kick anybody off for good. There isn't even a master switch that can shut it down in case of emergency. 'It's the closest thing to true anarchy that ever existed,' says Clifford Stoll, a Berkeley astronomer famous on the Internet for having trapped a German spy who was trying to use it to break into U.S. military computers.[18]

A Thirst for Bloodletting

The World Wide Web of Internet and on-line services, with all-seeing eyes, are already functioning in their formative stages, and the grand delusion can already be seen in the high-tech pleasures of computer-mesmerized people. Here is a shocking *Time* magazine story titled "The Wizard of ID":

> Computer-game freaks are watching breathlessly for QUAKE, son of the highly-addictive DOOM. In the $1 billion universe of computer games, these are days of feverish anticipation. The twitchy teenagers and addicted adults who spend hours at a time blasting away the phosphorous phantoms on their PC screens know that Quake is coming. It's more like a second coming: Quake's forebear, the virtual reality, blast-'em-up sensation called Doom, is probably the most popular PC game ever created.

> Countless fans are currently searching 75 Websites looking for signs of Quake as if it were a visiting comet.

Quake will arrive . . . when a fellow from id Software will quietly upload the game unto a secret Internet-linked computer. Within minutes, Quake will be copied to three dozen public computers nationwide. Then ravening game players, like mosquitoes attacking suntan-oiled vacationers, will suck the program into their home PCs. If they want a second course, they can transmit $50 to id's owners, four game jockeys in Mesquite, Texas, whose software skills and marketing smarts have made them richer than a lucky wildcatter.[19]

What followed was nothing less than high-tech pandemonium. Chaos in cyberspace! Although the writer of the article pointed out the astonishing impact the strategy had on Internet society, the author failed to grasp the ominous, even apocalyptic implications. Though the marketing ramifications, as the writer pointed out, are indeed staggering, the fact that mankind with more and more recreational time on its hands obviously lusts voraciously for violence (even if only electronic game violence) should remind us of God's warning that the end of the age will be like the days of Noah, when all the earth was filled with violence.

The *Time* article continued:

The cloak-and-dagger antics aren't just a publicity ploy.

When Doom was released to its waiting public on midnight of December 10, 1993, via the University of Wisconsin's computer system, the weight of 1,500 simultaneous download demands crashed the whole network. "Maximum overload," gloats Jay Wilbur, the marketing superego behind id. "We took the whole university out."

With Doom, id perfected a clever strategy. The company gave away the first third of the game over the Internet, hooking huge numbers of players who then later paid $40 for the rest. "Shareware" versions of Doom may have been copied 30 million times. Doom generated more than $30 million in sales, $15.7 million last year.

Doom's charm wasn't its almost non-existent plot line, which involved space marines—or something. The attraction was hunt-and-be-hunted action that put the player behind a shotgun barrel (or a chain saw or a nail gun) in a hellish 3-D world of demons and fire-ball-spitting ogres.

Quake has a similarly empty script, but by using a radically different "graphics engine," it will deliver mesmerizing 3-E modeling.[20]

Emotion-igniting music from the pit is added to the bloodlust, and the youth of America and the world are drawn ever-deeper to the cyberspace abyss. Can there be any question that the hearts and minds—the very souls—of the young are being ensnared in ever-increasing numbers by Satan's cyberspace worldwide spiderweb? The article continues:

Doom addict Trent Reznor of the rock band Nine Inch Nails has created Quake's heavy-metal sound effects. The enhancements make Quake much more realistic than Doom—and yes, bloodies. (Kids: heads fly off and roll around on the ground! Zombies actually pull chunks of flesh out of their hides and fling them at you, then explode like red water balloons when you shoot them with your nine-inch nail gun.) V chips aside, the public thirst for video bloodletting hasn't abated.[21]

The development of these kinds of video bloodletting perfectly fit the scenario as given in 2 Thessalonians 2:1-4 and 2:7-12:

> We beseech you, brethren, by the coming of our Lord Jesus Christ, and by our gathering together unto him, that ye be not soon shaken in mind or be troubled, neither by spirit nor by word nor by letter as from us, as that the day of Christ is at hand. Let no man deceive you by any means, for that day shall not come except there come a falling away first, and that man of sin be revealed, the son of perdition, who opposeth and exalteth himself above all that is called God or that is worshipped, so that he as God sitteth in the temple of God, showing himself that he is God. . . .

> For the mystery of iniquity doth already work; only he who now hindereth will hinder until he be taken out of the way. And then shall that wicked [one] be revealed, whom the Lord shall consume with the spirit of his mouth, and shall destroy with the brightness of his coming; even him whose coming is after the working of Satan with all power and signs and lying wonders, and with all deceivableness of unrighteousness in them that perish, because they received not the love of the truth that they might be saved. And for this cause God shall send them strong delusion, that they should believe a lie, that they all might be damned who believed not the truth but had pleasure in unrighteousness.

The Year 2000 Problem

The year 2000 is really 6000 years from Adam. New Agers and one-worlders seem to be greatly anticipating the year 2000, and accordingly are planning celebrations of diverse sorts. The computer scientists are possibly the only group not so excited. The following appeared in *USA Today*:

> Have you heard about the biggest, most totally absurd goof ever to bedevil business?
>
> It's become known as the Year 2000 Problem. It threatens to crash every computer in the world. To fix it, companies and other organizations are going to have to spend as much as $600 billion the next four years.
>
> Hard to imagine anything so big it would cost $600 billion to fix. That's three times what all U.S. communications companies expect to spend to rewire the nation with fiber optics. It's 6,000 times what it will cost Bob Dole to try to get elected the leader of the free world. There are only 100 billion lightbulbs in the world. Changing all of them would cost less.[22]

The problem, the article explains, is a "stupid" one involving the fact that almost all computers, when they read and write dates, use only the last two digits of the year. To the computer, 1996 is "96." The machines have no idea that 00 following the turn of the century should indicate the year 2000. They think the year 00 still refers to 1900. Every piece of data labeled 00 becomes totally fouled up if the 00 is supposed to indicate the year 2000. Everything stored in the computer that has a date on it—every document, credit card bill, financial statement, database entry—is thrown into total confusion because of the glitch.

One example cited: Every time a merchant scans a credit card with the date 00 for an expiration date, the store's computers will automatically stop the transaction.

The computer figures the card expired in the year 1900. The *USA Today* story continued:

> Fixing the problem on one computer is not difficult. We're talking about changing a little bit of software code. It becomes a $600 billion debacle when you look at the size and scope of the glitch.
>
> "It's across all our information technology infrastructure. It's in all our data. It's built into bank ATMs," says Kevin Schick of researchers Gartner Group.
>
> "So it's the sheer size and amount of labor to look at everything. It's amazing how much has to be spent just to see if you have a problem."
>
> At Anderson Consulting, Iain Lopata uses this analogy: Fixing the year 2000 Problem on a single computer is like moving one grain of sand from Africa to Chicago. That's not hard. Fixing the problem on all computers is more like moving the Sahara Desert to Chicago, one grain at a time.
>
> But companies have to fix it, and they don't want to because fixing it only keeps bad things from happening. It has no positive value. The $600 billion is wasted money.
>
> How did this happen? Basically, because of laziness and shortsighted cost-cutting in the computer world.
>
> The Year 2000 Problem had its beginnings in the 1960's, when computers started to be used on a large scale. At the time, costly computers the size of a refrigerator had a fraction of the power and storage of today's home PC's. The expense of storing data was enormous. Programmers tried to minimize what would be saved. By reducing dates on all documents by two digits—two bytes on a computer—programmers could dramatically reduce

storage needed. "It was a sensible trade-off at the time," Lopata says.

But even though companies constantly upgraded computers, they never wiped out all their old computers and started over. They integrated new machines with some piece of the old system, and stored old data on the new machines. The old data and old systems still would use two-digit years, infecting the next generation of computers with the Year 2000 Problem. In turn, the bug has been passed from one computer generation to another, like a faulty gene in a royal family.

There's another way to look at this. Says Gartner's Schick: "When you look at $600 billion, that's chump change compared to what will happen if we don't solve the problem."[23]

A "computer glitch" like this illustrates the possible need to address all of the computers in the world more or less simultaneously. Let's assume that the solution to a computer problem is made available in the form of software "fixes." The "fixes" are not distributed widely on disk, but rather are available free through the Internet.

Is it not possible that the "fix" could also include some other sort of software that could be installed in a clandestine fashion, or that would disable the operating system without the continued "assistance" of a computer on the Internet?

We must remember that Revelation 13:8 has yet to be fulfilled. Let's take a look at it: "All that dwell upon the earth shall worship him, whose names are not written in the book of life of the Lamb slain from the foundation of the world."

The implication of this verse is that Antichrist is exerting worldwide control. How is this possible without controlling the computers? Elsewhere we read that the Antichrist's religious officer, the false prophet, "... had power to give life unto the image of the beast, that the image of the beast should both speak and cause that as many as would not worship the image of the beast should be killed" (Revelation 13:15).

The only conceivable way for this to happen worldwide is through television and computers. TV stations worldwide are now gearing up for digital, computerized image acquisition and distribution. This will be implemented. Thus we see fulfillment of Bible prophecy now clearly possible!

No More Privacy

When the government, private citizens, and even some businesses are concerned, perhaps it's time to take stock of how little privacy we still have. A recent article in *USA Today* gives details of our losses:

> Suppose everything you bought was monitored. Very closely. So closely that the grocer knows that your dog prefers canned food to dry. Or that you recently switched from roll-on deodorant to spray. So closely that the hotel you stayed at last week knows what your favorite candy bar is and how many Kleenex boxes you want in your room— even though no one asked. Or that the last time you signed onto the Internet, someone could have watched what you did, what you said, or what you bought, and then shared the information with a curious marketer who wanted to know.

> This is not the future. Such windows to your private life are already open for those who know where to look.

> It has gotten so out of hand, some experts say, that the right to privacy has all but disappeared, sacrificed on the altar of customer service and corporate profits. Today if consumers do not take

extraordinary steps to shield their privacy, they end up with very little or none at all.

With so much information circulating about our personal habits, traits and desires, McKinsey & Co. consultant Mike Sherman says he expects to see the grand opening on a new chain: Psychic Pizza. "Your pizza is delivered 15 minutes before you order it, or it's free," he jokes.

Unknowingly, through things people do every day—get the car washed, go to the grocery store, order a sweater from a catalog—they leave electronic fingerprints that give marketers crucial information.

And the information collection is just the beginning. An invisible price tag hangs from every crumb [that] marketers gather about each of us, and the sale of that information has bloomed into a multbillion-dollar industry. For as little as a nickel, marketers [far] removed from the original transaction can find out who you are, where you live, how much you earn and what you like to buy.

Sound like Big Brother is watching? He is. But these days, Big Brother isn't just government. Big Brother is also Big Business.[24]

Today, electronic transactions are closely monitored and reflect "actual behavior" of the consumers on whom they spy. Powerful computers and high-tech scanners carefully record how, when, and where we spend our money. No matter how the consumer answers marketers' questions in surveys, etc., the computer has the absolute capability to faithfully track and record most consumer activities.

"It's the Wild, Wild West, so you've got to be Jesse
James to protect yourself," says Evan Hendricks,
editor of the *Privacy Times*. "Or, you can just pay
cash for everything."[25]

The *USA Today* article reports that the average consumer
is on at least 25 typical marketing databases. Some of us, the
article says, are on 100 or more databases. There are more
than 15,000 specialized lists containing 2 billion consumer
names.[26]

Privacy will certainly diminish as computer power and
scope increases. The potential for great abuse exists, a fact
which does not escape the U.S. Congress. Legislation is being
considered, for example, the Medical Records Confidenti-
ality Act, which would create heavy penalties for wrongful
use of of medical records. Another is the Fair Credit Reporting Act, which would strengthen consumer rights for quick
corrections to inaccurate credit reports and would require
all credit bureaus to have toll-free lines. The Telecommunications Reform Act would give the Federal Communications
Commission a mandate to look at privacy implications of
new technologies such as Caller ID.[27]

The Terrorism Bill, which passed the Senate but stalled
in the House, is feared by its opponents to smack of Big
Brotherism because it would relax some wiretapping and
search-and-seizure constraints. Additionally, the Federal
Trade Commission has held hearings that could, according
to the *USA Today* article, lead to standards about privacy
on-line.[28]

The article continues:

Just how deeply are marketers prying into our privacy?
If you've parked in a hotel parking lot lately, your license may have been videotaped by a new data-gath-
ering firm that sends workers into parking lots. They

videotape the plates and attempt to track them back to their owners. The information is then sold to other hotels.

And some retailers are expected to experiment with special shopper ID cards molded with transmitters that automatically alert store sensors that you are in the store.

"Smart retailers not only know what I consume, but also how many, how often, and what color," says Don Peppers, a marketing expert.

Perhaps no single industry tries to track its customers more closely than the tobacco industry. More than $100 million of the $500 million that the big tobacco companies spend on marketing will tie into their massive customer databases.

That's why a dozen cigarette makers give away products to customers who redeem coupons. This provides the most important information they can gather: Names and addresses of their best customers.

Few customers keep more detailed electronic files than Ritz-Carlton Hotels. "We go to any lengths to find out guest preferences," explains Tammy Hohensein of the Ritz-Carlton in Palm Beach, Florida.

At the Ritz-Carlton in Naples, Florida, each employee–from the bellman to the pool guard–carries around a "guest preference" notebook. While walking guests to their rooms or to pool-sized lounge chairs, employees are encouraged to find out individual guests' likes and dislikes. Even the smallest things are noted. Employees quietly jot down guest preferences on the scratch pads and turn the information into the front desks.

These are just a few of the guest habits recently added to the Palm Beach Hotel's database:

• A gift shop cashier noted one guest coming in to buy Kit Kat candy bars. Now, when this guest checks in to any Ritz-Carlton nationwide, he gets two bowls of Kit Kats.

• A housekeeper made note of a guest who kept asking for Kleenex boxes. Now, when this guest checks in, she arrives to seven boxes of Kleenex throughout her suite.

• A room service attendant noticed one marketing executive would always ask for a bowl of fruit and a bottle of mineral water when he stayed with his wife. But he requested home-made oatmeal cookies and Coke when he traveled on his own.

Now, the hotel automatically knows what to bring him without asking.

"We've been doing this since 1991, but we've never had a guest who said, 'You know too much about me,' " says Heidi Zingsheim, reservations manager at the Naples Ritz-Carlton.

How much is too much? Harrah's Casino knows the precise gambling habits of millions of Harrahs' Gold Card holders. "We know what you bet, how long you play and we can anticipate what you'll lose or win," says Reg Mallamo, vice-president of marketing operations.

How? Frequent gamblers place their Harrah's Gold Cards into slot machines or hand them to card table operators in order to earn gifts of meals or shows. The tradeoff: Every nickel they spend is tracked. But it isn't just five-star hotels and fancy casinos that are amassing database on their customer's habits.

All 12,000 customers of Speedy Car Wash in Panama City, Florida are tracked by their license plate numbers. When the car swings in the driveway, an attendant quickly punches the license plate number into a computer and then knows the customer's name, address and what they want done to the car.

"Greeting people by name is a big issue with customers," says owner Jimmy Branch. "Since I can't remember 12,000 customers names in my brain, there's a computer that will do it for me."[29]

Isaiah 5:8 reads, "Woe unto them that join house to house, that lay field to field, till there be no place, that they be placed alone in the midst of the earth!" Perhaps this is a prophecy for the last days and indicates that privacy will be a rare commodity. Certainly no one will be able to hide.

The Web of the Net

The Net is coming down the superinformation highway at breakneck speed and threatens to catch every one of us in its invisible web. There is no escaping the Net. It is expected to dominate 60 percent of the homes in America by 1999 and generate 6 billion dollars in revenue.

A recent article about Internet carries a real impact:

Like it or not, the Internet is coming at you—and in more ways than you probably imagined.

Up to now, Internet communications largely have been limited to telephone wires and, in a few much-heralded experiments, cable television lines. Consumers hook them to personal computers and typically pay $20 to $40 a month to

> send and receive electronic mail, information and entertainment.
>
> That's too expensive for a lot of people. And most Internet connections on phone lines are still agonizingly slow: Today's conventional 14.4 kilobits-per-second (kbps) modems can take half a minute or more to receive a single page filled with color pictures from the World Wide Web, the multimedia portion of the Internet.[30]

According to the *USA Today* article, only 10 million homes in America use the Internet global computer network. The size of that market will no doubt change vastly in the near future. Several companies say they can lower the price of the service and boost transmission speeds by broadcasting Internet data through local TV signals, microwaves, and satellites. The Internet will then become a mass medium of tremendous scope. Communications and commerce will then undergo a revolution perhaps unrivaled in the history of human progress.

> "This is a crazy world where information will be able to come from anywhere," says Richard Doherty, a researcher and consultant at the Envisioneering Group. "By the turn of the century, the majority of the Internet content that people get will come from the alternative services."[31]

This is a foreboding prospect for telephone and cable companies, according to the *USA Today* story. Those industries intend to dominate the web connection business–a business expected to generate 6 billion dollars in revenue by 1999.

According to the article, PC makers promise Intercast tuner cards in models that will sell for about 200 dollars each.

These should be available in just a matter of months. With the cards, computer owners can watch regular TV shows on their PCs by viewing the bottom of the screen. The owner can call up Web pages containing information about subject discussed on the air.

Say NBC's Tom Brokaw gives a report about the Israeli elections. A curious viewer might call up text and graphics from a biography of Prime Minister-elect Benjamin Netanyahu, a history of the Mideast peace process or an analysis of the new Knesset.

Most of that information will be instantly available. It already will have been sent to, and stored on, the PC. Intercast won't enable users to send their own e-mail or surf the Web at will. They'll only be able to see the pages broadcasters provide.

But that might be plenty. "Our research shows that people are excited by the Web but have no idea what to do when they get there," says Mariah Scott, who directs the Intercast Industry Group for chipmaker Intel.

WavePhore, a company working in Intercast, has even bigger plans of its own. It's talking about using TV signals—sent over the air or via cable—to broadcast any Internet pages that users want. Customers would communicate their choices and transmit some data, such as e-mail, via telephone modem.

The TV transmission method isn't perfect. It takes about 10 seconds to send a typical Web page. That's faster than most telephone modems but doesn't set speed records. To juice things up, WavePhore could transmit the most popular pages to users' PCs before they sit down to surf.

"Only 50 sites generate the bulk of the traffic," says Patrick Gilbert, WavePhore's vice-president for strategic business development. "And 1,000 sites constitute over 90% of Internet usage."

CAI President John Prisco touts his product's advantages. "It's fast to market. And the infrastructure costs are a fraction of the cost of wired services," he says. It only costs about $10 to install wireless cable service in a home. Cable companies often charge much more.[32]

The major obstacle to explosive growth is the limited number of homes that subscribe to wireless cable. Only 710,000 homes or so are currently linked to the system. Only people who can aim an antenna directly at the local microwave transmitter without interference from buildings or trees are candidates for the service. Some providers, such as US Satellite Broadcasting and EchoStar, already equip their TV-top receiver boxes with special plugs that could be used to connect with PCs. Currently, however, there are not enough satellites to accommodate the millions of requests to transmit different Web pages. According to *USA Today*, EchoStar plans to launch a new satellite in the fall of 1996 and another in 1997.[33]

WorldGate communications CEO Hal Krisbergh says he has a solution for the 62 million homes that subscribe to cable. And customers—who would pay $4.95 a month—wouldn't even need a PC.

Krisbergh introduced his plan in April to cable operators: Put the brains for the connection, a big computer, at the cable transmission site. It would send Web data through cable wires to the home set-top box at three times the speed of a conventional phone modem. The TV would essentially serve as the monitor.

Viewers would send messages to the operator's computer—for example, what Web page they want to see—with a keyboard that communicates via infrared waves to the set-top box.

"Just imagine if 60% of the population (roughly the number of cable subscribers) has access to the Internet," says Krisbergh. "You'll see a whole shift in communications, shopping—every aspect of how we see the world. It will have a major, universal impact."[34]

This article shows the frantic efforts to build up the Internet and make it universal. The race will continue until the Internet is available to every living soul.

Politics in Cyberspace

Politics is already being influenced by cyberspace. In coming years the Internet may have a dominant role in politics as does network television today. Notice a few paragraphs in the July 21, 1996, *Oklahoman*:

Computer-equipped voters, as never before, can arm themselves with the power of knowledge before stepping into the voting booth.

From candidates' campaign literature to in-depth campaign finance studies to raw data on campaign contributions, the World Wide Web is awash with free information about candidates and political issues.

All that is necessary is an Internet access account and Web browser software.

But voters who turn to the on-line world for political information must learn to be cautious consumers, says one of the suppliers of that information.

"If you don't know who we are and you don't know our track record over the last six or seven years, you shouldn't take what we say as gospel. It's not a newspaper of long-standing reputation," said Alex Benes of the Center for Public Integrity.[35]

Global Internet

If you think the Internet has developed quickly, it has! But the speed limit on the superinformation highway has just been raised. A new device that costs a few hundred dollars has been recently introduced in Oklahoma City, and now virtually anyone who wants to and has the bucks can turn on the Internet:

A new company has rolled out a low-cost device to browse the Internet's World Wide Web, blasting in front of computer industry veterans who have talked about the idea for months but not delivered.

WebTV Networks, Inc., a Silicon Valley startup firm, demonstrated its device publicly for the first time Wednesday and announced two powerful partners.

Sony Electronics, Inc. and Philips Consumer Electronics Co. will start selling devices based on the technology in September.

Nearly a dozen companies, including large ones like Oracle Corp. and IBM have talked about lower-cost Internet access devices in recent months.

WebTV Networks kept quiet, working with Sony and Philips for months and building their trust by adhering to design deadlines.

"We're late to get to retailers. They've already made a lot of their fall plans," said Ed Volkwein, senior vice-president and general manager of sales and marketing at Philips. "This could be the hottest thing for Christmas."

Indeed, if the product becomes available for just a few hundred dollars as expected, it could open up the Internet to a huge number of people who have been put off by the high cost of personal computers and the difficulty of installing software and signing up an Internet access company.

WebTV's machine uses a phone line and universal remote control to navigate the worldwide computer network. Logging on is as simple as pushing a green button marked "Web" on the remote. A wireless keyboard is optional.[36]

Knowest thou the ordinances of heaven? Canst thou set its dominion in the earth? Canst thou lift up thy voice to the clouds, that abundance of waters may cover thee? Canst thou send lightnings, that they may go and say unto thee, Here we are? (Job 38:33-35).

The Internet is closing in on the people of this planet, and all nations will soon walk in the shadow of the World Wide Web.

In the realm of cyberspace we are dealing with the natural and the supernatural—the physical world and the spiritual world. That is why when the Internet becomes full-blown as the World Wide Web, people will discover that they have entered the incredible world of Armageddon. It will be an unknown world with uncharted paths and a horrible nightmare without past or future.

Escaping the Dark Prince

The soul of Internet will be the pulsing powerful entity called the image of the beast. As the living tool of Antichrist, this huge and horrible instrument of death will direct all worship to Antichrist and ultimately the devil.

When the lights of Internet come on all over this solar system, the world will behold the shadowy form of the image of the beast—probably something like the silent metallic man of Daniel 2, which is described as a bright and horrible image. But in Revelation 13, this Frankenstein of all the ages comes alive and walks through the earth.

Consider a world totally dominated by the dark prince— the god of this world who will finally be able to control banking and business, commerce and trade, politics and principalities on high. This will be a world that man has never known before or will ever know again.

After the return and reign of the Lord Jesus Christ, the new heavens and the new earth will be unspeakably glorious and the Son of God will be worshiped by men and angels alike. The realm of the second death, the lake of fire (not in this solar system), will become the permanent exile of fallen angels, demon spirits, and unregenerate mankind.

God's Internet will direct the world of light and the redeemed. God's Net will enfold all nations into the glorious enjoyment of peace and prosperity.

Let us prepare to walk with Christ in white in a universe without war and where sin will become an obsolete word, a world where God will dwell among men and there will be no death. Believe John 3:16 and be ready to inherit the habitations of His praises!

PART TWO

The Coming Dictatorship

❖ ❖ ❖

6

Israel: Earth's Lightning Rod

Zola Levitt

Israel is the most important country in the world today. From a secular viewpoint, it is situated on the land bridge between the Asian and African continents, and it represents an island of democracy in an ocean of dictatorships. It is America's key ally in the Eastern hemisphere. Economically, it is quite a power for its size, having an economy ten times the size of that of Egypt, Jordan and Syria put together! Politically, it is front page news almost every day. The unbelieving world is indeed interested in Israel.

But for believers, its significance is beyond measure. The premillennial view of Scripture reveals that all believers will spend a thousand years in Israel with their King, and this could happen seven years from today! In the Second Coming, our Lord will not return to just any country, but as a matter of fact, "his feet shall stand in that day upon the mount of

Olives, which is before Jerusalem on the east" (Zechariah 14:4). He will reign on the throne of David from Jerusalem, ruling a world of believing nations. We who have trusted Him for our salvation will rule with Him. The Bride of Christ will become the Queen of the Kingdom to come.

But before all of those happy events, there is the day of God's wrath to contend with—"the time of Jacob's trouble" (Jeremiah 30:7). Little Israel is involved in close to 100 percent of End Times prophecy.

The Tribulation period, the seventieth week of Daniel, will transpire when the Antichrist makes a peace covenant with the nation of Israel. That simple statement has been uttered for quite a few years, but we happen now to live in a time when people are riding up on a constant basis with peace treaties for Israel to sign. This mere fact by itself is grounds to suppose that the time is very short before the entrance of the one who will ultimately betray Israel and the world. The improvement in the Antichrist's treaty, compared to today's peace agreements, is probably the guarantee he can give of Israel's security, presumably by his ten-nation confederacy in western Europe. He will be able to provide close-in land, sea and air defenses. Another attractive feature may be the seven-year span of the treaty, and possibly permission for Israel to rebuild their temple at last. Whatever the terms of the treaty, the Antichrist would be clearly recognizable to Bible readers by his lavish promises of peace on earth. This will be a false peace, of course, but are we not living in an age of false peace agreements? As we look at a world containing Chechnya, Bosnia, Lebanon, Ireland and South Africa, to mention a few smoldering fires, we hear of peace agreements being signed and abrogated all the time. It is actually rather remarkable to compare our times with the biblical descriptions of the Tribulation period. (This is to say nothing of the famines, pestilences, earthquakes, wars and rumors of wars, offenses, betrayals, etc., spoken of by the Lord in His Olivet discourse [Matthew 24] which is also addressed to Israel [see verses 13, 15, and 16].)

Where Israel is concerned, an uneasy peace will obtain for three and a half years, at which time the Antichrist will sense the Jewish people's suspicions of him, and will attempt to assert his authority. He will do no less than call himself the God of Israel, or in Paul's words:

> Let no man deceive you by any means: for that day shall not come, except there come a falling away first, and that man of sin be revealed, the son of perdition; who opposeth and exalteth himself above all that is called God, or that is worshipped; so that he as God sitteth in the temple of God, showing himself that he is God (2 Thessalonians 2:3-4).

Our Lord Himself, along with the prophet Daniel, foresaw the cataclysmic effects of this spiritual excess: "When ye therefore shall see the abomination of desolation, spoken of by Daniel the prophet, stand in the holy place, (whoso readeth, let him understand:) then let them which be in Judea flee into the mountains" (Matthew 24:15-16). In all probability, the Jewish people will bolt, having mistrusted the Antichrist right along. (Some teach that the Israeli leadership will accept him as a Messiah when he first comes. I do not believe they are that credulous. Having had bitter experience with false Messiahs in the past, they are far more careful than that. And after all, when the real Messiah presented Himself, they largely did not accept Him either.)

To continue our schedule of Tribulation period events, we have the mobilization of the world's armies, and particularly that of the King of the East and his force of 200 million men-at-arms, according to Revelation 9:16. It seems that the second half of the Tribulation is devoted to preparing for Armageddon, the world having heard enough of the Antichrist's peace plans. Perhaps when the Israelis bolt, the

Chinese and the others who are watching come to the conclusion that the Antichrist is not God after all, but is actually
quite vulnerable. Since he controlled the world, then those
who defeat him might control the world as well. And so the
fight commences as the King of the East's army literally
marches to Armageddon, robbing, raping and pillaging as
they go through the eastern hemisphere.

Where does a 200-million army march? Anywhere it
likes. And so the Antichrist's forces from western Europe and
the theatre nations designated as the King of the North and
the King of the South, arm to meet this invader in that quiet,
level valley in Israel surrounding the hill "called in the
Hebrew tongue Har Megiddo [Armageddon]" (Revelation
16:16). The rest of the Tribulation period is the story of battles at Armageddon and Jerusalem, about which the Lord
sadly observed, "And except those days should be shortened,
there should no flesh be saved" (Matthew 24:22).

The Lord's arrival at this point is, of course, the Second
Coming, which initiates the thousand-year Kingdom in Israel.
His first act is to judge the nations of the earth as to whether
they are sheep or goats; that is, whether each citizen had a
saving faith or not. He sets up a throne of judgment and uti-
lizes as His standard—and note again here the importance of
Israel—"Inasmuch as ye have done it unto one of the least of
these my brethren, ye have done it unto me" (Matthew
25:40). Most intensively "my brethren" refers to the Jewish
people, or at least to the 144,000 "of all the tribes of the children of Israel" of Revelation 7:4. Outlawed, they still testified of Christ in the world, despite the Antichrist's reign, and
those who helped them, fed them, clothed them, visited them
in prison, as the passage urges, demonstrate that they are
sheep. Those who did not help them are goats and are bound
with Satan for the duration of the thousand-year Kingdom.

If churches today who care little about Israel were put to
the test of these Tribulation period believers, one wonders if

they would qualify as sheep under the Lord's standards. One can only hope that believers in this age of relative freedom, prevalence of Bibles in many translations, and no Antichrist in power to contend with, would at a minimum be able to meet the test of the Tribulation period believers.

When the sheep have joined with the Old Testament saints and the church, the Kingdom has its population and it begins in earnest. It will last a thousand years, and while there will be some sin and some mischief in the world, it will be an upside-down society compared with what we have today. To believe in the King, who may be seen in Jerusalem from year to year at least on the Feast of Tabernacles (Zechariah 14:16-19), will be the choice of the vast majority of the world. The unbelievers in the Kingdom (the descendants of those who survived the Tribulation in their natural bodies and came directly to the Kingdom—the children of the "sheep," as it were), will be as those born of Adam. They will have a choice between belief and unbelief, but those who choose the latter will be bound by the onerous laws of the Sermon on the Mount: "If thy right eye offend thee . . . if thy right hand offend thee . . ." (Matthew 5:29-30). It is at that time that the meek shall inherit the earth, and those who mourn will rejoice.

With that summation of upcoming events, we can begin to consider Israel as we see it today, as a harbinger of prophetic fulfillment.

Israel Today

Writing about Israel at any given time is very difficult because that nation is in a constant state of change. Anyone who has visited the place will testify to the almost electrifying atmosphere in the streets, and the sense of spiritual forces, potential physical danger, and unmitigated energy that simply permeate the air in that unique place. After thinking about this chapter for a full year and collecting notes, I realize that a book could well be written, rather than just a chapter, on this particular year in Israel. Three events, especially, seem to stand out as regarding prophecy. They are the assassination of Prime Minister Rabin; the sudden acceleration of terrorism in the spring of 1996; and the election of Binyamin Netanyahu, which seemed to surprise everyone but those familiar with the Israeli population and their concerns.

The global news media bias against Israel and in favor of various Arab schemes and causes has given many people a false picture of the Holy Land. The Arabs, 200 million in number, are cast as the underdog to the 4½ million Israelis; and the Palestinians, the perpetrators of terrorism, are considered the victims in the press and electronic coverage. With the media, the U.S. administration, and almost everyone else rooting for Prime Minister Shimon Peres and the "peace process," the world was shocked when the Israeli population elected Netanyahu.

But this was easy to understand from the streets of Israel. The population was simply worried about giving away land to people who seemed to have no intention of making peace. Instead, the Palestinians have used almost any excuse to perpetrate violence against Israel. The Hasmonean Tunnel, which caused such grief and loss of life in September 1996, was used purely as a pretext. I personally went through the tunnel with the chief archaeologist, Daniel Bahat, in December 1996 and found the place completely quiet, especially the exit which was opened near the Arab stores on the Via Dolorosa. The only action around that exit was the business being done by Arab shop-owners, who enjoy streams of new customers now that tourists can exit the tunnel on their side of it.

The media was dishonest enough to call the election "razor-thin" and "hairline," when actually the Jewish vote put Netanyahu ahead 56 percent to 44 percent. The vote of the

Israeli Arabs, a monolithic one in favor of Peres, made the election seem close in the pure numbers, but ought not to be taken seriously as valid balloting in a democracy. No Arab nation is now or has ever been a democracy, and Arab people pretty much vote as a bloc or as they are told to vote.

Regarding the first of the history-making events of the past year, the Rabin assassination, I looked back at our ministry's coverage of that event. We were certainly asked a host of questions about what really happened and how we felt about it. I will draw below from the letter that I wrote in response to those questions.

Israel's first assassination is being widely misunderstood. Supposedly, those who want peace supported Prime Minister Rabin, and those who are opposed to peace criticized him. Or so we are told. And finally "the opponents of peace" escalated their protests until one of them finally killed the Prime Minister. And now it's simply a question of whether Israel will follow Rabin's policies to perfect peace or fall into his opponents' clutches and continuous war.

That is the construction of the U.S. media of a very complex and tragic event in Israel. Biblical people know better what's going on. In reality, this "peace process" has a terrible flaw. It violates a biblical imperative: the sanctity of the borders of Israel. In their time, Babylon, Persia, Greece and Rome, all mighty empires, changed the borders of Israel as they pleased. All of them are extinct. Israel is not an ordinary nation to be changed and manipulated according to the fortunes of men. It is God's land, and "God is not mocked" (Galatians 6:7).

Those who would seek political gain by this assassination are pointing out that the opposition in its protests called Rabin a traitor, and they say the invective is what killed him. But Israel is a democracy and necessarily has a divided government, as is ours in Washington, D.C. One part promotes a program and the other protests, and that is how it works both here and in Israel. As to the "invective," a cartoon in the *Jerusalem Post* the day before Yom Kippur showed Rabin in full worship dress making his Day of Atonement confessions for the things he had called his opponents. Listed were "pariahs, parasites, crybabies, cancers, cowards, liars, idiots" and the list went on. Israeli politics have always contained such invective, and it's not strange to other democracies either. The fact is, the Prime Minister was shot by an overzealous Israeli crusading to maintain the biblical borders of Israel, and it's difficult for biblical people to condemn that goal.

One writer in the *Jerusalem Post* does not use the term "peace process," but calls it "the government's unilateral give-away program." The "ultra-extremist group," of American media expression, actually represents a probable majority of Israelis. "The opponents of peace" are simply those who object to giving half of their arable land to their sworn enemies and then hoping they are not annihilated. So far as the current clash goes, one could just as easily say the government started it with its extraordinary program of giving up the precious land of Israel for what has proved to be no peace at all.

We conducted a man-on-the-street program for our upcoming Jerusalem 3000 series, and I personally interviewed about 15 people in downtown Jerusalem. Twelve or 13 of them expressed extreme misgivings about the land-for-peace idea. Americans should realize that the "West Bank" describes biblical Judea and Samaria, and is a huge portion of Israel, not just a riverbank. The King of Jordan coined the expression "West Bank" to make the area seem small and unimportant, but it is the heart and soul of the Holy Land, and one glance at a map will show that. Many people I talked to felt it was a mistake to give up land of such proportions to people like the PLO. David Bar-Illan, the editor-in-chief of the *Jerusalem Post,* said in our October interview that Rabin was simply mistaken in his policies. When I pointed out that Rabin had fielded great armies against these very people and ought to know what he's doing, Bar-Illan said that great generals can make great mistakes.

Despite its incredible giveaway program, the government has never conducted a real referendum, a vote by all of the people, to understand if they support its policies. One Rabin government official said the huge number of people coming out to the funeral is the referendum, but he was not right. Policy by a democratic government must be with the consent of the governed, and the present Israeli government has never obtained that consent. The enemies of Israel include virtually all Arabs and all anti-Semites in the world, and that's quite a number of people! (It is not usually stated that there are 200 million Arabs and only 4 million Israelis. Our media maintains the myth that the Arabs are somehow the underdog.) Looking at the Arabs, one finds the real "opponents of peace." Hamas opposes any peace agreement with Israel, and its charter says as much: "The Hamas is opposed to all international conferences and negotiations and to any peaceful settlements." There were Arab celebrations in Lebanon and among the Hamas over the death of a man who even the dictators of Jordan and Egypt came to appreciate for his steadfastness and his character. While the world hastens to establish a 23rd Arab dictatorship in Israel, the Israeli "right wing" (as it is called by the American media) struggles to hold a very small land together. As to the PLO and Arafat, the Chairman did not attend the funeral because "he didn't want to be a distraction," as he said on the first day. On the second day, prompted by some PR man one could clearly hear on TV, he stated that he wanted to say goodbye to his friend, but "they [the Israelis] didn't give me this chance." In reality, Arafat did not attend the funeral because there is no peace and he would not have been welcome.

I am almost sorry to have to write this strong a letter after so sad an event, but the American media is so ridiculously misinformed, or so partisan toward a certain point of view, that it's hard to get any true picture of what's going on. CNN asked, "Can a nation that has seen so much bloodshed. . . ." Well, I've counted 27 days of war in Israel since 1948, as opposed to our own country's eight years in Vietnam and three years in Korea. Israel has lost some 3,000 soldiers, while we have lost 100,000. And we weren't fighting about our own country, in any case. Ted Koppel solemnly intoned, "A vision of Israelis killing Israelis–of what their country may become" in answer to the first case anyone can remember of an Israeli killing an Israeli. The ABC affiliate in Dallas said that the anti-government groups pose the greatest threat to security, when actually giving away the land to a sworn enemy obviously poses a still greater threat. Israel is unfortunately becoming to the news media and America what Jackie Kennedy was to the tabloids–a constant source of delicious drama and controversy. And yet we are talking here about God's country. Mike Wallace of "60 Minutes," a reliable critic of Israel, had Kahane Chai members as interviewees, as if this tiny fringe group counted for something. To put such people on "60 Minutes" as representatives of Israel is to put Ku Klux Klan or neo-Nazis on television as representatives of America, and Wallace well knows it. About the only heartening American response to this terrible assassination was the presence of more than 100 Washington dignitaries at the funeral. Prime Minister Rabin had a warm personal relationship with a great many in the American government, and as a government we favor his party in Israeli politics.

So to wrap up all that I have said, Prime Minister Rabin was a fine Israeli gentleman, a distinguished soldier and a crusader for peace. His policies were extremely controversial and led in the end to his untimely death. Time will tell which side is right or wrong in this conflict–or the biblical

End Times will come on and show that there really was no solution to the Israeli dilemma.

At this time, looking back on the assassination, it has seemed to militate toward the End Times in a very direct way. We might describe the subsequent chain of events as follows: Peres takes over the government and accelerates the peace process; the people of Israel polarize and the "right wing" is accused of causing the assassination; the Palestinians also divide, with those not in favor of the peace process heightening their terrorist activities; the bombing of buses in Jerusalem and Tel Aviv causes a majority of the Jewish population to swing toward the right; Netanyahu wins the election. At the time of this writing, there is an uneasy silence in Israel, with both sides (the Israelis and the Palestinians) waiting to see what the policies of the new government really will be. The way in which this militates toward the Tribulation period is that the policies Netanyahu chooses to embrace could have the potential to bring on real conflict—a true shooting war. That is, if he refuses to go ahead with the peace process, the Palestinians will sooner or later escalate the terrorism until life in Israel becomes unbearable. They might also consider that they have enough of an excuse to attack Israel, with the help of Syria or whomever, and they would most likely have world opinion on their side. World opinion is created by the aforementioned media bias, which is invariably anti-Israel these days. If, on the other hand, Netanyahu goes ahead with the peace process and step-by-step gives Israel over to the Palestinians, the Israelis would find themselves on a relatively narrow coastal strip facing the populous West Bank high ground in the center of the country. The Palestinians would then be in a position to launch an attack against a much smaller Israel, which the Israelis might choose to repulse with nuclear weaponry.

Thus, in either case, the so-called peace process leads ultimately to war. Or then again, it might lead to the brink of war, giving the Antichrist his cue to enter the negotiations with his own "superior" peace plan. One can imagine the beleaguered Israelis, realizing that the use of nuclear materials in so small a space would be almost as dangerous to themselves as to their enemy, contemplating what to do and glad to have an alternative of a seven-year peace plan. I am purely speculating on the scenario that will bring the Antichrist on stage at last, but the peace process in Israel is extremely suggestive of the administration of the Antichrist. It bears all his characteristics: it is anti-Israeli, it is a false peace, and it leads ultimately to war.

I have touched on the media bias that has given Israel an undeservedly bad reputation in the minds of today's generation. We must bear in mind that most of the people alive today did not witness the founding of Israel, nor did they live as adults through the period when a young and brave Israel of kibbutzim and defensive wars sustained itself and grew into the nation it is today. Rather, university-age students and even Baby Boomers are conscious only of a strong Israel and its opposition to the Arabs. That unfortunate opposition means that petro-dollars and Israel are on opposite sides of an ongoing debate. Should we support our sister democracy with whatever blemishes it may have, or should we favor the Arabs and maintain an inexpensive, steady flow of oil to run our civilization?

The media, like any other business, give their best customers the most courtesy, and they are utterly ruled by oil money. The advertising of cars, plastics, gasoline, cosmetics, and a thousand other petroleum products, supports the for-profit media enterprises we mistakenly assume are neutral in their reportage. Obviously, they follow an invariably pro-oil-money line. The Arabs have even gone so far as to purchase certain news agencies, including the United Press International, in order to more effectively manage the news we get.

I have personally had the experience of speaking to newspaper editors who would not even correct misreported facts in Arab-released news; they simply accused me of bias. I pointed out to the foreign editor of the *Dallas Morning News* that the paper had reported violence in Manger Square in Bethlehem in December 1994, while my tour group, which stood in the square the whole evening, had seen no violence whatsoever. I also commented that the *Morning News* was running an Arab news release from Cairo, and they might want to correct their errors. I was told that the editor understood my bias. I replied that it was not a matter of bias but of eyewitness testimony, and that the *Morning News* was not reporting the facts. I asked if, since they had an Arab writer, did they perhaps have any Jewish editors to look at the copy and see if it was at least accurate. To that, the editor answered, "I consider that a racist question."

David Bar-Illan, executive editor of the *Jerusalem Post,* reported that the *New York Times,* "the newspaper of record," reported an influx of 200,000 Palestinians from Kuwait into Gaza during the Persian Gulf War. Nothing of the kind happened at all, but that august newspaper refused to print a retraction or even look into the matter, and this important misinformation is now there to be read by future generations as presumably a reason why the Palestinians needed more land. The news on television networks is equally biased. I personally find very repugnant the reportage of Mike Wallace, Robert Novak, Anthony Lewis, Thomas Friedman and Ted Koppel. They can all be counted on to criticize Israel virtually 100 percent of the time. They are also all Jews, though they might not like that fact to be generally known.

Jerusalem is a particular bone of contention right now, and that is how the prophets portrayed it in the End Times. Jerusalem is the most wonderful city in the world, not only in its beauty, but also in its significance. The prophets picture the millennial house of the Lord there on Mount Moriah, where the old temples of God once stood.

The book of Revelation also continues the career of Jerusalem beyond the kingdom and into eternity: "And I saw a new heaven and a new earth: for the first heaven and the first earth were passed away; and there was no more sea. And I John saw the holy city, new Jerusalem, coming down from God out of heaven, prepared as a bride adorned for her husband" (Revelation 21:1-2).

But Zechariah also chronicles tougher times for Jerusalem before all that good news, and I'm afraid we are now living in that turbulent period. "And in that day will I make Jerusalem a burdensome stone for all people: all that burden themselves with it shall be cut in pieces, though all the people of the earth be gathered together against it" (Zechariah 12:3). This is a case where what once was a prophecy to be interpreted is now daily news that anyone can see. Jerusalem and, indeed, all of Israel are becoming the center of the earth and the focus of all nations. The current peace process, which is still on track even after the recent assassination, prophetically will lead to that "covenant with death and hell" (Isaiah 28:15) warned about in prophetic Scripture. The Antichrist will eventually arrive with his seven-year treaty, and that will be the beginning of the end.

An ironic and rather sad feature of the worldwide notoriety of Jerusalem and Israel is that a major part of the church, the body of believers who will live there during the coming thousand-year Kingdom, is largely oblivious to the significance of ongoing events. The denominational churches see nothing of spiritual import going on in Israel. Only Bible readers are aware of the repercussions of recent events.

Indeed, Israel attracts violent reactions the way a lightning rod attracts lightning, and that is in keeping with prophecy. Practically the whole world is unified in its desire to force Israel to bow to this awful peace process, and this shows the widespread lack of understanding of the times. False peace will be the theme the coming Tribulation period, and we have obviously entered an era of false peace today. Yitzhak Rabin was a fine gentleman and a good soldier, but the peace agreement he set in motion will not last because it is not God's peace in God's timing. Ultimately, all the world's peacemaking will be done by that "Dark Prince," of whom Daniel, the clear-eyed forecaster of the End Times, remarks, "He shall magnify himself in his heart, and by peace shall destroy many" (Daniel 8:25). Our times parallel such warnings in Scripture as those who cry "peace, peace; when there is no peace" (Jeremiah 6:14) and "for when they shall say, Peace and safety; then sudden destruction cometh upon them, as travail upon a woman with child; and they shall not escape" (1 Thessalonians 5:3).

In the interviews that our ministry collected in Israel for our "Jerusalem 3000" television series, a number of spokesmen—believers and unbelievers, Jews and Palestinians—clarified all of the above. It is obvious from all that they told us that virtually no one believes in this "peace process" with all his heart. But according to their various motives, it is a means to an end for the Palestinians—the end of Israel—and for the Israelis it is a hope for the end of terrorism. For the American government, it is good PR, and for the United Nations, a sort of victory. For those who are biblically informed, it is the end of the age.

Obviously, Jerusalem will remain in contention for some time to come. At the time of this writing, the Netanyahu government has ordered all Palestinian offices in Jerusalem to be dismantled, in accordance with the Oslo agreements. The Palestinians were never authorized to place government offices in the Jewish capital, but they did so anyway, and the Peres government, despite many well-publicized threats, never closed these offices. I myself with my TV crew interviewed Faisal Husseini, the "Palestinian Representative for

Jerusalem," in the Orient House, an Arab mansion dating
from the past century that had been refurbished as a Palestinian governmental headquarters for receiving foreign dignitaries, many of whom have visited. I counted 25
"plainclothesmen" (thugs in jeans and T-shirts) surrounding
the building and in the streets on all sides. For me, seeing such
an ominous personality as Husseini seated in state in such
surroundings felt like an eerie prediction of the Antichrist
entering the Temple and declaring that he is the God of Israel!

Israel, the Churches, and the Seminaries

Besides the media bias, there is a kind of theological bias
against Israel going on in churches and seminaries today. The
liberal churches have always been a lost cause so far as biblical study is concerned, and they, of course, are blissfully
unaware of the relevance of Israel in prophecy, or of
prophecy in general, for that matter. But I refer to biblically
based churches and seminaries, who over time have seemed
to change positions concerning Israel. Dallas Theological
Seminary, Moody Bible Institute, and most of the other biblical seminaries admired the Israelis when they were heroes
in the media in the great days of the Six Day War and the kibbutzim and so forth. But as the media bias turned against the
Israelis, so it seemed did the seminaries and even some Bible
churches. As I put it recently during a speaking engagement,
my ministry started out explaining Israel to Christians, and
now I'm having to defend Israel to Christians.

In reality, the Israelis have not changed, but some peculiar anti-Israel theologies have come down the road. "For the
time will come when they will not endure sound doctrine;
but after their own lusts shall they heap to themselves
teachers, having itching ears; and they shall turn away their
ears from the truth, and shall be turned unto fables" (2 Timothy 4:3-4). If we are to expect teachers who will just tickle
the ears, we have plenty now.

The ultimate scriptural error is replacement theology, which seeks to establish that the church has replaced Israel. This is the reason for the departure of all of the liberal churches, including the Roman Catholic Church, from sound biblical understanding. It is madness to try to replace Israel in the Scriptures with a miscellaneous group of Gentile peoples scattered around the globe. If the church has replaced Israel in all of God's promises and covenants, then Israel no longer has a role in God's future plan. This would make nonsense out of such Bible passages as Romans 11:25-26, which states "that blindness in part is happened to Israel, until the fullness of the Gentiles be come in. And so all Israel shall be saved." If Israel is out of the picture, that verse should read "and so all the church shall be saved," which would be ludicrous because the church is composed of people who are already saved.

The original replacement theology was Islam, which sought to replace both Judaism and Christianity and thus take over the religious world. As a matter of fact, that statement should not be in the past tense, since that process is still going on with the Moslems. But in the Western world, we should be more alert than to put our Bibles away and follow in error some pastor or professor with anti-Israel or simply anti-Semitic biases. We will not take space here to analyze a bunch of odd doctrines, but will simply say that the Antichrist's religion is the final replacement theology. It will seek to dominate the entire religious and secular world, and even replace Almighty God Himself! Such contemporary doctrinal errors as "Kingdom Now," in which we need to elect the right officials in order to bring in the Kingdom by human endeavor, and "Progressive Dispensationalism," a teaching that mixes up the Church Age and the Millennial Kingdom, are ways of simply cutting Israel out of the picture and thus making the whole Bible nonsense.

The fact is, God chose one people, Israel, and has dealt through them since Abraham and will continue that dealing through them in the future. Thus when we read of the building of the Tower of Babel and the godless ways of mankind early on in Genesis, in the same chapter we see Terah and the birth of his son Abram. God's solution to mankind's apostasy seems to be the invention of a single people through whom all nations of the earth would be blessed (Genesis 12:3). He continued to deal with them through the long period of the Old Testament adventures until the coming of the Messiah, a Jew, who chose 12 Jewish disciples and 12 Jewish apostles. And likewise, as we have seen, He will choose again from among the Jews in order to have testifiers to Christ in the Tribulation period to come, namely the 144,000. If we interrupt that elegant design of four millennia with the idea that some global Gentile organization will take this mantle upon itself, we obviously interrupt a plan of great magnitude. When we teach that we can bring on the Kingdom ourselves without prayer or reference to Israeli affairs, as in Kingdom Now doctrines, we simply depart from God's plan. When we teach that Christ is already ruling in the Kingdom at this time (even though the Messiah Himself entreats us to pray "thy Kingdom come"), we confuse dispensations. We are not exactly getting the cart before the horse, but we are putting the horse inside the cart and cannot move forward. Bringing the Kingdom into the Church Age, as Progressive Dispensationalism does, goes in the direction of Amillennialism, a doctrine which utterly denies the thousand-year Kingdom in Israel.

The Bible is basically the story of one people, the Jewish people. All of its writers cover to cover are Jews, Old Testament and New. The Messiah is a full-blooded Israeli Jew whose genealogies on both sides are presented in Scripture. To show the extremes to which Islam seeks to replace Judaism and Christianity, consider Yasser Arafat's claiming that Jesus

was "the first Palestinian revolutionary." He made this extraordinary statement in Bethlehem in December 1995 as the
birthplace of Jesus Christ was calmly handed over to Moslems
while the worldwide church remained asleep. Or consider
the amazing claim by Hanan Ashrawi (a member of Arafat's
cabinet) on "The MacNeil-Lehrer Report" that "Jesus Christ
was a Palestinian prophet born in Bethlehem in my country."
When Ms. Ashrawi, who claimed to be descended from the
first Christians, was told that the original Christians were all
Jews and that Jews never turn into Arabs, she was a bit confused, but this did not prevent her from being celebrated by
the Episcopalian Church as a good Anglican in an article in
their publication. Such muddling of theological doctrine and
historical fact will play into the hands of the Antichrist, who
will ultimately make the most fantastic of all claims, as we
have mentioned. We are receiving a great deal of practice at
believing total spiritual nonsense.

I wish to quote a few paragraphs from my July 1996
newsletter, since it deals with the Israeli election and the Arab
conference on terrorism and other contemporary events.

> In reality, the so-called peace process has been a loss to
> all parties, including the Palestinians, the Americans, the
> Europeans, and certainly the Israelis. The Palestinians
> were saddled with a police state, and truthful observers
> among them admit that they are being more oppressively
> crushed by Arafat and his henchmen than they ever were
> by Israel. Americans lose because we picked the wrong
> side and were crusading for the destruction of a sister
> democracy, our only true ally in the region. The Euro-
> peans lose because their anti-Semitism has caused Israel,
> truly a leader among nations, to regard Europe as practi-
> cally an enemy. Arab friendship could not possibly be
> worth Israeli aversion.

> Terrorism anywhere disheartens all but the terrorists, and
> prejudices their cause. The church burnings in America

will hurt African-Americans far less in the long run than they hurt the hate groups that perpetrate them. Like Hamas and Hezbollah in Israel, the hate groups in America become outcasts. It will be a refreshing time when we can drop the term "peace process" and let those Arab nations who wish to trade with Israel do so, and those who don't can please themselves.

A corollary to the remarkable Israeli election is that 80 percent of all Israelis voted. In this country, we're lucky to have half that percentage vote. Why was the election of such importance to the international community? The answer is oil and the inappropriate belief that the price will go down if the Israelis give away their land.

It's possible that our ministry's television program got Netanyahu some important votes. A Jewish news agency carried a story of my interviewing him, and tried to paint Netanyahu as hopelessly contaminated since he had Messianic friends. I imagine that caused the opposite reaction.

The election was also a defeat for President Clinton, who heartily supported Peres, and it created a new term for the Holy Land, used over and over by CNN and the networks: "divided Israel." If we consider the candidates running in our own election, we should be embarrassed in front of this brave young democracy where nearly every citizen voted. The *New York Times* on May 31 called the election "breathtakingly close," although they certainly know that if we remove the monolithic Arab vote, Netanyahu won by 56-44 percent—what the Times itself would call a landslide. Also, what we call "illegal aliens" in this country got in quite a few votes in Israel, and they, being entirely Arabs, were practically 100 percent for Peres. At a recent speaking engagement, I had to spell Netanyahu's name and explain what it meant (gift of God) because he received so little coverage in the American media that people simply didn't know who he was.

The excellent newswatch agency CAMERA (Committee for Accuracy in Middle East Reporting in America) detailed coverage of the Israeli election by CNN, the *New York Times,* and specifically Robert Novak and Thomas Friedman, both famous as Jewish enemies of Israel. Without going into too much detail, the conclusion of writer Andrea Levin was simply this: "What makes Friedman's analysis and that of so many other media commentators sterile and ultimately useless to the public is its contempt for the facts and, in this instance, its contempt for the people of Israel." God has spoken on this subject: "I will curse him that curseth thee," He told his friend Abraham regarding his seed, Israel (Genesis 12:3).

The problem with writing about prophecy is that one is not really a biblical prophet and can only speculate about world events. Israel indeed is a lightning rod for more than prophetic developments; it seems that the whole world is focused on that very tiny nation. The North Koreans mutter that something must be done about Israel, although it is doubtful that many of them could find it on a map. In Japan, where there are virtually no Jews, the Jews are blamed for problems with the economy. And on it goes. Indeed, Israel is the center of the nations, and in the Kingdom it will take its prophetic place as the head of the nations (Zechariah 8:20-23).

But to recap what I have said about Israel in prophecy, I believe that the present climate of a false peace process will lead us down one of several possible roads to a Tribulation period situation. As to when this could happen, it is difficult to say, but in view of the very complete fulfillment of all of the Lord's prophecies in Matthew 24, the Olivet discourse, we could hardly expect so tense a situation to obtain for, say, another 50 years. World attention tends to shift from place to place, and since it is currently on Israel, I cannot help having the feeling that this would be an elegant moment to conclude this age. Everything seems to be in the right place except for the entrance of the Antichrist with his peace covenant of seven years. It is hard to think of any other piece of the prophecy puzzle that is not either in position for the End Times or on the verge so that it could rapidly fall into place.

Thus, I think that the Antichrist is alive today and mature, and calculating his entrance. And I think that the present climate of concern over the peace process can lead us very directly to that day of an offered contract that will start the Tribulation period.

I had to moderate that view in an open letter that I sent to Prime Minister Binyamin Netanyahu. Written just before I submitted this chapter, the letter was about the future of Israel, and I think it is relevant to our discussion here. I will close my chapter with a reprint of this letter.

Dear Mr. Netanyahu,

My sincerest congratulations on your victory. It is biblically possible that you will be the most important leader of Israel since King David. What lies ahead for Israel is very complex and it seems to be a little dangerous. I'm glad you are in office.

The American press is calling it a razor-thin majority by which you won, but of course it was truly a landslide. The appearance of being close was caused by the monolithic Arab vote, which really should not be counted in Israel's prime-ministerial elections. Since all Arabs vote exactly the same, having no free elections of their own from which to learn, we can assume they are directed by some force in opposition to Israel.

Since the time we talked in 1994, when you kindly granted me an interview for our "House of David" television series, I note that a great many of your predictions have come true. Your fears of Arafat and of increased violence were more than justified, and your conception of the previous government as operating almost a giveaway program in terms of the land was prescient. I know that you will be more careful than your predecessors.

You have already announced that there will be no negotiations about Jerusalem. Thank God for that! Even if you should have to fight a 100-year war, you must never give up an inch of the Holy City. Our ancestors made it the capital of Israel 3,000 years ago and we have prayed about it for all those 30 centuries. And no matter who has come and gone, the place is ours and ours alone. Thank you for your clear statements on that crucial subject.

With the West Bank, Israel must likewise hold onto as much territory as possible in order to create a buffer zone against an invasion from the east. This was necessary in 1967 and it is necessary today. "Israel is a good country in a bad neighborhood," Ze'ev Chafets, editor of the *Jerusalem Report,* remarked to me some years ago. I'm afraid he was perfectly right. The settlements we have established in the West Bank must be guarded well, and new ones established wherever there is a chance of an incursion. We must bear in mind that the West Bank was just as surely given to the Jewish people as was Jerusalem, and God well remembers "the mountains of Israel" (Ezekiel 36:8-12). Don't give up Hebron, the world's first Jewish city. As a matter of fact, no other people have any valid claim whatsoever to any part of Israel. Sojourners have always fought the Chosen People for our land, but Almighty God has invariably returned it to us.

As to our present residence in the land, Scripture affirms, "I will plant them upon their land, and they shall no more be pulled up out of their land which I have given them, saith the Lord thy God" (Amos 9:15). The French billeted their armies and many civilians in Louisiana, and they have left us their language and their delicious foods. The Spanish likewise occupied America from Texas to California. But neither France nor Spain tries to claim land on this continent based on their passage through, and neither should any sojourner in Israel make such an invalid claim.

As to Gaza, it should be peacefully restrained and helped economically, as long as its residents accept Israel as a good neighbor and appreciate the opportunity to be the only Arabs in the region to live in a democracy. The Golan Heights, Jewish since ancient times, should be held as a buffer zone against Syria as long as its dictator lives, it seems to me. That is a country in which one man owns all the land and all the people, and with whom it is pointless to try to reach an agreement. Biblical Israel must keep its total integrity. Hold on to the land, Bibi, whatever you do!

And finally, Mr. Arafat: personally, I don't trust him. From the Nobel Peace Prize to the White House lawn to the visits in European palaces, his performances have all been a fake. A terrorist is a terrorist, and they seldom really reform. In Arafat's case, he cannot even restrain himself from inflammatory speeches before screaming mobs, or a 21-gun salute at the funeral of the mass murderer called "the Engineer." If a maker of bombs that are designed explicitly to kill civilians is a hero in Arafat's eyes, then there is no hope for making peace with Arafat.

Once again, Prime Minister Netanyahu, I am glad that you are in office and I am hopeful that Israel will have many peaceful and prosperous years under your able leadership. Again, thank you for our interview and please feel free to call on us with any request you may have.

Sha'alu Shalom Yerushalayim,
Zola Levitt

7

Kings of the East Lust Westward

Chuck Missler

❖ ❖ ❖

During the ancient world empires, the locus of power—the center of gravity in the world economy—went from Persia, to Greece, and then to Rome.[1] It has remained in the West for the past 2000 years. In the sixteenth and seventeenth centuries, the center moved from the Mediterranean area to northern Europe, then crossed the Atlantic to America. The twentieth century turned out to be, as Henry Luce put it in 1941, the American Century.

The locus of power now appears to be continuing its move to the east. Based on present trends, the twenty-first century appears to be the Asian Century. In a little more than a decade, that region's share of world economic output has increased to 25 percent, and that figure is rising. The East's portion of the world's foreign exchange has leaped from 10 percent to more than 50 percent, and with national savings rates ranging from 30 percent to 45 percent, the East is generating more savings each year than the U.S. and Europe combined. Lest we forget, it is savings—the creation of capital—that generates economic growth. To this add 36.5 billion

1997 Oct. Big Chg.

189

dollars per year—more than 100 million dollars per day—of capital investment flowing in from Western nations. China has attracted more foreign investment in the past five years than Japan has in the 50 years since World War II.[2]

However, a smooth and peaceful transition is highly unlikely. Some are predicting that the twenty-first century may be the most convulsive period in all of world history. A number of factors are conspiring to make the Far East increasingly unstable over the coming decade. These factors include:

1. China's inexorable rise to superpower status

2. The retrenchment of the U.S.

3. The existence of numerous potential causes for war

4. A burgeoning arms race.

Emergence and Retrenchment

With more than 1.2 billion people, China claims 22 percent of the world's population. Although the country is poor on a per capita basis, China's economy is growing by more than 10 percent per year. If the U.S. continues its growth of about 2.5 percent per year and China continues to grow at its present rate, the two economies will reach approximately equal size of about 8 trillion dollars in the next decade.

(It could take China a century to overtake the U.S. in *per capita* income, but this statistic is largely irrelevant geopolitically. The significant statistics are those indicating aggregate resources which China can command rather than the individual wealth of its citizens.) China's rapid rise to superpower status will change the balance of power in the Far East, inevitably destabilizing the region.

The inevitable retrenchment of the United States as the protector of the status quo is another aspect of our relative economic decline. Following World War II, the United States accounted for 40 percent of the gross world product (GWP). This share has now declined to 22 percent and is likely to drop still further.

Total U.S. military expenditure accounts for 30 percent of the world's military budget. For a country with 4.7 percent of the world's population and 6.3 percent of the world's land mass, it is unlikely to maintain its former level of dominance.

History shows a 20-year decline in the United States' commitment to the Pacific region:

- In 1975, the U.S. was forced out of Vietnam and the Communist North Vietnamese took control of the American-built naval base at Cam Ranh Bay.

- In 1976, all U.S. bases in Thailand were closed and all troops withdrawn.

- In 1990, the U.S. announced a reduction of U.S. military forces in the Pacific from 135,000 to 100,000.

- In 1992, the U.S. closed its naval base on Subic Bay in the Philippines, its largest base in the region. Clark Air Base was also closed.

- In 1996, the U.S. announced that it would pull out of some of its bases in Japan.

These moves all point in the same direction, and the message that Asians are receiving is that they can no longer rely on America for their security.

Potential for War

Serious potential for war threatens the Far East, including the exploding population growth, numerous disputed islands, continuing border disputes, and strong ideological tensions.

Mainland China contains 22 percent of the world's population on 7 percent of the world's land mass, while arable land resources are declining at the rate of 725,000 acres per year due to erosion and other factors. Obvious targets for potential seizures include the Russian Far East, Siberia, and Central Asia. China's continuing assertiveness toward the resources in the South China Sea is also highly probable.

China's energy needs have risen by more than 50 percent over the past ten years, and the country is now the second-largest user of oil outside the U.S. Over the next two decades, China's demand could exceed three times its current production. Speculative hopes in the South China Sea will strain relations on all fronts.

Thousands of tiny islands in Asian waters are subject to competing claims. For example, six countries—China, Taiwan, Vietnam, the Philippines, Brunei, and Malaysia—claim all or part of the Spratly Islands, which are located in the sea lane connecting the fast-growing economies of Asia with the oil-rich Middle East. One Japanese military expert predicts that whoever controls the Spratlys will gain regional hegemony in the next century.

Other islands at the center of disputes include the Paracels (Vietnam versus China and Taiwan), the Tokto Islands (Japan versus South Korea), the southern Kuriles (Japan versus Russia), the Senkaku Islands (Japan versus China and Taiwan), the Natuna Islands (China versus Indonesia), Pedra Branca (Singapore versus Malaysia), and the Sipadan and Ligitan Islands (Malaysia versus Indonesia).

Border disputes also persist between China and Vietnam, China and Laos, Indonesia and Papua New Guinea, and Cambodia and Vietnam. Each of these areas could flare up with the heightening of insecurities in the region.

Overshadowing these tensions in recent times is the pressure that China is placing on Taiwan and the potential conflict between North and South Korea. The displays of military force intended to intimidate Taiwan resulted in the U.S. moving two aircraft carrier groups into the region in March 1966. Defamatory rhetoric included threats by China to nuke Los Angeles. Despite the standoff, Beijing declared that military action against Taiwan would follow any declaration of independence, any foreign invasion of Taiwan, and any unsavory foreign military alliances.

The Korean situation also deteriorated significantly during 1995 and 1996. The movement of a North Korean force of over a million men with combat planes to the demilitarized zone between the two Koreas has positioned North Korea for a tactical surprise that could, along with its nuclear weapons, shatter the South Korea-Japan-U.S. solidarity during any initial breakouts.

Arms Race in the Pacific

The new prosperity in Asia, the shifting and uncertain balance of power, and the numerous tensions are all fueling an arms race in the Pacific that almost rivals that of the Middle East.

China has 5.4 million troops comprised of 3 million forces in active duty, 1.2 million in reserves, and 1.2 million in the People's Armed Police. It has 10,000 tanks, 18,300 heavy artillery pieces, 50 submarines, 55 warships, 500 bombers, 5000 fighter planes, 1040 support aircraft, and 17 ICBM nuclear missiles capable of reaching the Western

United States. The Dong Feng (East Wind) 31 is a solid-fuel ICBM with a 5000-mile range and is launched from mobile launchers.

The Chinese navy, previously the least important figure in China's military lineup, is now prioritized as the senior service. In purely numerical terms, it is remarkably large, with 1150 ships in inventory. That is more than 3fi times the number of ships operated by the U.S. Navy. China maintains an aggressive commitment to converting its costal-patrol navy into a *jinhai* ("green-water") navy and a blue-water navy by 2020. (A green-water navy is described as one able to operate from Vladivostok in the north to the Strait of Malacca in the south and out to the first island chain.) A world-class blue-water navy is China's scheduled goal.

China has operated up to 100 submarines over the last 30 years. In addition to substantial purchases of Russian Kilo-class submarines, the Chinese navy also boasts the *Xia* nuclear ballistic missile submarines, which look very much like the USS George Washington or the Russian Yankee-class boats. These subs originally carried 12 JL-1 submarine-launched ballistic missiles—called CSS N-3 in the West. These single-stage, solid fuel missiles resemble the Polaris A-1 and are credited with a range of 2500 nautical miles. China's multiple independently targetable re-entry vehicle payload missiles, the CSS-4, are presently being sea-tested, with a more advanced CSS-N-4 also under development.

The Chinese navy also boasts its *Han*-class nuclear powered attack submarines. While not as quiet as the Russian or U.S. boats, these vessels are highly respected among professionals.

China is presently negotiating the purchase of an aircraft carrier from the Ukraine, in addition to as many as 20 Kilo-class submarines. Experts do not believe that Russia has sold any wake-homing torpedoes to China, but *Kilos* are reported to be so equipped. U.S. surface ships still do not have any anti-wake-homing torpedo capability.

China launched its first communications satellite on a new Long March-3 rocket in April 1984. At least nine communications satellites are now available for naval links as needed. China has been using downlink data from the Japanese GMS and the U.S. Landsat, Nimbus-1, and National Oceanic and Atmospheric Administration satellites to provide critical oceanographic data to support their submarine operations.

The Neighbors' Response

In response, Japan, with Asia's largest navy, intends to equip its four oceangoing fleets with advanced Aegis air defense ships by 1998. Japan is buying a multiple-launch rocket system from the U.S. and plans to launch its own spy satellites within the next five years. Taiwan is buying six Lafayette-class frigates and 60 Mirage fighters from France, and has ordered 150 F-16 fighters from the U.S. It plans to buy 100 M60-A3 tanks from the U.S. and 150 other light tanks to go with the 160 M60-A3 tanks it bought last year. It is buying shoulder-fired Mistral missiles from France and Stinger missiles from the U.S. as well as a 188-million-dollar hi-tech communications system from the U.S.

North Korea is developing missiles with a range of more than 500 miles in view of being able to strike against U.S. bases in Japan. South Korea plans to build a new class of 4000-ton destroyers with advanced antiaircraft and anti-submarine weapons to accompany its 3000-ton destroyer to be commissioned in 1998.

Southeast Asian countries have committed to military purchases totaling approximately 50 billion dollars over the past two years. Thailand took delivery of its first aircraft carrier from Spain, is specifying a billion-dollar communications satellite system, and is negotiating with the U.S. for the purchase of advanced medium-range air-to-air missiles (AMRAAMs).

Malaysia has set aside 1.6 billion dollars for the purchase of offshore patrol vessels and two 650-ton corvettes, and has allocated 2 billion dollars to buy tanks, armored personnel carriers, naval patrol vessels, and helicopters. Singapore has bought five Dutch Fokker-50 patrol aircraft and has announced plans to purchase a submarine from Sweden in 1997. Vietnam has recently taken delivery of two 455-ton corvettes from Russia. In 1994 Indonesia acquired a 39-ship fleet from Germany, including frigates, landing ships, and minesweepers. Even the Philippines' small navy has increased to three frigates, six corvettes, and 12 offshore patrol boats.

The Pacific region is home to the fastest-growing economies in the world, but high risks accompany high returns. The region's balance of power is being upset by the decline of the U.S., the rise of China, and the ample availability of potential flashpoints, all fueling a vigorous arms race with the means to pay for it.

U.S.-China Relations

The U.S.-China relationship is clearly becoming the most geopolitically important one in the world, replacing the old U.S.-U.S.S.R. rivalry. Unfortunately, U.S.-China relations have reached a low point and are getting worse. Diplomatic strains involve disputes of human rights, trade, and America's involvement with the affairs of Taiwan.

The abuses of human rights in China are beyond imagining. It has been estimated that over 60 million people have been slaughtered by the Communists.[3] The harvest of body parts and organs from political prisoners and other abuses have been the subject of major concerns to the West. More than 3100 slave labor camps are presently exploiting tens of millions of slave labor prisoners to produce much of the 45 billion dollars in Chinese goods exported to American markets.

China is the fourteenth-largest export market for American goods; U.S. exports to China reached 9.3 billion dollars in 1994 (yet our trade deficit with China last year was 35.9 billion dollars). To exacerbate an already strained relationship, the CIA has concluded that China has indeed recently delivered important components for missile systems to Iran and Pakistan. These components are believed to improve the accuracy of the North Korean Scud missiles already in Iran's arsenal and will enable it to build such missiles on their own. Further, in the past three months China has delivered M-11 medium-range missiles and parts to Pakistan, in violation of an international accord.

Russian Fears

Moscow, in its desperate search for funds, has been transferring vast quantities of arms and high technology to China. This can lead to Russia's worst nightmare: an authoritarian neighbor with an economy roughly the size of America (ten times the size of Russia), but with a population four times as large, sharing a land frontier impossible to defend. Experts indicate that by 2010 China will have between 70 and 75 ground-force divisions, around 3000 combat aircraft, 60 to 70 major surface vessels, and 50 to 60 submarines. Russia's Pacific Force, on the other hand, will consist of just 15 to 20 ground-force divisions (down from the current level of 34 and the 1980 level of 46), 400 to 500 combat aircraft (down from 965 today and 1300 in 1980), 40 major combat surface vessels (down from 80 in 1980 and 50 today), and less than 20 submarines in the Pacific (down from the current figure of 35).

Russia's Far East has a history of trying to break away from Moscow's control, and in 1917 it was one of the first regions to do so. It took five years before Moscow regained control (during which a small expeditionary force of U.S. and Japanese troops landed at Vladivostok to assist the White Army against the Bolsheviks in 1919).

The massive influx of over 25 million Chinese migrants[4] is a growing and intolerable threat to Russia's Far East. A Department of Defense study attaches an 85 percent probability to the rolling disintegration of Russia, yielding China an opportunity to encroach on the Russian Far East.

Biblical Implications

In the table of nations in Genesis 10 we find a reference to a tribe called the Sinites.[5] *Sinim* is derived from a root suggesting "thorns." This suggests a people living at the extremity of the known world; some believe it is identified with the inhabitants of China. This probably derives from Ch'in, the feudal state in China from 897–221 B.C., which unified China in the third century B.C. and built the Great Wall. In later eras the Ch'in boundaries were always considered to embrace the indivisible area of China proper. It is from this dynasty that the name China is derived. (Also note the Greek *sinae* and the French Late Latin *sinae.*)

Thus we have *sinology*, the study of Chinese, especially with reference to their language, literature, history, and culture. The Sinitic (Chinese) languages have in common a number of features, many of which are typological in nature: monosyllabicity, tonality, affixation, indistinct word classes, use of noun classifiers, and strict word order. Phonological correspondences in shared vocabulary have been important evidence in the argument that all Sino-Tibetan languages derive from a common source.

During the Ch'in dynasty, the first governmental standardization of characters was instituted and involved some 3000 characters.[6] The Ch'in characters have to a large degree remained the standard to the present day.[7]

Archaeological researchers in Central Asia have disclosed extremely ancient seats of culture east of the Caspian Sea and have suggested the possibility of migrations from what is now Sinkiang and Mongolia (and possibly from farther west) and also of very early transmission of art forms from western Asia and southeastern Europe.

In the second half of the first millennium B.C., to protect itself from the Hsiung-Nu, a powerful group of nomadic tribes which then occupied the lands now in northern China, the Ch'in began to build the Great Wall along their northern frontiers in the late fourth century B.C. The Muslim writers in the eighth century refer to the Great Wall of China as *Sud Yagog et Magog,* "the ramparts of Gog and Magog."[8] The Muslims refer to Gog and Magog as *Vadjudj wa madjudj* in the Koran.[9]

Prophetic Implications

In Isaiah 49:12 we also find a provocative reference: "Behold, these shall come from far; and, lo, these from the north and from the west, and these from the land of Sinim."

In Revelation 16:12 we also find the Far East joining the Armageddon conflict: "And the sixth angel poured out his vial upon the great river Euphrates; and the water thereof was dried up, that the way of the kings of the east might be prepared." It is interesting that the phrase "kings of the east" translates literally from the Greek as "kings of the rising sun" (*avnatolh/j h`li,ou*). This is, however, the classic way of speaking of the East, so one might make too much of this. (Or could the Holy Spirit be hinting at something more precise than we generally suspect?)

The current rapprochement between Japan and China is extremely provocative from a prophetic viewpoint. The combination of Japan's capital and technology with the labor and raw materials of China is expected to spark, during the next decade, the biggest economic boom that planet Earth has ever seen.

The Continuing Signs

Our horizon continues to be moving toward the lineup that fits the classic biblical scenario—in Europe, the Middle East, Russia, Israel, and now also the Far East. We are indeed in the times of the signs!

I personally believe that you and I are being plunged into a period of time about which the Bible says more than any other period of time in history—including the time that Jesus walked the shores of Galilee and climbed the mountains of Judea.

Each of us as believers has a twofold challenge: 1) to find out what the Bible predicts about these times; and 2) to find out what is really happening in our world today. Both are essential.[10]

"Behold ye among the nations, and regard and wonder marvelously, for I will work a work in your days which ye will not believe, though it be told you"(Habakkuk 1:5).

"The prudent man foreseeth the evil and takes refuge, but the simple pass on and are punished" (Proverbs 22:3; also 27:12).

Sources

Intelligence Digest, Islamic Affairs Digest, and other publications of intelligence.

International Ltd., The Stoneyhill Centre, Brimpsfield, Gloucester, GL4 8LF, U.K.

Jane's Intelligence Review, Jane's Information Group, Sentinel House, 163 Brighton Road, Coulsdon, Surrey, CR5 2NH, U.K.

Signal, official publication of the Armed Forces Communications and Electronics Association, June 1995, pp. 75-77.

Strategic Trends of the 90's, briefing package published by Koinonia House, Coeur d'Alene, ID.

Chuck Missler, *The Magog Invasion* (Western Front Ltd., Palos Verdes CA, 1995).

The McAlavany Intelligence Advisor, P.O. Box 84904, Phoenix AZ 85071. (See the April 1996 issue for an in-depth review of China.)

Aviation Week, July 8, 1996.

Forbes, July 15, 1996.

U.S. News and World Report, July 17, 1995, p. 32.

Newsweek, October 31, 1994.

New York Times, March 17, 1996.

Los Angeles Times, October 7, 1994.

Personal UPDATE, a monthly intelligence newsletter published by the author.

Encyclopaedia Britannica, Encyclopedia Judaica, other standard references, and private sources.

8

The U.S. and Other U.N. Serfdoms

Christopher Corbett

You had to look closely at your TV screen to detect it. You had to read several paragraphs down in your local newspaper story to pick it up—if it was even mentioned at all.

And if indeed you had noticed it, would you have been curious, disturbed, or even angry that on December 22, 1994, when the body of U.S. Army helicopter pilot David Hilemon was returned from North Korea (where he had been shot down when he veered off course) his coffin was draped not in Old Glory, but in *the flag of the United Nations*?

Or what if you had been a family member at the funeral of the 14 U.S. servicemen killed in a tragic "friendly fire" accident over Iraq in 1994? Would you have blanched when Vice President Albert Gore stated, "I would like to extend my condolences to the families of those who died in service to the United *Nations*"?

Not in service to the United *States*.

In service to the United *Nations*.

U.S. troops under foreign commanders? Foreign troops training on U.S. soil? GATT, WTO, and other strange acronyms signaling U.S. submission to multinational treaties and courts of law? What's happening to the United States? How long will the United States *be* the United States?

Truthfully, some people *are* noticing these trends and asking such questions. There are probably not enough people to reverse our course, but still, there are some. Yet few have any idea of why these things are happening or of the greater spiritual significance they portend. Few grasp the fact that the prophetically driven sand is shifting under our feet at this very moment.

What the Bible Says About America

A few years ago, in a huge exhibition hall of a major religious conference, I stopped at a booth for missionaries to Roman Catholics. One of their tracts was entitled "Everything the Bible Says About Purgatory." Intrigued, I picked it up and opened it, only to find myself staring at two blank pages. My initial reaction was "A printer's error—how incompetent!" Then I paused, chuckling at the implicit message that had been so cleverly delivered.

I got the point.

That's the same feeling I get when I search the Bible for direct references to the United States. Although the Bible says much about America *indirectly*, such as when it talks about Gentile nations in generic terminology such as "the coastlands," it says very little—in fact, probably nothing—about America *directly*.

Why not? The sad truth is that the United States is probably destined to be submerged into a globalist order in which our sovereignty will be compromised, if not erased, by the greater objective of world unity. Many historians note that America is a cultural appendage of Western Europe, which will likely become the center of the revived Roman Empire foretold in prophecy. Certainly there is no hint that the U.S. is this coming empire or even its center. Certainly there is no hint that America will even actively resist this empire.

Indeed, with the prevailing moral and political climate, why would we resist?

America is becoming populated by people who are devoid of basic Judeo-Christian ethics, suffer from functional, cultural, and economic illiteracy, and are cut off from the generational roots of patriotism which guided their ancestors.

Confused, ill-educated, and unable to bear the burdens of freedom, millions of Americans are ripe for the siren song which tells them that peace, security, and escape from ecological holocaust are attainable only at the price of forsaking such "outdated" notions as nationalism. Like other nations and regions, the United States is being drawn under the wing of the New World Order and likely will be submerged into its identity, just another spoke in the wheel.

What's So Bad About Globalism, Anyway?

Globalism is a term used to describe the movement in which national sovereignty and dominion are de-emphasized, while preeminence is given to the authority of planetary institutions and alliances—the New World Order. This is happening in areas such as economics, government, and culture, including religion. Powerful figures who operate in these spheres are working to build a consensus which views mankind's future in terms of planetary institutions.

Christians who are theologically conservative have earned a reputation for opposing globalism. But it is important for Christians to understand *why* globalism deserves to be viewed with skepticism. Christians are called to bring "every thought into captivity to the obedience of Christ" (2 Corinthians 10:5 NKJV)*–that is, into harmony with Christ's Scriptures. Mere knee-jerk patriotism isn't the standard for the Christian, who reasons on a higher plane.

So what does Scripture say on the matter? The Bible lays out with surgical precision the reasons why globalism as it exists today is incompatible with a mature Christian worldview. The overarching vision of modern globalism presents a Utopian scheme that is directly at odds with the Bible's doctrines of the nature of man, the role of nation-states, and the function of government. At best, globalism is unwise political theory with a few short-term advantages. At worst, it supplies the blueprint for tyranny on a nightmarish scale.

But isn't such an accusation unfair? After all, many globalists insist that their aims are nothing less than to alleviate unspeakable human suffering, to promote enduring peace, and to ensure the survival of the human race. How then could Christians, who allegedly serve the Prince of Peace who loves the world, possibly be against an effort to bind up the wounds of the planet?

Biblical Answers

The political reality is that today's globalism as practiced by the United Nations and its hangers-on is closely connected with efforts to eliminate nations as the principal political entity of mankind–or if not to outright eliminate them,

---

* All scripture quotations in this chapter are taken from the New King James Version. Used by permission. See credit line on copyright page.

then at least to supersede them with global agencies which would plunge the nation-state into irrelevancy. This is global Utopianism, and it is strictly prohibited by the Bible.

Only a few chapters into the Bible we learn that nations are the invention of none other than God Himself. This is found in Genesis 11, and is reiterated by Paul in Acts 17:26. God instructed mankind to disperse and fill the earth, but man refused, and God responded.

Consider the Genesis 11 account. The vast testimony of human investigation into history, archaeology, theology, and even linguistics points to this passage as an accurate depiction of a historical event. To deliver man from political tyranny and occultic bondage, God forced a dispersion by dividing the race into different languages and thereby into distinct nations. In Genesis 9:1 God commanded Noah and his sons, "Be fruitful and multiply, and *fill the earth.*" But by Genesis 11 we see just the opposite. Congregating in the plain of Shinar, the now-prolific populace says:

> Come, let us build ourselves a city, and a tower
> whose top is in the heavens; let us make a name
> for ourselves, *lest we be scattered abroad over the face*
> *of the earth* (Genesis 11:4).

Historical commentators such as Henry Morris present sound evidence to suggest that the Shinar movement was a hotbed of astrology and what we know today as "Eastern" and "New Age" religion. Even worse, the unity was a breeding ground for unbridled sin. The language was one, the economic system was one, and the political system was one. And man, sinful to the core, was going to abuse these "advantages" to defy God's rules and probably enslave himself by perverting technological advancement into a tool for tyranny. God's act of parental mercy is recorded:

> "Come, let Us go down and there confuse their
> language, that they may not understand one an-
> other's speech." So the LORD scattered them
> abroad from there over the face of all the earth,
> and they ceased building the city (Genesis 11:7,8).

And that was that. The prideful tower of Babel was left behind and the humble work of civilized nation-building began.

Of course, international relations by themselves are no more sinful than learning a foreign language. But today's globalists, as we will see, go much further. Today's globalists are trafficking in wholesale eradication of key aspects of national sovereignty. This is nothing more than an attempt to resurrect the Tower on a grand scale, and the effects of their foolishness could be devastating to our nation and posterity. Indeed, one group, the Council of Europe, used a painting of the Tower of Babel as a *positive* image in its advertising campaign![1]

Nations Are a Blessing

A further reason that God decentralized the human race into nations is obvious from another key Bible doctrine–the depravity of man. God understands what we often won't admit, which is that "the heart is deceitful above all things, and desperately wicked; who can know it?" (Jeremiah 17:9).

Can humans be trusted with the kind of awesome political muscle which would be possessed by a world government? God answers no. The existence of sovereign nations provides a buffer to this kind of power, much as the checks and balances of the United States Constitution work to restrain sin within our borders. No such checks and balances would work in a global government, nor have many globalists seriously proposed any.

A third strike against globalism is that the tyranny unleashed by a one-world government would violate another doctrine of the Bible—man as God's image-bearer. Man is fallen, but he is not trash. Each individual is special and is to be respected. A government with no inhibitions is likely to violate man's God-given "inalienable rights." This principle argues forcefully against global government.

In general, then, nations are a blessing, and their absence would be a curse. Paul refers to the advantages of nationalism in Acts 17, speaking to the Greek philosophers:

> He has made from one blood *every nation* of men to dwell on all the face of the earth, and has determined their preappointed times and the *boundaries of their habitation* . . . (Acts 17:26).

He even connects nationalism to God's mercy: ". . . so that they should seek the Lord, in the hope that they might grope for Him and find Him" (verse 27). Nations are God's blessing. Although imperfect, although fallen, although often falling short, *national* governments provide a framework of order for people to live free from chaos. Governments—*national* governments—are ordained by God to restrain evil and promote justice (Romans 13:1-7; 1 Peter 2:13-17). Within this framework of order mankind may sew and reap, plan and build, love and be loved, raise a family, contemplate eternal things, and perhaps find God. (Interestingly, nations will exist even in the millennium, according to passages such as Zechariah 14:16-18. That is how firmly imbedded God has made this principle.)

The truth is that globalists are blind. Ignorant of biblical truth (or, more often, disdainful of it) globalists today are proposing unbiblical views of the role of nations, the nature of man, sexuality, economics, charity, and spirituality. Opposing them in the name of God—and proposing

Christian solutions to the world's ills—is a valid ministry for the church.

Building the Worldview Tower

Given such a biblical framework, how should Christians view the United Nations, since it is the current touchstone for globalism? Once thought a powerless joke, the U.N. is today making a bid for greater power than any world body in history. But perhaps the most significant heavy lifting done by the U.N. has been the construction of a pseudo-world-view (that is, a *false* worldview).

This "ideological construction project" can be seen in five major U.N. conferences which took place between 1992 and 1996, each one putting into place a major part of the pseudo-worldview which must be injected into the minds of the world population before the New World Order can be offered as a credible alternative for the human race.

Earth Summit, Rio de Janeiro, 1992

At the Rio Earth Summit in 1992 the U.N. outlined a pseudospirituality backed up by a pseudoscience, and vice versa. Leaders came from every nation. These included President Bush, scores of federal department heads, and a full congressional delegation lead by then-Senator Albert Gore. Indeed, it was hailed in the press as the largest meeting of world leaders in human history.

The aim of the conference was to have every nation sign a legally binding Biodiversity Convention ("Convention" meaning treaty) and other commitments which would have obligated the U.S. and developed nations to pay billions of dollars to "clean up" the planet and avert an ecological holocaust. The payments would also have prohibited substantial scientific, medical, and industrial development from taking place in Third World nations. These nations, while "protected" against alleged ecological pillage, would have been compensated royally by developed nations, with a well-heeled U.N. bureaucracy overseeing and enforcing the transfer of wealth.

Fortunately, the U.S. didn't bite.

Despite pressure from environmentalists like Al Gore, President Bush received even more heat from conservatives and businesses at home who wanted no part of the treaty, and scientists who were appalled at the warping of environmental research to push a political agenda. Bush refused to sign the Biodiversity Treaty.

Yet the Conference still produced Agenda 21, an 800-page strategic plan for national and global regulation of "everything from forests, deserts, oceans, and rivers to women's rights and health care."[2] Several commissions were established, many aimed at using supranational agencies to protect the environment, redistribute wealth, study the ecosystem, and line the pockets of power-hungry diplomats. As conference executive secretary Maurice Strong said, "This is a launching pad, not a quick fix."[3]

The scientific element at the Rio conference was one familiar to almost every parent of a child in an American public school today: Our planet is ecologically dying, and nationalistic capitalism is the cause. Despite a plethora of scientific reports convincingly attacking notions of "global warming," "ozone depletion," "deforestation," and a litany of alleged disasters, the only science allowed at the Earth Summit was tilted toward the sky-is-falling theme. (A good summary of the overwhelming research refuting popular "chicken little" environmental theories is *Trashing the Planet*, by renowned scientist Dixie Lee Ray, former head of the U.S. Atomic Energy Commission and also former Governor of Washington.) The conclusion of each report was the same:

Because disaster is at the door, Western nations must submit a portion of their sovereignty and their money to U.N.-operated institutions.

The spiritual element was even more alarming. Pantheistic earth-worship dominated the conference. Maurice Strong opened the conference with a reading of the Declaration of the Sacred Earth. Nature was called "Divine." The opening ceremony featured a Viking ship named *Gaia*, the name of the Greek earth goddess and a popular New Age term for the pantheistic Goddess talked about even by many scientists. (Pantheism means "all is God, and God is all.")

Christianity was blamed by many delegates for ecological horrors due to its doctrine of a Creator separate from His creation, its doctrine of nationalism, and its teaching that man was given dominion over the earth to wisely steward it, not worship it.

The verdict, expressed by influential international activists such as Willy Brandt, Lester Brown (president of the organization Worldwatch), and Hilary F. French (author of the Worldwatch study, *After the Earth Summit: The Future of Environmental Governance*): "A more broadly defined concept of security corresponds to a more narrowly defined concept of sovereignty."[4] According to various accounts by journalists, attacks on sovereignty echoed throughout the committee meetings and addresses.

How the U.N. Is Building a "Pseudo-Worldview"

"Pseudo" comes from a Greek word for "false." The five U.N. conferences held in this decade can be seen as steps to building a false view of reality—a pseudo-worldview which opposes a realistic worldview based on the Bible. Here is a brief chart to illustrate the points.

U.N. Conference	Stated Goal	Spiritual Impact
Earth Summit, Rio de Janeiro, 1992	Protect the environment	**Pseudospirituality and Pseudoscience:** Distorted scientific data employed to support a pantheistic, Eastern view of God and creation.
Human Rights Conference, Vienna, 1993	Protect human rights	**Pseudopolitics:** Government and rights seen as defined by man rather than defined and revealed by God. The danger: Rights defined by one group of people can always be redefined (and destroyed) by a subsequent group, whereas rights defined and revealed by God are absolute.
Population Conference, Cairo, 1994	Prevent starvation and poverty	**Pseudosociology:** "Solve" poverty by authoritarian abortion and birth control rather than promoting economic growth through free markets, national autonomy, a work ethic, and faith in a rational God whose laws bless technological productivity.
Women's Conference, Beijing, 1995	Protect women's rights	**Pseudosexuality:** Feminist ideology downgrades the heterosexual family, legitimizes homosexuality, and undermines the created functional order of male leadership.
Habitat Conference, Istanbul, 1996	Provide global housing for all	**Pseudoeconomics:** Marxist emphasis on "sustainable development" means limiting productivity of "rich" nations and giving their "excess" to global bureaucracies and favored "poor" nations.

The Tower Grows Taller

According to journalist Joan Veon, who has attended most of the U.N. conferences in the 1990s and researched them all, the Earth Summit set the agenda for every other U.N. conference: Dire global emergencies require planetary solutions which must dispense with national sovereignty, property rights, and outmoded (Christian) theology and ethics.

Human Rights Conference, Vienna, 1993

If the Earth Summit established a pseudoscience and pseudospirituality, the Vienna Conference laid the ground-work for a pseudopolitics–a false view of government. This conference was an effort to build upon the U.N. Declaration of Human Rights.

Covered by the nearly unassailable mission to combat grisly human-rights violations across the globe, the Vienna Conference made great strides in reengineering the concepts of national sovereignty and individual freedom. But two especially bad assumptions crept along under the cover of the high-profile noble causes: first, that human rights emanate from government, not a transcendent Creator; and second, that all human rights must be legally harmonized across the planet, defined and enforced by a planetary agency.

These concepts are part and parcel of U.N.-based human rights action. The U.N. Declaration of Human Rights, in Article 29, paragraph 3, states:

> These rights and freedoms may in no case be ex-
> ercised contrary to the purposes and principles
> of the United Nations.

Compare that to Thomas Jefferson's statement that "man is endowed *by his Creator with inalienable rights....*" In one case, the political foundation of government is God, and immovable. In the other case, the foundation is the highly movable earth of international government.

The U.N. Convention on the Rights of the Child, for example, has planted within its many admirable goals some provisions which, if strictly interpreted, give children the right to determine their own sexuality *autonomously from parents*, the right to watch any entertainment (even, presumably, pornography), the right to refuse religious instruction, the right to associate with whomever they prefer (Does this include gangs? Drug-dealers?), and other such implications. Such interpretations are exactly the agenda of many children's rights activists in America and Europe. In a Denmark U.N. Summit in 1995, the head of the U.N. Children's Fund (UNICEF), Richard Jolley, remarked, "The state is the custodian of the rights of children." Dr. Jolley stated that he considered spanking children to be child abuse.[5]

The pattern is clear: Broad, vaguely defined "rights" are written into international documents which can be used as an excuse for governmental invasion (today national government, tomorrow international) into areas which God reserves for families and churches.

Population Conference, Cairo, 1994

The Cairo Conference established a pseudosociology. The premise: The world is racked by overpopulation which is causing starvation in underdeveloped countries. The solution: universal access to abortion and proactive birth control, and huge transfers of money from developed nations—managed by the U.N.

The premise, of course, is incorrect. Numerous studies show that starvation is not caused by too many people, but by too little food. Food shortages, in turn, are almost always caused by totalitarian governments, tribal warfare, pagan superstition, or resistance to modern agricultural methods. The highest population density on earth is in Singapore, where nobody starves. The lowest population densities, on the other hand, are in areas where starvation is rampant. (One of the many excellent books refuting the overpopulation scare is *Prospects for Growth*, by E. Calvin Beisner [Crossway Books, 1990]. Also see numerous articles and books by Julian Simon.) Yet the myths of pseudosociology cut no ice with internationalists, whose true agenda is global messianism.

At Cairo, the U.S. was embarrassed by the leak of a State Department cable which informed diplomats that a "priority" item at the conference was "assuring . . . safe access to abortion . . . a fundamental right of all women." This came after statements for public consumption that the U.S. would not support international abortion rights. Yet only a year earlier, Conference organizer and U.S. Undersecretary of State Timothy Wirth—a man who is well-known to have kept a glass bowl of condoms, instead of candy, in his office to punctuate his fervor for the "safe sex" message—made a speech in which he stated:

> A government which is violating basic human rights should not hide behind the defense of sovereignty. Difficult as it is, we must also discuss thoroughly the issue of abortion. . . . Our position is to support reproductive choice, including access to safe abortion.[6]

One of the conference organizers was Planned Parenthood International, the world's leading supplier of abortion and birth control. Of course, no one suggested looting Planned Parenthood's immense wealth to provide free services. Indeed, Planned Parenthood would likely benefit from the expansion of international "family planning."

African delegates to the conference complained of U.N. relief agencies which typically understocked lifesaving penicillin but never seemed to run short of free condoms. Fortunately, the attempt to enforce a universal right to abortion was thwarted by extreme public resistance from the Catholic Church, evangelicals, and Third World Muslims.

Yet the conference kept the momentum going for the pseudo-worldview being built, brick by brick, with the hands of the U.N. and its powerful allies in governments across the world.

Conference on the Rights of Women, Beijing, 1995

The Beijing Conference outlined a pseudosexuality in which men were portrayed as villains, patriarchy (including biblical male headship) assaulted in seminar after seminar, lesbian rights pushed with no official resistance, and access to abortion and birth control promoted with zeal.

The writing of the platform document for the Conference was supervised by former U.S. member of Congress Bella Abzug. An archfeminist, Abzug also led a workshop in Beijing which was observed by a reporter from the *Washington Times:*

> Mrs. Abzug, in one of the more than 350 workshops on the second day of the forum, joined hands with other women in a prayer tribute to "Mother Earth" that mocked orthodox Christian belief. "Give thanks for the fruits of life," said a Brazilian delegate who led the group in prayer. "Thanks to Mother Earth, for you give life. Thanks for water. People from my community decided no more Crucifixion. We believe in life. We celebrate life, not the Crucifixion. We are power." Mrs. Abzug and several dozen women

218 ❖ Christopher Corbett

holding hands then thrust their hands into the air, chanting, "I am power. I am power. I am power."[7]

This, remember, was not the action of a fringe attendee, but of the *author* of the guiding document of the Conference!

Hillary Clinton also attended, along with 125 U.S. government representatives. Of the 46 official U.S. delegates, not one was prolife, evangelical, or conservative. For public consumption in most of the American media, reporting on the conference dwelt on innocuous projects like stopping international prostitution. But the numerous Christian or politically conservative observers reported an overwhelming emphasis on "empowering women"—meaning an overthrow of the biblical view of the family and gender roles.

Workshops included:

- Lesbianism for the Curious
- Spirit and Action: Lesbian Activism from an Interfaith Perspective.
- Lesbian Flirtation Techniques
- Beyond the Trinity Creator

Clearly, the building of the U.N. tower includes the placement of a pseudosexuality, backed up by a feminist pseudotheology.

Habitat II Conference, Istanbul, 1996 (also in conjunction with the U.N. World Summit on Social Development, Copenhagen, 1995). The Habitat II Conference, building on the foundation of the Copenhagen Development Summit, laid out a pseudoeconomics. The premises of these conferences were socialistic and globalistic: The Third World countries are underdeveloped due to exploitation by the United States and other Western nations. To redress this imbalance, internationally binding treaties with international enforcement agencies are necessary.

The Istanbul conference championed the concept of "sustainable development" as a planetary goal. Sustainable development, according to conference leaders such as Maurice Strong, means the *minimum* development required to sustain *all* life on earth. In other words, the United States might have limits—caps—on its gross national product. These caps would be determined by a formula dictating how much each person really needs to sustain himself. Anything over the sustainable limit would be sent to nations who are under their sustainable development levels.

Of course, such concepts were couched in more polite terms. Yet behind the velvet jargon lay the steel fist of globalist demand-based economics. This flies in the face of a biblical concept of property rights, individual initiative, national sovereignty, and voluntary charity toward those outside one's own borders. True economics is increasingly coming under fire from globalist pseudoeconomics.

How They'll Guard the Tower

A worldview is necessary for building a new world. But ideas aren't enough. To be a legitimate governing authority, the New Order needs an enforcement mechanism. Is there one on the horizon?

Although dim, it is possible to discern the embryonic stages of what appears to be a global army of potentially awesome proportions. We already know that this is a goal of Boutros Boutros-Ghali, who until 1997 was Secretary General of the United Nations. In the Winter 1992/1993 globalist-leaning journal *Foreign Affairs*, Boutros-Ghali noted the "expansion in demand" for U.N. "peacekeeping services." He noted that troops "would be under the command of the secretary-general." The initiative was received warmly by President Bush, and plans were made to train U.N. forces at

American military bases. By 1996 there were scores of U.N. operations across the globe.

Yet Boutros-Ghali's *Foreign Affairs* article was demure compared to his June 1992 speech *An Agenda for Peace.* As reported by John McManus:

> As Boutros-Ghali stated at the time, he wants the nations of the world to supply him with personnel, equipment, and funding to create an armed force to be at his disposal "on a permanent basis."... But the efforts of the U.N., according to this Egyptian bureaucrat, "must encompass matters beyond military threats." Boutros-Ghali wants a U.N. army to be involved in "securing justice and human rights," "promoting social progress and better standards of life in larger freedom," and attaining "sustainable economic and social development."[8]

Of course, to implement such a scheme the U.N. would need help from nations who already have large military forces. The U.N. would need willing accomplices who could, inch by inch, condition their population and their armed forces for such a transition. If such a script indeed existed, recent American leaders would seem to be playing their roles with relish.

Consider the following items.

Fact: Strobe Talbott, Deputy Secretary of State in 1993, wrote an essay just a year earlier when he was Editor at Large for *Time* magazine. Published on July 20, 1992, the article, entitled "The Birth of a Global Nation," was a straightforward plea for one-world government. "I'll bet," he wrote, "that within the next hundred years...nationhood as we know it will be obsolete: all states will recognize a single, global authority." Talbott toys with the idea of some kind of checks-and-balances system, but gives nothing concrete. Within a year this man was appointed as the second-most-powerful figure in the U.S. Department of State. He was also the President's college roommate.

Fact: In only one fiscal year, 1993-94, the President shrank the U.S. Army from 790,000 to 570,000 troops, a cut of four divisions; cut the Navy by 100 ships, including a full Carrier Battle Group and two Carrier Air Wings; cut the Air Force by eight tactical fighter wings; cut the Army Reserve by 28 percent. These were considerably more than President Bush had recommended, and not explainable by the end of the Cold War. Defense analyst Loren Thompson of Georgetown University claimed, "U.S. defense capabilities are dropping like a rock."

Fact: The shrinkage of U.S. capabilities mirrors the growth of the U.N. "Blue Helmet" forces. The U.N. army grew by 800 percent–from 10,000 troops to 80,000–from 1988 to 1993.

Fact: In November 1993 President Clinton invited Secretary General Boutros-Ghali to review the Corps of Cadets at West Point–an honor normally reserved only for the U.S. Commander-in-Chief.

Fact: Over the objections of General Colin Powell (then Chairman of the Joint Chiefs of Staff), President Clinton in 1993 signed two Presidential Decision Directives (PDD 13 and 25) which put U.S. troops under foreign U.N. commanders and took away their right to refuse orders which American field commanders deemed unwarranted or incompetent. Since then, U.S. troops have served under commanders from several nations in U.N. peacekeeping operations.

Fact: In 1996, Army corporal Michael New was court-martialed and discharged for refusing to don the Blue Uniform of the United Nations. New claimed his oath of allegiance was to the U.S. Constitution, not the U.N. Charter.

In the mid-1990s, however, Congress was not so willing to go along, proposing measures to keep U.S. troops from serving under non-U.S. commanders. Yet the Executive Branch continued the trend through its executive order capacity, and international pressure for use of American troops increases every time a new "multilateral" peace agreement is hammered out, whether it be in Eastern Europe, the Mideast, or Asia. There is never a lack of crises which the U.N. does not seem to think it can solve through third-party police efforts.

Can the United Nations really knit together a fighting force with enough autonomous power to govern the globe? That remains to be seen, but the trends are ominous. For true globalists, those who command the political and financial resources to invest in globalism, this could be the acid test telling them whether the United Nations is a viable structure for global government, or whether some new and more powerful agency is needed. Either way, for those who want to build the Tower, they will have to find a way to defend it and allow it to project military power.

How They'll Pay for the Tower

In 1995 the U.N. was criticized in *Reader's Digest* for wasteful, extravagant spending. Then the U.N. itself admitted that not only was inefficiency a problem, but that it did not have the money to operate. Although the plea of poverty was met in many quarters with skepticism, no one doubted that the U.N. had plans—big plans—to increase its income.

Two emerged. One was to get loans from the World Bank. The other, more compelling, was to institute a world tax. Not only was such a tax publicly suggested by U.N. Secretary General Boutros Boutros-Ghali in an interview published in 1996, but his comments were an extension of the Copenhagen World Summit held in March 1995. And although the initial reaction from American leaders was publicly negative, there is good reason to believe that a global tax is in the cards, even if it will take some time.

On January 15, 1996, U.N. Secretary General Boutros-Ghali proposed a sweeping global tax on numerous daily activities in which American citizens and businesses participate.[9] With this tax the United Nations would finally have the money to get itself out of its growing multibillion-dollar debt and fulfill its stated ambitions to police the world and expand its "social development" programs.

Of course, nationalists fear this would go far beyond feeding the hungry. They see a global tax as virtually legitimizing world government.

According to Inge Kaul, top U.N. strategist, the world would need to be softened up to the idea of a global tax. Indeed, as alien an idea as it might seem to the public, a global tax has long been a dream of one-world planners in the U.N. The plan is to start with a tax on currency exchange, sold to the American public, in the words of one of its proponents, as "a tax on Wall Street, not Main Street."[10] But it wouldn't stop there.

At the high-level World Summit (attended by Hillary Clinton, among others), the plans for imposing the global tax emerged. Key members of the influential Council on Foreign Relations joined with U.N. officials and other "insiders" in discussing taxes on:

- all overseas travel expenses

- satellite communications

- ocean fishing
- international phone and computer communications
- currency exchange
- postage
- fossil fuels and nonrenewable energy.[11]

At the meeting, U.N. official Kaul estimated that "a global tax on nonrenewable energy . . . could generate $66 billion per year."[12] Other estimates went as high as 300 billion dollars per year. The irony of such suggestions is that through 1995 U.S. taxpayers had already paid the U.N. 30 billion dollars since 1945, funding a quarter of its budget.[13]

The U.N. clearly has designs on what to do with the money it craves. As stated above, Boutros-Ghali in a major address in 1992, and again in an article in the Council on Foreign Relation's *Foreign Affairs* magazine, has called for establishment of a permanent U.N.-operated global army. CNN lauded this proposal for what it called a "Planetary Police."[14] Bella Abzug, the matron of the Beijing Conference, was also in Copenhagen. There she spoke of the need for a global tax on private corporations to finance the U.N.'s feminist programs.

Finally, with the 300 billion dollars per year from world taxes, many defenders of sovereignty worry that the U.N. will be free to pursue socialism and world government. The U.N. could gain control by using environmental scares and bogus disease control—contrived "crises" employed to declare global emergencies and impose U.N. law.

How They'll Get There from Here

Will the New Order come in through slow absorption of the U.S. and other nations, or will sovereignty be lost in a climactic, possibly orchestrated, event? The slow absorption route seems the most reasonable, but let us not be hasty in reaching this conclusion.

Let's go back to Maurice Strong, organizer of the Rio Earth Summit. Strong is one of the world's wealthiest men. A Canadian industrialist, he rubs elbows with other wealthy globalists such as David Rockefeller. He has been head of Dome Petroleum, Power Corporation of Canada, the Canadian International Development Agency, and, at the personal request of Prime Minister Pierre Trudeau, first CEO of Petro-Canada. He not only staged the Earth Summit, but in 1987 headed the U.N. Environmental Program (later called the World Commission for Environment and Development).

The World Commission issued a report which introduced the concept of "sustainable development" (i.e., limited development by Western nations), and called for a "green" police force under the sole authority of the U.N. with access to enter *any nation.* Strong's report said that this police force should not be limited "by yesterday's notions of national sovereignty; that human survival may not be secured save by the reach of enforceable law across environmentally invisible borders."[15] Strong also has stated, "The United States is clearly the greatest risk to the world's ecological health."[16]

But remember Strong's comments opening the Earth Summit? How he spoke of the earth as "sacred" and nature as "divine"? The truth is that Maurice Strong is a committed adherent to New Age, pantheistic mysticism. According to a profile in the May 1990 issue of *West* magazine, Strong's wife, Hanne, is an occultist who claims to speak with disembodied spirits. Christians recognize this activity as demonism. In 1978 the Strongs purchased a ranch in Colorado of several thousand acres. After several mystical experiences, the Strongs established Baca there—a retreat community for New Age experiences, frequented by the likes of Shirley MacLaine and visited by "Henry Kissinger, the World Bank's Robert MacNamara, and the presidents of corporations like IBM, Pan Am, and Harvard University," as well as being the home to some of the more prominent and radical New Age think tanks like the Aspen Institute.

The Strongs intend to make Baca a model for harmonizing all the world's religions. Hanne says, "This place will have a key role in the future of mankind."

Near the end of the *West* article, Strong tells of his yearning to write a novel:

> Each year, he explains as background to the telling of the novel's plot the World Economic Forum convenes in Davos, Switzerland. Over a thousand CEOs, prime ministers, finance ministers, and leading academics gather in February to attend meetings and set economic agendas for the year ahead. With this as a setting, he then says, "What if a small group of these world leaders were to conclude that the principal risk to the earth comes from the actions of the rich countries? And if the world is to survive, those rich countries would have to sign an agreement reducing their impact on the environment. Will they do it?" ... Strong resumes his story. "The group's conclusion is no. The rich countries won't do it. They won't change. So, in order to save the planet, the group decides: isn't the only hope for the planet that the industrialized civilizations collapse? Isn't it our responsibility to bring that about?"
>
> "This group of world leaders," he continues, "form a secret society to bring about an economic collapse. It's February. They're all at Davos.

These aren't terrorists. They're world leaders. They have positioned themselves in the world's commodity and stock markets. They've engineered, using their access to stock exchanges and computers and gold supplies, a panic. Then they prevent the world's stock markets from closing. They jam the gears. They hire mercenaries who hold the rest of the world leaders at Davos as hostages. The markets can't close. The rich countries. . . ." And Strong makes a slight motion with his fingers as if he were flicking a cigarette butt out the window.

I sit there spellbound. This is not *any* storyteller talking. This is Maurice Strong. He knows these world leaders. He is, in fact, co-chairman of the Council of the World Economic Forum. He sits at the fulcrum of power. He is in a position to do it.

"I probably shouldn't be saying things like this," he says.

Can Strong "do it"? Maybe, maybe not. And how many others would join him, even if he were willing to suggest it?

But the mere fact that such a man (possibly influenced by the demonic realm) even considers such a course is enough to make a reasonable person wonder whether the birth of the New World Order will be like the proverbial frog in the kettle, or whether it will come like a blast of scalding water in the face.

What Can Christians Do?

What should Christians think and do about the attacks on their faith and their nation's sovereignty?

First, we should put things into perspective. We know a lot, but there is a lot we *don't* know. At best, all we can say is that the current trends suggest the stage may be in the process of being set for something that resembles the reign of the Antichrist in the tribulation. How long God will allow the stage to be set, and at what pace, is His to know. We are merely to be ready—as ready today as Christians were to have been at any time in the almost 2000-year history of the church.

Second, wherever we may think we are on the prophetic timetable, we can agree that globalism, especially as it is practiced today, is a false and unbiblical solution to the world's ills. It may do some good (just as a typical cult may do its adherents *some* moral good), and that limited good should be acknowledged. But in the overall picture globalism does not contribute to human good. In fact, the closer you look, the more negative the system appears.

Third, Christians should point out the U.N.'s false promises and instead hold out *authentic* solutions to the world's problems. *We* know what the real solutions to starvation are. *We* know what the real answer to tyranny is. *We* know how to take care of the earth without worshiping it. *We* know how to use our God-given rationality to employ science for good, not to distort it for political purposes. *We* are called to go into the world and be "salt" and "light" to glorify Him. *We* can fulfill Jesus' command to "do business till I come" (Luke 18:13).

Finally, while we may grieve for the world's folly, we can with confidence withstand the encroaching evils of globalism and New Age impositions, knowing the ultimate conclusion of the story and our share in the victory. But material comfort and emotional ease may not be in our future if events move swiftly. All the more reason to study, pray, seek fellowship with strong believers, and obey the Scriptures from the heart, walking with the Savior of our souls, and, one day, of the world.

Ultimately, globalism will triumph—but not the false globalism of the Antichrist and today's spirit of antichrist. Even in the tribulation, he will have a difficult time keeping his domination together without rebellion (see, for example, Daniel 11:40-45). But the kingdom of Christ will truly triumph. All nations will bow before His throne as He rules from His capital in Jerusalem. That is a true globalism which every Christian will enjoy.

9

The Soviet Phoenix Arises

Dave Breese

No nation in our time has presented so fascinating, dangerous, cruel, or problematic a picture to the world as has Russia in this century. She has kept the world on pins and needles while the onlooking nations have armed themselves against the possibility of cruel aggression on the part of this monster from the North. Russia's warmongering threats to the nations of the world have certainly been the main reason for the trillion-dollar-a-year military defense expenditures by the nations of earth. Russia has certainly been the cause of the Cold War, and as a consequence has engendered a military policy in the United States and Europe called "containment." And except for that containment program, many more nations might well have become Communist states than is the case today. No military policy decision has been made since World War II without the question "What will the Russians do?" being raised. The present massive amount of Russian military power has precipitated many an anxious conference attended by nervous diplomats sitting around the polished tables of our major cities. A look at history might explain this anxiety.

Fascinating History

Russia came out of the last century feeling a sense of isolation from the other nations of the world. It had a monarchy under the czars who lived in costly splendor and a peasant class which had existed for centuries on the brink of ruin. There seemed to be little prospect of that system improving under Russia's circumstances at the time.

After the turn of the century there began to be preached within Russia a strange new doctrine which came to be called Communism. The promises of this novel and revolutionary point of view became a thing of special appeal to the working class. One cannot help being curious about the dictates, the theology, and the promise of Communism when one notices that this ideology conquered 150 million people in Russia and another 100 million in Eastern Europe. Add to this the 1 billion population of China and the curiosity grows. What was the magnetic promise that made Communism the influence that it was (and is) in the world? What was it that made people shout until hoarse the slogan "*Workers of the world, unite; we have nothing to lose but our chains. We have a world to win*"?

These kinds of slogans were first heard in the days of the French Revolution. In that revolution came the preaching that finally led Louis XVI, King of France, and his bride, Marie Antoinette, to the guillotine. Hundreds of thousands of others finally died in pools of their own blood because of the Utopian promise of a changed world that came out of the French Revolution. That revolution also cleared the way for a clever military genius tyrant by the name of Napoleon

Bonaparte. Under his program of world conquest, France lost 2 million of its handsome sons, and similar statistics of death were inflicted on the great powers of Europe. Even a fool should look at the results of the French Revolution and cry, "Never again!"

But the ideology of the French Revolution—which came largely from Jon Jacque Rousseau—was destined to live again in modern Russia.

The Three Points of Communism

The main points of the preaching of the Communist revolutionaries were three, the first of which was atheism. The Communists insisted as the basis of everything else that "there is no God." They then proceeded to produce a state that became a perfect, grisly illustration of the outcome of denying the existence of God. Alexander Solzhenitsyn was once asked the question "Sir, why did things degenerate to the place in Russia where its leaders killed 60 million of their own people? What possible and terrible attitude could have come over the Russian people and leaders for them to do such things?"

Solzhenitsyn's answer is most instructive. He explained the Russian catastrophe in just four words: "They have forgotten God."

And so we see the truth of Scripture worked out in daily life. The Bible says:

> The fool hath said in his heart, There is no God.
> They are corrupt, they have done abominable
> works, there is none that doeth good. The Lord
> looked down from heaven upon the children of
> men to see if there were any that did understand
> and seek God. They are all gone aside, they are
> all together become filthy; there is none that

doeth good, no, not one. Have all the workers of iniquity no knowledge, who eat up my people as they eat bread, and call not upon the Lord? (Psalm 14:1-4).

The Bible teaches that atheism produces abominable works. In fulfillment of this prediction of the result of atheism, Russia became one of the most vicious, murderous, hateful societies that has existed in all of history.

Russia became this kind of nation despite the thousand-year influence–indeed, *dominance*–of the Russian Orthodox Church. Few religious institutions were more characterized by form, ceremony, tradition, crosses, candles, liturgy, and pealing music played in dark brownstone churches. It can also be said that few religions have had less positive influence upon the surrounding culture. Religion, as Russian Orthodoxy proves, is one thing, while the preaching of the cross, producing its transforming effect upon society, is quite another.

The second point of Communist ideology is materialism. Under the influence of Karl Marx, materialism was asserted to have an almost living, religious form. It was therefore called "dialectical materialism." This means that there is within material a life force, an *elan vital*, that gives it the power to transform individuals and societies. Consequently, Communism taught that Marxism was "the wave of the future," the last surge of dialectical change that would come upon the world. Be sure that there is still a residue of these views in Russia today.

The Soviet ideological structure also embraced economic determinism. This is the view that we are what we are because of our economic environment. Therefore, under the ideas of this determinism, capitalism was credited as being the number one problem of the world. People, in the Marxist veins, became selfish and vindictive because they were members of the proletariat and therefore were slaves. By contrast, the members of the bourgeoisie were seen as owning the means of production and taking the profit to themselves.

Therefore only economic revolution, no matter how bloody, could create the brave new world that the Communists promised. And so there came, first upon Russia and then the satellite nations, the bloody embrace of Marxism-Leninism, which arrogated to itself the right to control the lives of everyone.

Soviet Expansionism

After years of scheming, Communism came to power in Russia in 1918. It was then that dictator Nikolai Lenin promised, "First we will take Europe, then Asia, then America, and it will fall like a ripe plum into our hands." After the Communists captured Russia in 1918, it looked like they were destined to fulfill that boast.

They were tremendously helped during the days of World War II in the supply of money, arms, ammunition, airplanes, and military resources in gigantic amounts. They emerged from World War II a powerful nation. As a consequence, they embarked on a program that has filled 50 years with efforts to produce, however violent, conversion to Communism and conquest of the world. Happily, we can report that this boast of world conquest has not yet come to fruition.

In fact, in our generation an unexpected and dramatic change has taken place. In the 1980s Russia recovered a small bit of its sanity and began to change from hard-line Communism. Subject to the economic and ideological pressure of the Reagan administration, "the Evil Empire" appeared to renounce its boast of world conquest. It set free the satellite nations of Eastern Europe and worked diplomatically to produce a rapprochement with the United States. So the latter years of the 1980s and the early years of the 1990s brought a relaxation of tensions between the United States and Russia. In fact, the U.S. soon began investing billions of dollars to help the Russians in the reduction of their intercontinental ballistic missiles and their nuclear forces. Relatively free elections were held in Russia, and the world continues to look with astonishment at the apparent dramatic changes in the Soviet Union.

Not the least of these is the changes that came about under the leadership of Mikhail Gorbachev, who did quite a bit to loosen things up. Nevertheless, he was defeated in the nationwide elections. His successor, Boris Yeltsin, was escalated to power as acting president, and then was elected in the much-more-organized free election in May and June of 1996.

Yeltsin's story is most fascinating.

The Present Scene

Something of the situation in Russia is encapsulated for us by an August 1996 *Los Angeles Times* report on Yeltsin's inaugural ceremonies at the Kremlin:

> A gaunt President Boris Yeltsin was inaugurated Friday as the first Russian leader elected in the post-communist era. The strangely mournful ceremony was marred by his slurring delivery of the oath of office and overshadowed by a calamitous setback for Russian forces fighting separatist rebels in Chechnya.
>
> The President, appearing in public for the first time since June 26, spent just 16 minutes in the ceremony, delivered no inaugural remarks and barely acknowledged the other dignitaries around

him before he walked slowly offstage, ashen and unsmiling.

Yeltsin was shown on Russian television on Friday evening raising a glass and telling 1,100 guests at a banquet in the Grand Kremlin Palace following the inauguration: "The people's support gives me the authority to act decisively and firmly. I shall use this honorable authority in the interest of all people living in Russia."

Informative also are the paragraphs that follow:

The 65-year-old Yeltsin, who was hospitalized twice last year for heart disease, has been working from a government dacha since his reelection on July 3. He had not made a public appearance since June 26.

Some of Yeltsin's aides said he would benefit from a bypass operation; one aide recently hinted that his coming vacation would be an appropriate time for him to have it.

Millions of Russians who watched the day's dramatic events on television were shocked no less by Yeltsin's drawn appearance and labored diction than by the fresh humiliation of Russian forces in Chechnya.

Before dawn Friday, Chechens who are fighting for independence from Moscow overran heavily armed federal forces defending the main government building in the Chechen capitol of Grozny. The building was destroyed and on fire Friday evening. It was the climax of a devastating counteroffensive launched Tuesday that has left about 120 Russian troops dead, 400 wounded and

50 missing. Separatist spokesmen claimed several hundred Russian troops were killed. Rebel and civilian casualties are unknown.

The rebels' thrust came after several weeks of attacks by Russian forces, which unleashed an offensive a week after Yeltsin was reelected.

In spite of the news from Chechnya, the Kremlin went ahead with a gala luncheon banquet after the inauguration, in which Yeltsin sipped champagne and Prime Minister Viktor Chernomyrdin toasted his health.

So the present time brings a picture of Russia as militarily weak, ideologically confused, and led by a sick man as its president.

How different is the present picture from the promise once made by the arrogant Communist cadres! Again and again they named Russia as "the greatest nation on earth" and predicted that the wonderful results of Communism in this land would soon be the example that would bring the whole world into commitment to Marxism-Leninism.

Not content with simple persuasion, Russia built an army of more than 4 million and equipped it with modern weapons for what they thought would be the final assault on the world.

In addition to its land army, the Russians moved strongly in modern aircraft and submarine-led navy that could carry deadly nuclear force into the heartland of any nation on earth. As a result of its nuclear capability, Russia became the most feared nation on the face of the earth.

A vast new development, however, has come upon Russia in these recent days. This astonishing thing is called "the end of the Cold War." The Soviet Union as a true unity of nations has ceased to exist. The nations of Eastern Europe are on their own, and China goes it alone without thinking of itself as being a part of the Communist unity of the world. Indeed, the end of the Cold War has posed enormous new considerations for Russia.

One of these demanding considerations has been the call to devise a capitalist system in succession to the Communist economy. The leaders of Russia are now discovering that this is not easily done. It is difficult on the face of it, but that difficulty is greatly complicated by the rise of one of the most efficient and cruel Mafia organizations in the world. In the confusion of government weakness, the Russian Mafia has established itself as a major force in Moscow and other major cities of Russia. Whoever may be the person in opposition, if he disagrees with the Mafia, he will very likely be executed on a public street. Consequently, an "economy of fear" has settled upon the Russian populace, and they wonder if a just economy can ever be developed.

So effective has been the success of the Russian Mafia that it has established branches of this cruel system in the United States. In and around New York City, the Italian Mafia, the Jewish organized crime groups, and the Oriental syndicate have been pushed upon by the Russians.

Who would have dreamed that the time would come when a Russian Mafia would become a decisive force in one of America's major cities? Indeed, the Russian situation testifies to the fact that history is filled with dangerous surprises.

The Hunt for Purpose

A recent call has been raised by Boris Yeltsin which could not have been expected from Russia in days gone by. Concerning this, the Associated Press presented an article titled "Russia is on a hunt for its purpose in life." The article is subtitled "Yeltsin asks Russians to describe what should be the country's mission."

This is followed by a report from Moscow which says:

> Boris Yeltsin thinks Russia needs a new national vision. So he is asking his compatriots to come up with one. Something, perhaps, to rival the American Dream. Something so inspiring it would erase all memories of "Glory to the Communist Party of the Soviet Union."

> Yeltsin assigned his advisors and the country's intellectuals to the task, giving them about a year, and the government-run *Rossiiskaya Gazeta* newspaper this week began soliciting suggestions. It offered a prize of nearly $2,000 for the best "Idea for Russia."

> No need for American-style brevity in the contest—letters and faxes are allowed to run as long as seven pages. In the land that gave the world Solzhenitsyn and Tolstoy, asking for 25 words or less seemed inappropriate.

> The ideas are rolling in, but they don't exactly lend themselves to the catchy slogan or soundbite. Many are rambling, personal meditations on themes such as individual and collective fate.

> One doctor thinks Russia's spirit can only be healed by the Russian Orthodox Church. An artist says that Russians have to take personal responsibility for the country's future.

> A geologist from the Far East says people mainly need money and food.

> "If all that fits into the national idea, then I'm for it," wrote Lev Lushnikov of Magadan. "But at this point it still seems premature, we talk too much."

> Russia has always had national slogans, from the czars' "Orthodoxy, Autocracy, Nationhood" to the Soviet's "Dictatorship of the Proletariat."

But since the 1991 Soviet collapse, Russia's old red Communist banners have been replaced mainly with advertising, and many Russians of all political stripes feel the country is adrift.

The New Call

This new call in Russia is certainly to be observed with astonishment. For the last 80 years, Communism has been the arrogant boaster that it knew it all. The Communists have considered all the other nations of the world—especially the United States—as confused, selfish, hypocritical, and stupid. They have anticipated the day when capitalism would collapse under its own weight and religion, and "the opiate of the people" would simply wither away. Few nations in world history have been so vocal in their contempt for other peoples as has Russia. This nation, under its myopic succession of leadership, has asked no one for advice and has presented itself to the world with a know-it-all attitude.

With what final result? Present-day Russia is conducting a contest to answer the question "Who are we?" "What are we supposed to be doing in the world?" The old Communist slogans like "Workers of the world, unite; we have nothing to lose but our chains; we have a world to win" are gone. Now everything is in a state of flux and there remains nothing but questions.

We suggest that when the attitude of lost identity takes over in a nation, that nation is in great peril. All too often, government and academic bewilderment is the prelude to anarchy. One could ask, "How long will the students of Russia live without purpose and exist with no direction in life?"

Russia has come through a most turbulent past. This century for this troubled land has been one of ecstasy and agony on the part of its oppressed people, for the promise of Utopia in the future is much easier said than done. Many books could be filled to tell the story of nation after nation that has hurled itself into great battles with the promise of Utopia ahead. The result has never been Utopia; instead, blood-filled presumption gives way to reality and the nation attempts to find itself again.

It is totally fascinating to watch a great anomaly unfold in Russia. On the one hand, an obviously ill president is inaugurated and gives the promise of peace and tranquility for the days to come. At the same time, the Chechen secession groups mount a bloody offensive which is seen by all the world as evidence of the weakness of Soviet military power. It is a most amazing thing to behold.

The New Attitude

Out of this the onlooking world is developing the attitude that Russia is weak. The suggestion is that purpose is gone and discouragement has taken over. This, along with the touted reduction of Russia's military forces, is an attitude that attempts to write off Communist capabilities in the days to come.

We would not, however, be wise in accepting this evaluation at face value. While weakness appears to be the story of the present, that story is not the real truth. No, the Russian phoenix will rise again to power, and it has not in fact even disappeared today.

Despite all the talk about Russian weakness, this nation still retains a military force that places it number two in the entire world. The array of infantry forces, naval vessels, aircraft, and especially rockets is still a genuine threat to the world.

"But isn't this in the process of being destroyed?" some will ask. It is true that we are treated by the press to pictures of rockets being decommissioned and their fuel burned away. Such photographs are presented on American television as proof that Russia is working at reducing its nuclear force to zero.

But to believe this is to be amazingly shortsighted. Nuclear materials have a relatively short life, probably less than ten years (although don't plan on it). It is therefore necessary to destroy older weapons on a regular basis because they become unstable. The Russians would certainly not be above giving us pictures of the routine destruction of aging weapons as evidence of a large reduction of the nuclear force-in-being.

We do not, however, have any serious evidence of a real reduction of the 30,000 nuclear warheads that Russia is known to have. It is frightening to imagine the potential of this force in the hands of a bewildered and unstable government.

In fact, such a situation practically invites the ascendancy of a strong ruler who steps to the fore to bring purpose and goals once again to a bewildered and wondering people. The present Russian situation is an open invitation to exactly such a ruler.

To think further about this, two names should be kept in mind. One is Gennady Zyuganov. Zyuganov is a powerful vote-getter, but we must remember that he is a dedicated Communist. He is *totally* unreconstructed by the new spirit of Russia and believes that Communism, in its most powerful form, still represents the answer to the future.

The *Wall Street Journal* reports on this Communist leader's campaign, showing that it featured such Bolshevik-era slogans as "power should be returned to the people" and "women will raise children with confidence in their future." With these slogans, Zyuganov produced something of a Communist revival in Russia and garnered for himself a 40 percent vote. It is frightening to think that 40 percent of the voters in Russia, despite their personal experience with the cruelty of Communism, were willing to vote for such a leader.

The second provocative name is Alexander Lebed. Virtually unknown up until now, he has emerged into—indeed skyrocketed into—a national significance, standing at the side of Boris Yeltsin. This man is young, purposeful, and possessed of a stern military background. He cannot be expected to opt for Russian weakness, but can in the last analysis be expected to push for military strength. Should the situation in Russia grow any more shaky, we can certainly count on Lebed to call for a new era of rearmament to increase national strength.

Given the Communist response to Zyuganov, we can also expect that a high percentage of Russians would respond affirmatively to such a call. After all, these people have known nothing in all their lives save the Russian-stated propaganda that diplomacy rose out of the mouth of a cannon. Stalin himself established this pragmatic Russian philosophy, and Lebed, by this time facing a disillusioned nation, can certainly be expected to say "Amen" to the revival of that point of view.

We can see that Russia, then, has within it the components of a revival of Communist expansionism, militarism, and ideological resuscitation. These components cannot be ignored by the West. Yet the West appears to be falling asleep in the face of such a threat.

Future Changes

The components of marked change in days to come already exist in Russia today. These consist of: remaining vast military power, an unstable government, and powerful leaders ready at any time to take over. Let no one therefore succumb to the notion that Russia is to be totally discounted in any power move in the immediate years to come.

Quite obviously the current scene in Russia is one of continued internal provocation and a sizable threat to the peace of the world.

Many of us are familiar with the fact that the Word of God refers to this vast "king of the North" in no uncertain terms. One of the fascinating occupations of our time is to read the reports which come from the news and then check a comparable source of information as presented in the Word of God.

The news may change and kingdoms may rise and fall, but the Word of God is changeless and enduring. About this Scripture says:

> For all flesh is like grass, and all the glory of man like the flower of grass. The grass withereth and the flower thereof falleth away, but the Word of the Lord endureth forever. And this is the Word which by the gospel is preached unto you (1 Peter 1:24,25).

What then does the Word of God indicate about this phoenix of the North that has a way of rising again? We have a remarkable report in the words of the Prophet Ezekiel:

> The word of the Lord came unto me, saying, Son of man, set thy face against Gog, of the land of Magog, the chief prince of Meshech and Tubal, and prophesy against him, and say, Thus saith the Lord God: Behold, I am against thee, O Gog, the chief prince of Meshech and Tubal; and I will turn thee back, and put hooks into thy jaws, and I will bring thee forth, and all thine army, horses and horsemen, all of them clothed with all sorts

of armor, even a great company with bucklers
and shields, all of them handling swords: Persia,
Ethiopia, and Libya with them; all of them with
shield and helmet; Gomer and all its hordes; the
house of Togarmah of the north quarters, and all
its hordes; and many people with thee (Ezekiel
38:1-6).

Here we have the opening words of one of the most dramatic passages of the Bible. Ezekiel takes two chapters,
starting with Ezekiel 38, to describe a fearsome battle. The
description that follows ought not to be ignored by anyone
who would be aware of today's possibilities in the development of the prophetic Word.

We can learn a number of lessons from this chapter. The
first is that there will be a tremendous invasion from the
North that will come upon the Middle East and the nation
of Israel. Scripture says that the invasion will come "against
the mountains of Israel" (Ezekiel 38:8). So once again Israel
will be the provocative center of a tremendous military confrontation.

Second, this passage tells us that the invading army will
consist of Gog and Magog and will be led by "the chief prince
of Meshech and Tubal." This expression, "the chief prince,"
is actually "the Prince of Rosh, Meshech, and Tubal." So what
do we have? Here we have Russia moving with powerful
forces in a program of conquest of the South.

We also learn that Russia will take to itself certain allies
who will be a part of this attempted program of conquest.
Especially do we note that Persia will by an ally of Russia
(verse 5). One of the frightening developments of our time
is the furnishing of nuclear weapons and materials to
modern-day Iran—once known as Persia. The recent leaders
of Israel have frequently said, "Our real concern in the

Middle East is not with Syria or Lebanon or the Saudis but with Persia. Persia, or Iran, is considered a rogue nation steeped in Islamic fundamentalism and led by near-insane leaders who would stop at nothing.

Intervention from Above

This passage also tells us that this stupendous invasion from the North will be successfully countered by divine intervention. God says:

> I will call for a sword against him throughout all my mountains, saith the Lord God; every man's sword shall be against his brother. And I will enter into judgment against him with pestilence and with blood; and I will rain upon him, and upon his hordes, and upon the many people that are with him, an overflowing rain, and great hailstones, fire, and brimstone. Thus will I magnify myself and sanctify myself; and I will be known in the eyes of many nations, and they shall know that I am the Lord (Ezekiel 38:21-23).

As a consequence of this divine intervention, the armies that invade from the North will be virtually exterminated. Yes, the end of Russia's armies will be on the inhospitable northern mountains of Israel.

We are also told in this passage that the defeat of the king of the North will be a great testimony as to the existence of God for the whole world to see. Yes, the astonished nations of earth will see in the defeat of the northern armies the power of God in His ability to intervene at will. What is the result of a nation rebelling against God and becoming His enemy on earth? God says:

> I will smite thy bow out of thy left hand, and will
> cause thine arrows to fall out of thy right hand.
> Thou shalt fall upon the mountains of Israel, thou
> and all thy hordes, and the people that are with
> thee; I will give thee unto the ravenous birds of
> every sort, and to the beasts of the field to be de-
> voured. . . . And I will send a fire on Magog, and
> among those who dwell carelessly in the coast-
> lands; and they shall know that I am the Lord
> (Ezekiel 39:3-6).

Further, God says, "I will set my glory among the nations,
and all the nations shall see my judgment that I have executed, and my hand that I have laid upon them" (Ezekiel
39:21).

Yes, the Russian phoenix will arise and move once again
in an attempt at world conquest. However, this endeavor
will be a classic illustration of the total futility of fighting
against God.

The Future of the United States

Out of all of this the question is frequently asked, "Where
is the United States at the time of this battle?"

The question grows out of the fact that the United States
is a well-known supporter of the nation of Israel. In fact, the
U.S. has been Israel's only major friend in this modern era.
The Middle East could have been conquered by the Russians at any time over the last 20 years were it not for the
United States. Our nuclear capability and presumed will-
ingness to use it has deterred this total aggression described
in the Word of God. Because America has been Israel's great
protector, people do ask about the situation of America in
that tremendous end-time confrontation.

We think there are several possibilities. The first is that America will have been destroyed. The leadership of America persistently votes against the antiballistic-missile-defense system. Consequently, today Russia has an ABM protection system around its major city, Moscow, whereas America does not. This is an invitation to destruction which our leaders should surely know. One wonders.

A second possibility is that America will have been blackmailed into nonparticipation. One of the interesting developments of our time is that growing Russian expertise at near space is not exactly matched by the American program. They can put astronauts in orbit for a year and even carry American visitors. Near space could be the perfect platform for nuclear blackmail. It in effect says from on high, "Give up or we will destroy Washington or New York." Could we stand against such an ultimatum? The answer is not clear.

The third possibility is that America may have simply been discounted and considered a paper tiger. The moral situation in America today as reflected in many walks of American life is not good. America may simply lose its prestige, acceptance, financial leadership, and many other things in the world because of its present inattention to moral things. There is little doubt that America has been in the process of forsaking the Lord, much as the Russians did 80 years ago. The Russian situation teaches us that the outcome of such an attitude can be the evaporation of the nation's capability.

Another possibility may also be the rapture of the church. The rapture of the church would take a high percentage of the leadership class out of the United States. This is true of almost no other nation of the world. If 50 million Christians were taken out of the United States in one day, there would be a crisis of leadership in America that could be governmentally fatal. In fact, in the current political campaigns, Christianity is coming to the fore in a real fashion. In the election of 1992, the Christians garnered 33 percent of the vote. This has to be respected. Any political individual who can represent 33 percent of the electorate is bound to gain a certain amount of respect. If that group suddenly disappeared, what would the outcome be? The outcome would at least recast the power structure of the world into a new mold.

Parenthetically, we need to remember that the fate of a nation is dependent not on politics or economics but on godliness. "Blessed is the nation whose God is the Lord," says the psalmist in Psalm 33. Conversely, Scripture announces that "the wicked shall be turned into hell, and all the nations that forget God" (Psalm 9:17).

Two Crucial Factors

At any rate, we can surely conclude that the protection of America over Israel is not in place at the time of this Russian invasion. This emboldens the king of the North to move with dispatch, thinking that his victory is sure. In order to have aggressive war, at least two components must be present: One is a desirable prize and the other is a presumed absence of effective resistance.

The Middle East is certainly a desirable prize. It represents the oil of the world and therefore the major source of the world's wealth. This is worth taking, and a presumably strong nation, seeing the Middle East as the key to world leadership, could become arrogant enough to give it a try.

The absence of effective resistance would certainly be assumed if America were taken out of the picture. In fact, the absence of American influence may well precipitate an alliance between Israel and the leadership of Europe. This could certainly become the covenant predicted by the prophet Daniel (Daniel 9:27). Given this development (and it is certainly being thought of by Mideast leaders today), we have come very close to the fulfillment of Daniel's prophetic picture.

There is no doubt that the rise of the Russian phoenix from the ashes of the failures of the past will be a most important global development. The very people who would like to see this happen are in positions of power in Russia today. The person who would advocate continued friendship with America—Boris Yeltsin—is a fading power in Russia today. We have developing before our very eyes the components that could bring to pass the fulfillment of the prophetic picture as given to us from the Lord. We must therefore remind ourselves that we have a more sure word of prophecy, unto which we do well to take heed (2 Peter 1:19).

A final question remains: We who see these things coming to pass—what shall we do? Christ spoke very pointedly to this question when He said:

> There shall be signs in the sun, and in the moon, and in the stars; and upon the earth distress of nations, with perplexity; the sea and the waves roaring; men's hearts failing them for fear, and for looking after those things which are coming on the earth; for the powers of heaven shall be shaken. And then shall they see the Son of Man coming in a cloud with power and great glory (Luke 21:25-27).

After this Christ takes the time to answer our question "What shall we do?" "When these things begin to come to pass, then look up and lift up your heads, for your redemption draweth near" (Luke 21:28).

Yes, it is time to look up. We who know Christ as personal Savior should look up for that marvelous event, the rapture of the church. Yes, Christ is coming for His own according to His wonderful promise.

Upon being reminded of the nearness of the return of Christ, we should renew our determination to become artic- ulate witnesses for the Savior. The world has heard rumors that all is not well for the days to come. Consequently it is asking as never before, "Who can I trust?" We alone who know the gospel of Jesus Christ have that answer. Let us therefore announce to a disturbed world with new force and new concern the marvelous message that Christ is able to save to the uttermost those that come unto God by Him.

The Prophetic Word

Considering all that is taking place in our present time, the prophetic Word becomes increasingly important. That Word says, "Seeing then that all these things shall be dis- solved, what manner of persons ought ye to be in all holy living and godliness?" (2 Peter 3:11). That's the way to live in times like these.

The situation in Russia is changing fast. Even as we observe from a distance, titanic forces are moving in the Russian culture, promoting riptides in one direction or another. The volatility of this powerful state produces the possibility of revolution, assassination, further division, and dramatic political change from many a corner. This volatile and unsettled situation could produce new considerations overnight. We therefore recommend that each reader keep a careful eye on the Russian scene, for such observation is bound to see surprising new developments.

Bear in mind that Russia has killed 60 million of its own people, a ghastly policy concerning which the Lord has surely taken notice. Russia will certainly not be allowed to speak to the international community and excuse itself by merely saying, "Sorry about that!" No, as God is just, a fearful retribution from heaven will come upon this nation. The events that the Bible predicts will come upon this prince of the North will be so telling that all the nations of the world will take notice of the fearful results of forgetting God.

In the meantime, we call all the nations of the world, especially the United States, into a posture of national repentance. While there is still time, this nation must turn to God and thereby be spared the wrath to come. In the meantime, let every individual see the wisdom of receiving Christ and thereby gaining the hope of eternal life, which God, who cannot lie, promised before the world began. The current provocative politic developments on every hand should cause each one of us as believers to even now look up for the redemption that draws nigh.

10

The Mideast March to Megiddo

Paul Feinberg

Those who live in the Western world tend to think that the most important world events happen in Washington D.C., Ottawa, London, or at least in the United Nations. But serious Bible students have long realized that this is simply false. From a divine perspective the Middle East, in a very real sense, is the center of divine activity in human history. It was there that God chose a small nation from which the Messiah and Savior of the world was to be born. And it is there that the events which mark the end of human history will take place. Therefore, whenever social, political, or economic unrest takes place in that part of the world, serious Christians observe the activity with close attention.

In this chapter I would like to tell the biblical story about what is to take place there in the future and also examine current events in this area to see what light they might shed on what the Bible says.

Daniel's Seventieth Week

Daniel 9 reveals a very important and fundamental prophecy,[1] one which has to do with a time after the church has been taken out of the world to be with her Lord in heaven.[2] Daniel is told that this revelation is about His people, Israel, and His city, Jerusalem. Daniel 9:2 and following states the occasion for the giving of this prophecy: Daniel, who is studying the prophecy of Jeremiah (25:11,12; 29:10), in which God says that the desolation of Jerusalem was to last 70 years because of Israel's sin of idolatry, becomes concerned; he wants to know when this period will be completed. He is uncertain as to when the 70 years of exile will be over because there were three sieges of Jerusalem, the city falling only on the last.

God does not answer Daniel's question directly, but gives him a related revelation. It is not about 70 years in which idolatry will be ended, but about 70 "weeks" or heptods (490 years) in which all iniquity, transgression, and sin will be put away from the nation of Israel and eternal righteousness will be established (Daniel 9:24). Sixty-nine of these "weeks" are now past; they ended with the coming of Messiah, the Prince, at His baptism and entrance into the messianic office (Daniel 9:25). After the first 483 years and before the last seven years, two things will happen that are related to God's people Israel (Daniel 9:26): Messiah will be cut off and have nothing (the word translated "cut off" is used of a violent death) and the city of Jerusalem will be destroyed, an event which we know occurred in 70 A.D.

That brings us to verse 27, the most important one for the topic at hand. Some interpreters believe that week 70 immediately follows the end of the sixty-ninth week. The antecedent of the "he" which begins the verse, in this view, is Messiah, the Prince, of verse 25. This interpretation states that the covenant which the Messiah makes with many is the new covenant of Jeremiah 31 and Hebrew 10. This covenant was established by Christ's death on the cross. The most serious objection to this view—and a decisive reason for rejecting it—is the fact that the new covenant is not a seven-year covenant, but an eternal one.

The correct interpretation of this verse identifies the antecedent of the "he" with the ruler who will come. If this were not the case, then it would be impossible to explain why "he" is in the text. Verse 26 makes perfect sense without his mention. Again, the only explanation for his inclusion is that "he" is the antecedent of the pronoun that begins verse 27. Therefore the seventieth week of Daniel is not about the Messiah, but Antichrist. Daniel's seventieth week will be the week of Antichrist. On the basis of this text, Christians talk about a time of trial or tribulation which will last for seven years before Christ returns to the earth.

A Counterfeit Trinity

Satan, the great counterfeiter of God and God's truth, will present a counterfeit trinity to the world during Daniel's seventieth week. Revelation 12 and 13 describe this trinity. Chapter 12 reveals the motivator and central figure—that old dragon, Satan, who has two masterpieces described in chapter 13: the beast from the sea and the beast from the earth, or land. Since the sea often symbolizes the nations of the world, it is fair to say that Antichrist will be a Gentile. Moreover, this deceiver's functions will be political (Daniel 2, 7). The second beast will be from the earth or land. I think he will be an apostate Jew, as the land of Israel is often referred to as "the land." This beast's functions will be religious (Daniel 8,11; 2 Thessalonians 2:3ff.).

This trinity, then, will consist of Satan himself, a Gentile political leader located in Rome, and an apostate Jewish religious leader who will operate from Jerusalem. Some refer to the first beast as the Antichrist or the beast; others call the first beast the Antichrist and the second the false prophet. Therefore it is helpful to observe each one's function and location to avoid ambiguity. The two will try, however, to establish a worldwide rule during the tribulation period.

Peace at Last?

We are now able to identify the "he" of Daniel 9:27. He is the first beast of Revelation 13, the political leader. We learn that this final week of Daniel's prophecy will begin with a covenant that this leader will make with many in the nation of Israel for one "week" of seven years. This agreement will guarantee Israel's political and religious sovereignty and autonomy. The Jews will be allowed to build a tribulation temple and establish a sacrificial system. Scriptures indicate a brief period of peace for the first 3½ years, although some of the judgments of Revelation 6–19 will begin to fall on the earth.[3]

A number of things will happen at the midpoint of the week to radically change what will take place. First, Satan will enter heaven and make war with Michael the archangel. Michael will prevail against Satan and his followers, who will be cast to the earth. Satan will immediately turn his rage and anger against the nation of Israel, pictured as a woman. It is clear that without God's supernatural intervention and protection of the woman, Satan would destroy her (Revelation 12:13-17). The temple worship of sacrifices and oblation will cease (Daniel 9:27).

Although some would disagree with this, I think that this time frame will roughly be the time of the revelation of the second beast, the world religious leader who will come into prominence with the destruction of the harlot of Revelation

17 and the end of temple worship in Israel. Jesus taught that what will follow will be a time of great distress, unequaled from the beginning of the world and never equaled again. As a matter of fact, if the days of the severest trial were not shortened, no flesh would survive (Matthew 24:21,22). We can see what Jesus meant. The number and severity of the divine judgments spoken of in Revelation 6–19 will intensify. This counterfeit trinity will take power and try to subject the entire world to its authority (Revelation 13:15-18). There will be the abomination of desolation in the holy place (Daniel 9:27; 12:11; Matthew 24:15; 2 Thessalonians 2:3,4; Revelation 13:11-15).

It is difficult to identify precisely what is meant by the abomination of desolation, but this phrase often refers to idols or idolatry, which would indicate that an idol—most likely of the first beast who was wounded, died, and rose again—will be placed in the temple. This world religious leader will try to establish the final form of apostate religion, the worship of Satan as God. Failure to comply will be met with the most severe physical, social, and economic sanctions (Revelation 13:15-18).

The Meeting at Megiddo

Within this context, the nations of the world will march to a meeting with Almighty God at Megiddo, or Armageddon. The relationship between these two terms is not entirely clear. In fact, the name "Armageddon" appears only once in the Bible, in Revelation 16:16, and it does not appear in any Hebrew text that we possess, leading some interpreters to suggest that this refers not to a geographic locality, but rather to an event. Others believe the word "Armageddon" is a corruption in the language, and really means "city of desire" or "his fruitful mountain." If so, it might refer to the city of Jerusalem. However, the most popular explanation—and the one that I think is correct—is that Armageddon refers to Mount (Ar) Megiddo (Magedon), a military stronghold (Joshua 12:21; 17:11; Judges 1:27; 2 Kings 8:27)[4] which occupied a strategic position on the southern rim of the Plain of Esdraelon in the north of Palestine.

Megiddo is mentioned often in the Old Testament. It was a royal city for the Canaanites (Joshua 12:21), and after the conquest of Canaan by the Israelites, it was given to Issachar (Joshua 17:11), although it later became the possession of the tribe of Manasseh (Judges 1:27). Megiddo did not become secure within the land until the time of Solomon, who built fortifications in the area and placed 12 deputies over Taanach and Megiddo (1 Kings 4:12; 9:15).[5]

A number of significant Old Testament historical events occurred in this locality. It was here that Barak was victorious over the king of Hazor, whose army was under the command of Sisera (Judges 4:13-15). In addition, Gideon defeated the Midianites here (Judges 7), Saul died here (1 Samuel 31:6-8), and Ahaziah, king of Judah, fled to this place and died here (2 Kings 9:27). However, the primary historical interest in this area lies in the death of Josiah, who attempted to stop Pharaoh Neco of Egypt as he passed through Carmel into the plain of Megiddo. Unsuccessful in his attempt, Josiah was shot by an Egyptian archer as he tried to escape. He died on the road to Jerusalem (2 Kings 23:29,30; 2 Chronicles 35:20-24; Zechariah 12:11).

Megiddo is identified with the modern archaeological site of Tell el-Mutesellim. This site has been extensively excavated, and is one of the most important sites in Palestine.[6]

Mount Megiddo or Armageddon is important not only historically but prophetically as well. This is where one of the climactic battles of human history—a conflict between the forces of God and the forces of Satan—will be fought. The

Bible tells of a period of time called "the day of the Lord" that precedes the return of the Lord to this earth. This will be a time when a multinational war will take place (Joel 3:9-15; Zechariah 14:1-5; Zephaniah 3:8; cf. Mark 13:7,14ff., 24ff.). For premillennialists, this will come before Christ sets up his kingdom on this earth for a thousand years.

Armageddon: Battle or War?

As I have already said, there is some disagreement over the scriptural meaning of Armageddon. One problem facing the biblical interpreter is that it seems difficult to present a coherent picture of all that is said on this subject. For this reason some commentators think that Armageddon symbolically represents this final conflict. They caution against taking the prophetic, apocalyptic imagery too literally.

However, I believe there is a better way of dealing with the interpretive problem: *We must recognize that Armageddon is not a battle, but a war.* This can be supported by two considerations. First, the only actual mention of Armageddon in the New Testament is in Revelation 16:16, and it is in the context of a battle on the great day of God Almighty (Revelation 16:14). This Greek word may be translated either as "battle" (NIV) or "war" (NASB). I prefer the NASB rendering. That is, Armageddon will not be a single battle, but a full-fledged war.

Second, as we gather all the texts that relate to this conflict, we see fighting throughout the land of Palestine. Revelation 14:20 speaks about blood flowing out of God's winepress as high as the bridles of the horses for the distance of about 180 to 200 miles—the distance from Dan in the north to Beersheba in the south. Having said this, the Bible describes three principal areas of conflict: fighting to the south of Palestine (Daniel 11:40-45), which is said to occur in Egypt, Edom, Moab, Ammon, and Ethopia, as well as in the south of Israel by the Dead Sea; fighting in the north (Ezekiel 38, 39; Daniel 11:40-45); and conflict in the city of Jerusalem and the Kidron Valley (Joel 3; Zechariah 12, 14).

If this is the correct understanding of the teaching of Scripture, then Armageddon will not be just a battle, but a war—with three major areas of fighting—that will ultimately engulf the entire land of Palestine. And it gets its name from one of the major battles or areas of conflict.

All the Nations of the World

Not only will this war involve the whole land of Israel, but the Bible teaches that all the nations of the world will also become embroiled in it (Zechariah 12:3; 14:2; Revelation 16:14). These nations quite clearly will form four power blocks or alliances: nations to the south of the land of Palestine; a confederacy from the West; armies from the East (Revelation 16:12)—mounted troops will number 200 million (Revelation 9:16); and finally, nations from the north of the land of Israel (Ezekiel 38, 39; Daniel 11:40-45).

When the Bible speaks of all the nations of the whole world, does this mean that every country in existence today will do battle in Armageddon? Obviously not. Just within the last decade, we have seen some nations come and go. None of us can say for sure just what nations will be in existence at the time this prophecy is fulfilled. Will the nations of the Western Hemisphere—the U.S., Canada, and Mexico— be a part of this final conflict? They are not mentioned by name anywhere in the Bible. This does not mean that they will *not* be in existence, but neither would any prophecy be falsified by their absence.

While certain nations are not specifically mentioned in any way in prophecy, other nations are clearly named as participants in Armageddon. Some of the nations named fall under general designations. Daniel 2 and 7 clearly indicate a Western confederacy of nations, although the exact nations included in that alliance are not clear. These two chapters speak of four world powers that will arise one after another. Though not all Bible students agree, it seems best to identify this fourth kingdom with Rome, which we know will exist in prophetic times. During Daniel's seventieth week a little horn will arise and take power. He will be the world political leader.

We are not certain which nations the symbols of ten toes and ten horns signify. Some have tried to identify this prophecy with the creation of an European Common Market in our time. It is difficult to say whether this is correct. If Christ were to return for His church today, it could well be that this Common Market would be used in the fulfillment of this prophecy. However, if Christ's coming is some years off, even centuries into the future, we cannot say what the case will be. Recent history teaches us that nations making up the Common Market have changed; nations have come into and out of existence. What we can say with confidence is that, if we are correct in our interpretation of the Daniel texts, God will raise up a confederacy of nations in this general area to participate in the event of the end times.

Similarly, Revelation 16:12 indicates that a group of nations will come from the East to Armageddon. The nations are not named, but the size of their troops is enormous. This fact, in addition to the fact that the Euphrates River is dried up to aid their march to Megiddo, precludes this as a reference to the nations to the *immediate* east of the land of Palestine: Saudi Arabia, Iran, and Iraq. So some interpreters identify this contingent with nations such as India and China.

Other nations named specifically as participants in this conflict include: Ammon (Jeremiah 9:26; Ezekiel 25:1-7;

Daniel 11:41); Assyria (Isaiah 14:24-27); Egypt (Isaiah 19, 20; Ezekiel 29, 30; Daniel 11:41); Libya (Daniel 11:43); Moab (Isaiah 15, 16); and Syria (Isaiah 17), to name just a few. There is also the possibility that Babylon (Isaiah 13, 14, 21) will be rebuilt. Ancient Babylon is modern Iraq and part of Iran. The Bible speaks of its absolute destruction, and this seems never to have occurred historically. While we do not know exactly what nations will be in existence at the time of Armageddon, the Bible states clearly that all those nations which do survive until eschatological times will participate in the meeting at Megiddo.

Battle Plan for Armageddon

So far we have seen that Armageddon will involve all the nations of the world and will be fought over the entire land of Palestine, but exactly what will happen? Three passages in Scripture help us understand the battle plan for Armageddon: Daniel 11:40-45; Revelation 16:12-21; Revelation 19:11-21. This war will begin with simultaneous invasions into the Holy Land from the south and the north. The invaders will be successful at first, with many countries falling. While the power blocs mentioned before will fight one another for their own self-interests, they will arrive at the city of Jerusalem, where they will decide to unite against God and His people, Israel.

But God will respond to the challenge of the nations against his people Israel. Christ will return to the earth in great power and glory with the armies of heaven. From His mouth will come a sharp sword, with which He will strike the nations of the world. Christ Himself and the armies of heaven will make war against the ungodly trinity. The seventh bowl of judgment will be released. This will include flashes of lightning, rumblings, thunder, and a great earthquake which will cause the City of Jerusalem and the Mount of Olives to its east to be split. The enemy will be struck with panic and madness. Islands and mountains will disappear. God will hurl from the sky huge hailstones that weigh a hundred pounds. The political and religious leaders who have deceived the world will be caught and cast into the lake of fire.

It is not hard to imagine what this will do to the nations of the world who have come against the Jews: They will do their best to get away from the destruction. At this time God will destroy the armies that flee to the south (Daniel 11:42-44) and to the north (Ezekiel 38 and 39). While some students of prophecy understand Ezekiel 38 and 39 to take place in the middle of Daniel's seventieth week, I think it is better to place it as a part of Armageddon. Since this speaks of the destruction of armies on the mountains of Israel in the north, this may explain the significance of the battle and why the war is called Armageddon.

I place the prophecy here because of the completeness of the destruction. It will take seven years to put out the fires God has sent forth from heaven, as well as seven months to bury the dead. This seems out of keeping with something that will take place in the middle of the tribulation period. Further, Ezekiel says that this conflict was spoken of in the former days by the prophets. I think these prophets speak of God's wrath in connection with the return of Christ, not with the events in the middle of the seventieth week of Daniel.

Can This Be True?

What I have just described is what I call the biblical story, or at least an important version of that narrative. At this point some would argue that we have a compelling reason for rejecting the Bible as true and relevant to our lives today.

This is an ancient book, some 2000 years old, they would say. *It may have been written by people who were spiritually sensitive, but they could not possibly have known anything beyond their own historical horizon. How could a writer of 800 B.C. or A.D. 95 know anything about the geopolitics of the final generation? To think that they might is foolishness of the highest order.*

We conservative, evangelical Christians have a ready and correct response to such claims. The Bible is indeed a human book. It has human authors who wrote using their own personalities, style, and vocabulary. But the Bible has dual authorship; it is not just a human book, but a divine Book as well. The Holy Spirit superintended the genuinely human authors so that they were kept from error and had access to knowledge that transcended their time-bound place in history. The Bible is not *ahistorical,* but what is expressed in it transcends the writers' place in history because God is also its Author (2 Timothy 3:16; 2 Peter 1:16-21). Therefore, when the Bible predicts what will take place in the future, we have a good reason for believing what we read. This point has been substantiated concretely, for the Bible not only tells us what we should expect at the return of Christ and afterward, but it told us what would happen at Christ's first coming. Christians have always pointed to fulfilled prophecy in Christ's first advent to justify our confidence in what is said about the second advent.

There remains, however, another question, one which comes not from those who reject the Bible's authority but from those who accept it and believe that whatever the Bible teaches is true. The question they raise is about the interpretation of prophetic literature. They would respond to my description of the biblical story with accusations that I have taken the texts I have discussed too literally. Their position would be something like this: The Bible does teach that there will great evil on the earth before Christ returns. However, we should be careful in taking what is said too literally. Prophetic literature is full of symbolic depiction of events, and thus Armageddon is a name given by biblical writers to an end-time conflict between good and evil. God is victorious, but care should be exercised in the description of the details.

At this point a look at current history will show that while the geopolitics of the world have certainly changed over the nearly two millennia since the close of the canon of Scripture, the Middle East still plays a critical role in the modern world. That is, though we may think that Washington D.C. or the political centers of Europe are the center of politics in our world, our attention continually returns to events in the Middle East. Before I turn to examine some of these events, a word of caution seems in order. The student of prophecy should avoid two mistakes when thinking about current events. The first is to ignore the events as if they have no significance in relation to what the Bible has to say. To do this is to allow the events spoken of in the Bible and unfolding in history to overtake us without our proper preparation!

Second, prophecy students should avoid identifying events as explicit fulfillment of prophecy. If the rapture of the church is the next event on God's prophetic calendar and if it is not preceded by any signs, then we should be very careful about talking about the *fulfillment of signs* which show that Christ is coming for His church. Closely related to this point is the fact that *Scripture does not tell us the time of Christ's coming,* which is imminent; that is, it can occur at any moment. Jesus could have come for His church in the first century A.D. or He could come many years, even centuries, from our time.

Current events might look strikingly similar to those prophetic signals which God's Word says will precede Christ's *second advent*–that is, His literal return to earth to set up His millennial kingdom. However, since Scripture teaches that there are no signs that precede Christ's coming *for His church in the air* (i.e., prophecies yet to be fulfilled before the *rapture* of the church), we must be careful not to dogmatically proclaim that events we see occurring today are signals of the imminent rapture. We should not pass over this point rapidly. We need to understand that attributing to current events prophetic significance pointing to the rapture is an error that might cause the unsaved, who so desperately need Jesus Christ, to go even deeper into unbelief.

With this in mind, let us turn to what I have called the facts of current history in the Middle East.

Armageddon and Oil

Clearly, a major reason for the importance of this region is related to its oil reserves. Many readers remember the gasoline shortage of the early 1970s. Since almost everything in highly industrialized societies runs on petroleum products, anything that can upset the free flow of oil from the Middle East poses a serious threat to the industrialized nations of the world.

Even more of us remember the events of 1990, when, while much of the world was either on vacation or asleep, Saddam Hussein took Kuwait by force. That act placed under Hussein's control 20 percent of the world's known oil reserves. Within two weeks the price of gasoline at the pump rose by 50 percent; in two months the price increased by 100 percent.[7] Hussein was then in a position to control navigation on the Persian Gulf, a means of transporting 40 percent of the oil from the region. The nations of the world could not stand idly by and watch 46 percent of the world's oil reserve threatened.[8] Seldom has the world witnessed such unity among the world's leaders. They met at the United Nations and voted sanctions against Iraq.

The abundance of oil in Arab countries has resulted in a redistribution of the world's wealth. In those countries where oil is plentiful and the population is not dense, per capita income can be as high as 17,000 dollars, as in the United Arab Emirates.[9] Oil revenues are so great that they could make it possible to buy the Bank of America in six days and IBM in 143 days. Given the oil reserves of this area and the economic power that comes from the redistribution of the world wealth to this region, it is not hard to imagine the prophecies of the ancient seers coming true. Though many regimes seem grossly out of step with our modern, high-tech societies, there is wealth and power enough to send all the nations of the world there to protect what they see as their own self-interests.

Longstanding Hatreds

Give peace a try! This popular slogan certainly seems to be good advice. With oil and wealth come economic prosperity. Why resort to war? All of this might make perfect sense to the rational mind, but irrationality is the order of the day in the Middle East. Hatreds there are longstanding and run deep. Israel is a small nation surrounded by hostile neighbors, some of whom are sworn to drive her into the sea. The hostility that rages has a very long history, one that we can trace back to Isaac and Ishmael in the book of Genesis. So when Yitzhak Rabin and Yassir Arafat shake hands and make peace on the lawn of the White House, it is no small accomplishment.

As if the hostility between Jew and Arab were not enough, little unity exists among the Arabs themselves. While it is true that the Arab League has been formed, old and deep hostility remains among Arabs. We can see this in two ways. First, leaders of Arab states who try to make peace with Israel are in danger of losing their lives. For example, when Egypt and Israel made peace, Anwar Sadat paid for this courageous act with his life. Lest we think the Jews are exempt from similar acts, just remember the murder of Yitzhak Rabin. Second, even where a peace accord has been reached, radicals who oppose the peace resort to violence to overturn it. Peace seems eminently rational for this region, but though it sometimes seems within our reach, it always eludes our grasp. Hatred makes this area unstable.[10]

The Supernatural Factor

No analysis of the Middle East is complete unless we recognize that supernatural forces are at work. Human history is an arena in which the struggle between God and Satan is played out. This is where the conflict between good and evil stages its last act. Almost every passage that gives us the biblical story shows this supernatural factor at work. In Revelation 16:12-16, the New Testament passage in which we see the word "Armageddon," John sees three evil spirits that look like frogs come out of the mouth of the dragon. These evil spirits went out to the kings of the whole earth to bring them to Armageddon. Great deceptive power was given to these demon spirits so that they could perform miraculous signs. In Zechariah, it is God who says that He will make Jerusalem a burden to all the nations of the world (12:3), and that it is He who will gather all the nations to this city (14:2). Ezekiel puts this same point in striking language. He says that God will put hooks in the jaws of the nations of the world to bring them to Armageddon (38:4), and that He will turn them around and drag them along (39:2). The nations have hated God and His people Israel. Now the nations are brought supernaturally to the valley of Jehoshaphat so that God can enter into judgment against the nations (Joel 3:1-3).

Supernatural forces are not only responsible for the nations coming to Armageddon, but repeatedly we are told that God sets the limits on the success of wickedness. Daniel says that God's court will sit in judgment of this end-time world political leader, and that his power will be taken away and he will be completely destroyed (7:26). Concerning the end-time religious leader, God says that his end is decreed (9:27), and that he will come to his end and no one will be able to help him (11:45). Ezekiel teaches us that God does this to show His greatness and holiness (38:23) and that throughout the punishment of the nations God will display His glory among them (39:21).

God is at work through human means to accomplish His plan. Everything is transpiring right on time, and victory is assured both for Him and for those who are His.

What Can We Do?

Sometimes all of this seems so abstract and beyond our control. *What difference does it make to my everyday life?* More importantly, *What can I do to make any kind of difference?* As Christians we are never taught to acquiesce to circumstance or to give ourselves over to despair. We are clearly commanded to do certain things.

1. Pray for the peace of Jerusalem and this region. The Holy Spirit says through David that we are to pray for the peace of Jerusalem among its neighbors (Psalm 122:6). Notice that we are never commanded to pray for the wrath and judgment of God to fall on the nations. These things will come; that is certain. However, we are to be peacemakers. We are to pray for peace. This is something that we know we should do, but too often we

think our prayers will be ineffectual; even worse, we forget to pray for peace at all. Only heaven will show how the prayers of God's saints have changed the course of human history. Let us not be so fainthearted that we lack the faith to believe that God may grant peace, even in our time.

2. Share the gospel with precious Arab and Jewish people. Again, this is something that most of us would consent to in theory but fail to put into practice. Paul says that the gospel is the power of God. From a human perspective it seems as though there is no hope for peace in the Middle East. However, with God anything is possible! We realize that if relationships between nations and within nations are to be changed, it will only come through a change of heart, and only God can do that. Evangelism among Arabs and Jews is not easy; it takes some preparation on our part, and it seems even more difficult because many of us can travel to the Middle East only for a short visit, if at all. Thus we need to provide means for mission agencies as extensions of our feet and our lips in the carrying of the good news to these needy hearts in these nations.

3. Support attempts to bring peace and justice to the nations of the Middle East. Sometimes our eschatology has been used to justify our inaction. We say that we are really happy that things look bleak, because then it is more likely that the Lord will return soon. And we want Him to come. But Christians are to be peacemakers, not warmongers. Peace will not come and it certainly will not last where there is no justice or fairness. Justice is difficult to describe for the Middle East. The Jews are God's chosen people. But the Arabs for the most part are also the descendants of Abraham. So when God says that He

will bless those who bless Abraham and curse those who curse him, that principle applies to both Arab and Jew. While the land of Israel has been promised to Israel, that is after the return of the Messiah. Furthermore, the reason the Jews have been in exile is because of disobedience and disbelief. Though God holds nations responsible for their actions toward Israel, in an important sense they are His chastening rod. Therefore, as informed Christians, we need to be fair. We need to find and support justice for all parties, realizing that there is a time when the Judge of all the earth will set things in order and see that His will is done on earth as it is in heaven.

4. Rest in the assurance that God is in control of human history, and He will be victorious. His glory will be displayed to Israel and the nations. The study of prophecy is practical indeed. We already know the end: God is victorious. Nothing can defeat His glorious will. We are on the winning side. A healthy appreciation of God's activity in history allows the saints to rest in the serenity of eternity while still living in the chaos of time. Grace and peace to you from our Lord and Savior Jesus Christ!

11

United Europe's Power Play

Arno Froese

Since the founding of the European Common Market in 1957 (based on the Treaty of Rome), Europe's significance has grown year by year. Although various scholars have argued Europe's biblical prophetic significance and some have presented the idea that the world's last power structure is to be centered in the United States, I feel it is essential that we determine why Europe is the only candidate for end-time world rulership.

In this chapter I will present six points which reinforce the notion of a united Europe power play. For a better overview, permit me to mention these six in headline style: First, Europe (Rome) ruled the world during the crucial time when Christ was born. God gave His only begotten Son during the time when Rome occupied Israel.

Second, the European system of civilization has ruled the world ever since, even to our present day.

Third, we will follow in detail how Europe imitates Israel, attempting to replace God's chosen land and chosen people.

Fourth, Europe's future and potential is virtually limitless in comparison with all other nations. Today's European Union is only the beginning of things to come.

Fifth, based on prophetic Scripture, the "ten kings" that will rule the world will be a creation that comes forth from Europe.

Sixth, the final kingdom incorporating democracy, freedom of religion, a free market society, a global financial system, and a world economy is now being established throughout Europe.

The Bible concerns itself mainly with the nation of Israel and its surrounding neighbors, and distinguishes three categories of people: Gentiles, Jews, and the church. Let us take a closer look at how these three groups of people came about.

Abraham the Chosen

Before the Lord God called Abraham, all people on the earth could be considered Gentiles. Then, through this one man who had a wife that was barren, the Creator planned to bring forth a nation. Here we recognize how God pleases to work with seemingly impossible odds. Biologically speaking, it was impossible for Abraham and Sarah to have descendants. This is clearly documented in Genesis 18:11: "Abraham and Sarah were old and well stricken in age, and it ceased to be with Sarah after the manner of women." Right here in the beginning we see God's method, which negates the capabilities of man—in this case, of Abraham and Sarah. They surely could not pride themselves in their accomplishment. They did receive the promise, but by themselves, without God's supernatural intervention, nothing could have been fulfilled. Thus we learn that God's promises do not depend on man's actions. God maintains total control at all times and in all situations.

The simplicity of this promise is overwhelming: "I will make of thee a great nation" (Genesis 12:2). Not just another nation among many, but "a great nation." Later God's faithful servant Moses wrote the following about this special nation: "Thou art a holy people unto the Lord thy God, and the Lord hath chosen thee to be a peculiar people unto himself, above all the nations that are upon the earth" (Deuteronomy 14:2). No one can deny the superiority of these people. This is true even today, before the final fulfillment of this Scripture. No group of people has played such a major role in our civilization as have the Jews. Whether in politics, science, the arts, or finances, the success of these people is overwhelming. The Lord simply tells us that they are to be above all the nations on the face of the earth. It is therefore a great error to compare the Jews with any other people.

This choosing, however, incorporates a specific purpose—namely, that these people should be "a holy people unto the Lord." When we search the Scriptures, we find that this has never fully taken place. Therefore it is a prophecy which will yet come to pass.

The Chosen People Reject the Chosen One

When God in the fullness of time intended to fulfill His promise for His people to be "a holy people," He sent His Son, the Lord Jesus Christ, the Messiah. He proclaimed loudly and clearly, "Repent, for the kingdom of Heaven is at hand!" But we all know the result: They rejected Him. John testifies, "He came unto his own, and his own received him not" (John 1:11). Through the parable of an unnamed nobleman, Jesus predicted this rejection: "We will not have this man to reign over us." Israel simply rejected the fulfillment of Bible prophecy.

This denial was not some kind of accident that occurred in the heat of a debate or conflict; the rejection had been

278 ❖ ARNO FROESE

prophesied long before. More than 700 years before the birth of Christ, the coming of the ruler of Israel was announced, including geographic details of where He was to be born and from which tribe: "Thou, Bethlehem Ephratah, though thou be little among the thousands of Judah, yet out of thee shall he come forth unto me that is to be ruler in Israel, whose goings forth have been from of old, from everlasting" (Micah 5:2). The birth of Jesus was not a coincidence but fulfillment of prophecy.

Now we come to an extremely important point–namely, the acceptance of the substitute. If we are not willing to receive the truth, we are forced to accept a lie. In plain words, if we do not follow Jesus, we will follow the Antichrist. It is therefore no surprise that the Jewish people–who had suffered greatly under the occupational force of the Roman Empire but rejected the Messiah–accepted foreign rulership by exclaiming, "We have no king but Caesar!" With the rejection of the Messiah, Israel lost her opportunity to be "a holy people" for a certain period of time.

During this period of temporary rejection, God created a new "holy nation," the church of Jesus Christ. Similar to the choosing of Israel, the church consists of a peculiar people: "Ye are a chosen generation, a royal priesthood, a holy nation, a peculiar people, that ye should show forth the praises of him who hath called you out of darkness into his marvelous light" (1 Peter 2:9). These are important fundamentals to understand in order to avoid confusing the Gentiles, Jews, and Christians. God chose the Jews for His earthly inheritance and the church for His heavenly inheritance.

Israel the Eternal

Although Israel has been set aside for a period of time (for all practical purposes, it was not a nation for about 2000 years), from God's eternal perspective it never ceased to be a nation. As a matter of fact, God bases Israel's perpetual existence as a nation on the universe: "Thus saith the Lord, who giveth the sun for a light by day and the ordinances of the moon and of the stars for a light by night, who divideth the sea when the waves thereof roar; The Lord of hosts is his name: If those ordinances depart from before me, saith the Lord, then the seed of Israel also shall cease from being a nation before me forever" (Jeremiah 31:35,36). If you see the sun by day and the moon by night and hear the waves roar, then you may know that Israel is still a nation!

In Romans 11:1, the apostle Paul asks the question "Has God cast away his people?" The answer is crystal-clear: "God forbid, for I also am an Israelite, of the seed of Abraham, of the tribe of Benjamin." He thereby confirms Israel's eternal existence. This chapter carries great weight because the apostle specifically emphasizes that he speaks to the Gentiles: "I speak to you Gentiles, inasmusch as I am the apostle of the Gentiles" (Romans 11:13).

The statement which the apostle Peter makes does not mean that we are now replacing Israel. Some have said that all the promises of the Scripture now belong to the church. Such teaching, however, does not correspond to the collective message of the Holy Scripture.

We must take careful notice that Romans 11 reveals the time frame of the church of Jesus Christ. Although the process of fulfillment of Bible prophecy for Israel was interrupted, it will continue at a given time. To be precise, the time frame of the church corresponds to Israel's rejection and reacceptance as a nation on earth.

Romans 11:25 gives us the answer: "For I would not, brethren, that ye should be ignorant of this mystery, lest ye should be wise in your own conceits: that blindness in part is happened to Israel until the fullness of the Gentiles be come in." It cannot be said more plainly. Israel's salvation depends on the "fullness of the Gentiles." For that reason we should do everything in our power to preach the gospel of our Lord Jesus Christ to the uttermost parts of the world. When the last one of the Gentiles is added, the church will be complete and thereby the time of salvation for Israel will have dawned.

So how does this relate to Europe? The answer is that Rome was in power at Jesus' first coming. In the following pages we will see how Rome will also be in power when Jesus comes again.

Four Gentile Empires and Europe's Civilization

Virtually all serious Bible scholars agree that the entire history of the Gentile nations is pictured in the image that King Nebuchadnezzar of Babylon saw in a dream. Daniel, the Jewish youth in captivity in Babylon, was inspired by the Holy Spirit to reveal four world power structures: 1) Babylon, 2) Medo-Persia, 3) Greece, and 4) Rome.

We have already established that Rome ruled Israel and much of the then-known world when Jesus was born. Prophecy, however, indicates that the final Gentile power structure is the fourth and last one, the resurrected Roman Empire.

At the arising of the Antichrist, as described for us in Revelation 13:3, "...all the world wondered after the beast." Then in verse 4 we see total support expressed by the people of the world in two questions: 1) "Who is like unto the beast?" and 2) "Who is able to make war with him?"

Not only will the masses of the world's population admire this wonderful, benevolent political leader, recognizing him as an absolute genius in politics, economics, and military policy, but "all that dwell upon the earth shall worship him" (verse 8).

Does this passage really mean *"all"* the people who live on earth, or does it only mean "all from a certain geographical area"? We find a clue in Revelation 7, just before the last seal is being opened. Verse 9 reads, "After this I beheld, and, lo, a great multitude, which no man could number, of all nations and kindreds and people and tongues, stood before the throne and before the Lamb, clothed with white robes, and palms in their hands." This certainly describes the global family. "These are they which came out of great tribulation, and have washed their robes, and made them white in the blood of the Lamb" (verse 14b). Therefore the last Gentile world empire will be truly worldwide.

Europe Worldwide

To prove that all other continents and nations are excluded from the *leadership* of this end-time world dominion, note the following:

1. Geographically, Europe lies in the center of the world between the East and the West.

2. Europe is the center of the philosophy that has shaped the progressive civilization of the world.

3. Today, Europe is again the center of world trade, commerce, and finance.

4. Europe is the center of religion, with the Vatican being the most powerful religious organization in the world.

Of the five internationally recognized continents— Europe, Asia, Africa, America, and Australia—three of these—Europe, America, and Australia—are built exclusively upon European philosophy and civilization.

Our early American and Canadian immigrant forefathers were virtually all Europeans. This applies to Australia as well. Central and South America are equally dominated by European civilization, including business, religion, and language. You won't find any significant activity in North, Central, and South America that resembles any native culture.

More than 50 percent of the African population speaks French and approximately two-fifths speak English. No African country would have a chance to even sell a pound of coffee beans unless they did it the European way. The entire political, economic, and social structure of virtually the whole of Africa is exclusively based on the European system.

What about Asia? Analyzing Japan, Korea, Hong Kong, India, Taiwan, and other progressive Asian countries, we find that they too are based on the principle of Western European civilization.

We rarely see a person from China or Japan traveling the world in his or her traditional costume or using ancient methods of communication while he attempts to sell his wares. People from these countries are forced to do business the European way. Colonial rulership by European nations has solidly installed fundamentals such as democracy, the educational system, language, metric measurements, agriculture, finance, and a functioning industry. None of those things, as they are now, originated in Africa or Asia.

You may search the records, but you will not find any evidence of African people going to Asia in the attempt to establish colonies, or American Indians going to Europe claiming territory. Neither will you read of Asian people being successful in establishing colonies on other continents.

New Guinea, Australia, and New Zealand, on the doorsteps of Asia, were left untouched and virtually empty by Asians for millennia. Only Europeans were successful in establishing their culture and civilization in other places. Only Europeans sailed around the world, leaving their mark that is clearly visible today.

The entire industrial revolution as we know it must be credited to the creativeness of the Europeans and their descendants.

For these and many other reasons I have steadfastly opposed the theory that the last world empire, called Mystery Babylon, will be established in its historic place in Iraq or in the United States of America.

Europe's Imitation of Israel

An additional, convincing fact that the European system will dominate the world lies on the religious level. Four characteristics demonstrate Europe's intention to replace Israel as the chosen nation.

1. Not Europe, but Israel is in reality the center of the earth. "Thus saith the Lord God: This is Jerusalem; I have set it in the midst of the nations and countries that are round about her" (Ezekiel 5:5). The Hebrew Bible reads, "living at the center of the earth." Luther translates this "Jerusalem in the midst among the heathen surrounded by countries." Ezekiel 38:12 confirms, "dwell[ing] in the midst of the land."

2. While Europe claims to be the center of philosophy that has shaped the progressive civilization of the world, we read in 1 Kings 10:24 that real philosophy is an outgrowth of wisdom and originates in Israel: "All the earth sought to Solomon, to hear his wisdom, which God had put in his heart."

3. Although Europe is becoming the world center of trade, commerce, and finance, the original promise was given to Israel: "The Lord thy God blesseth thee, as he promised thee; and thou shalt lend unto many nations, but thou shalt not borrow; and thou shalt reign over many nations, but they shall not reign over thee" (Deuteronomy 15:6).

4. Religious dominion was not given to Europe either. To Israel, the following promise was made: "There was given him dominion and glory and a kingdom, that all people, nations, and languages should serve him; his dominion is an everlasting dominion, which shall not pass away, and his kingdom that which shall not be destroyed" (Daniel 7:14).

The European flag, comprised of 12 stars formed in a circle, does not represent 12 nations. Presently, 15 nations are full members and many more are yet to be added. But Europe's constitution requires that only 12 stars should represent all the nations that will be gathered into the Union. Why? I believe that unconsciously they are imitating the 12 tribes of the children of Israel and the 12 apostles of the Lamb. We must not forget to mention that Europe [Rome] had a superior influence upon God's chosen people Israel even 2000 years ago.

U.S.A.–Part of Europe

America's European heritage has often been forgotten or hidden in the minds of the average citizen, but we are more attached to Europe [Rome] than we may think.

Our government is based on Roman principles. The supreme council of ancient Rome was called the Senate. This identical system is used today in the U.S. and Canada.

This also applies to Italy, France, Ireland, South Africa, and Australia, just to name a few countries.

Take a look at the various government buildings throughout the U.S.A. and you will see striking similarities to the Roman architecture found in the Vatican. Virtually all major government buildings are crowned with a cupola, a dome just like the one on top of St. Peter's Cathedral in Rome.

During a recent trip to Washington D.C. I visited the Capitol. In the long line of people waiting to get into the building, I asked five individuals three questions: 1) Are you an American? 2) Were you educated in the U.S.A.? and 3) What is the significance of the many Roman statues that can be found all over Washington? The answer I received from four was "I really don't know." One person, apparently well-educated, answered, "During the design of the Capitol, the popular artistic expressions were Roman-based, and thus our forefathers chose Roman symbols to represent America." This reinforced the statement I have made throughout the years that the climax of glory of virtually all European nations was the Roman world empire. America is the result of 37 million European immigrants whose ancient background is Roman.

I took great pains to read many of the inscriptions in Washington. From the Capitol to the Lincoln Memorial, from Arlington Cemetery to Union Station, the inscriptions I read over and over again across the entire city were strictly Roman. What do I mean by "Roman"? The name of God, Jesus, was nowhere to be seen. Therefore Christians, Jews, Moslems, Hindus, Buddhists, and especially Freemasons could easily interpret any and all inscriptions for their own religions. That is typically Roman.

Much more could be said about America's relationship to Rome, but these few facts show that America will have to return to the roots of her European founding fathers.

Only three or four decades ago, Europe was not taken seriously in the United States. It was simply brushed off as the "old country." This has changed drastically. Today, to be European is "in." Although we still use the old weights and measurements in America, sooner or later we will change to the European metric system which is now used globally.

Less than a decade ago, European nationals had to obtain a visa when traveling to the United States. That has been changed. The U.S.A. has become a tourist attraction due to the cheap dollar. Americans no longer can afford to travel to Europe as easily as Europeans can to the U.S.A.

The Roman "Taxing" Law for Today

While the nations are moving closer to each other due to the communications explosion, we are witnessing that the various groups of people, races, and nationalities are eager to identify themselves and be recognized because all races and groups of people must be accounted for just in the same way people had to be "taxed" before Jesus' first coming. Luke reports, "It came to pass in those days that there went out a decree from Caesar Augustus that all the world should be taxed. (And this taxing was first made when Cyrenius was governor of Syria.) And all went to be taxed, everyone into his own city" (Luke 2:1-3). The word "taxed" means to be counted. In modern language this was a population census. This caused a great commotion in the Roman one-world empire. Everyone had to return to his or her roots to be accounted for. All had to go back to where they came from. It took place just before Jesus came to the world the first time.

The real reason, however, for the population census was the fulfillment of the prophetic Word. Mary and Joseph resided in Nazareth, but the Savior of the world needed to be born in Bethlehem, so God moved Caesar Augustus to do His population census so Jesus would be born in Bethlehem, according to the Scriptures.

We should not be surprised to see the accounting of the nations taking place in our days before the second coming of Jesus. Not only the U.S., but all other governments on the face of the earth as well, are gathering information about each individual citizen more than ever before. Why? Because Jesus is coming!

America to Become Catholic

Asked in 1967 if America would become Communist, Dr. Wim Malgo, founder of Midnight Call Ministry, stated, "America will not become Communist, but rather Catholic." That statement was significant because during those years, Communism was the threat to world peace. The Communists took possession of one country after another. The West's military arm was effectively weakened through the effort of various peace groups.

What did Dr. Malgo mean by "America will become Catholic"? "America's strength does not lie in her military force," he explained, "but this undefinable power is due to the existence of a strong, independent church. As the years will go by, powerful deceptive movements will sweep the nation with the aim to bring the church back to Rome." We are witnessing this movement even today as some of the most vocal Christian groups openly proclaim that there is no difference fundamentally between Protestants and Catholics. This spirit of unifying with Rome is evident in virtually all major denominations and is being reinforced by new movements which do not distinguish between Roman Catholicism and Protestantism.

We see America looking toward Europe not only on the religious level, but on an economic level as well. An article in *Money* magazine in July 1994 stated that 250,000 Americans are leaving the country for good in the attempt to seek fame and fortune somewhere else.[1] This is only the beginning!

When traveling across Europe, as I often do, I sense a new awakening that is grounded in the hope for unity among the nations on the continent.

When listening to the younger generation, quite frequently I hear references to "we Europeans" instead of hearing them identify their nationality. When crossing the border from one European Union country into another, travelers don't see a border traditionally marked by the flag of that country; instead, they see the European flag, under which "Welcome to Belgium," for example, might be stated.

Europeans seem confident in their absolute assurance of a great future while Americans, in contrast, look back to the so-called "good old days." History tells us that no nation ever repeated its former glory. Europeans do not look back, except historically; rather, they look forward to a much greater power structure—to be precise, they look forward to the greatest power structure in the history of mankind.

Europe's Modern History

To understand Europe's potential, let us review what has transpired during the last four decades. The early stages of the European Union is described in a publication entitled "European Integration":

> The first stone in the building of the European Community was laid on May 9, 1950, when Robert

Schuman, the French foreign minister, put forward a plan worked out by himself and Jean Monnet for France and Germany to pool all their coal and steel production under a joint High Authority, within an organization open to any other country in Europe. His plan thus took up the idea put forward by Winston Churchill in his famous speech in Zurich on September 19, 1946, when he had called for the creation of a United States of Europe, singling out the essential need for Franco-German cooperation. Churchill, however, had envisaged the United Kingdom's role as a promoter rather than as an active participant. Thus on April 18, 1951, Belgium, the Federal Republic of Germany, France, Italy, Luxembourg and the Netherlands signed the treaty establishing the European Coal and Steel Community (ECSC) and on July 23, 1952, when it came into force, the Schuman Plan became a reality. The new Community's founding fathers hoped that it would be the seed from which further European political integration would grow, culminating in the emergence of a European Constitution.[2]

France, in the meantime, proposed to establish a European Defense Community, but the idea was abandoned due to lack of interest. Then, in 1956–

A committee chaired by the Belgian Foreign Minister, Paul-Henri Spaak, was asked to consider possible moves for further integration. In 1956 the committee concluded its work, and its report served as a basis for negotiations leading eventually to the treaties establishing the European Atomic Energy Community (Euratom) and the European Economic Community (EEC), which

were signed by the six in March 1957 and entered
into force on January 1, 1958.[3]

Economics was the key word at the beginning stages of
success on the way to realizing the dream of a united Europe.
"Encouraged by their initial success, especially in the economic field, the six returned in the early 1960s to the goal
they had never completely abandoned: Closer political integration."[4]

The original six founders were 1) Belgium, 2) France,
3) Germany, 4) Italy, 5) Luxembourg, and 6) Netherlands.
That was the beginning of the fulfillment of Europe's dream
to be unified that has existed for 2000 years. Europe's potential was now built on the population of 220 million people
as a foundation.

In January of 1973, three more nations were accepted:
1) Britain, 2) Denmark, and 3) Ireland. Thereby 66 million
additional consumers were added to Europe.

In 1981 Greece was added. Europe then counted 297
million people.

Two more nations were added in 1986: 1) Portugal and
2) Spain. Europe had now grown to 336 million people.

On January 1, 1995, three more nations were admitted
to the Union: 1) Austria, 2) Finland, and 3) Sweden. The combined population of the European Union was now 362 million.

It is important to understand that these developments
have been taking place at a time when Soviet Communism
has fallen into shambles in the East and American capitalism
is no longer absolutely superior in the West. Any argument
against that fact is silenced by the testimony of our own
national debt staring us right in our face.

The amazing growth of the European Union has not
come to an end but is only beginning.

In the early stages under the Treaty of Rome, the European Common Market tried to establish trade and commerce for the well-being of the Europeans, but the aim of Europe today is nothing less than total integration, forming one solid power bloc to reach world unity.

At this moment, East European nations are desperately knocking on Europe's door asking for admittance. In 1994 the first application for membership was received, as the *Daily Mail* of April 2, 1994, reported:

> Hungary was the first former Communist Bloc country to apply to join the European Union, saying it needed membership to "Guarantee security and integrity." Hungary's bid to move into the Western economic system is likely to be followed this month by Poland and later by the Czech Republic."[5]

The Ten Kings

At the time of the beginning of the European Common Market, speculation was made that when ten nations joined the Common Market it would constitute fulfillment of Revelation 17:12. Here is what that Scripture says: "The ten horns which thou sawest are ten kings, which have received no kingdom as yet, but receive power as kings one hour with the beast." This corresponds precisely to Daniel's prophecy: "The ten horns out of this kingdom are ten kings that shall arise" (Daniel 7:24). While today we can see plainly that these "ten kings" do not represent ten European nations, I want to quote Dr. Wim Malgo, who made this statement in 1967 regarding the ten kings:

> Let us not look for ten countries being members of the European Common Market, constituting

the fulfillment of Revelation 17:12. Rather we must look for ten power structures that will develop through the European initiative but will be worldwide.[6]

I have always fully agreed with this statement because the Bible specifically says *ten kings*. A king is not a nation. He is an individual person. The uniqueness of a person is that he is distinctly different from another. What then is the meaning of the "ten kings"? This simply means that we should expect the world to be categorized into ten different economic power structures.

In the last few years a number of nations have formed economic cooperation in the East and the West, in the South and the North. Two important treaties recently signed are *GATT* and *NAFTA*. Many others have been signed or are in the process of being established. In South America, *Mercosul,* something similar to the Common Market of Europe, is being formed. The same is true for Africa and many parts of Asia. I therefore propose that the world could be divided into the following ten economic power structures:

1. Europe
2. Far East
3. Mideast
4. North America
5. South America
6. South Asia
7. Central Asia
8. Australia and New Zealand
9. Southern Africa
10. Central Africa

These power structures reflect my personal opinion and no doubt will change. However, we know one thing for sure: Power no longer lies in the ability to manufacture and use weapons of war. The time when one country invades another, subdues its citizens, and incorporates territory of the vanquished is past. The "weapons of war" today are found in the banks, financial institutions, and currency markets. The battles are fought in the boardrooms of the executives running global corporations.

The predominant political system is democracy: a product of Rome, popularized by the French Revolution, and solidly implemented by Britain and the United States. Today there is no serious opposition to democracy.

We Are a Global World

A one-world global system is not something we should look for in the distant future; it is a reality here and now. This is not due to some mysterious conspiracy, as some claim, but rather it is an evolutionary process of the democratic free-market system.

Let's look at one example. More than 50 percent of a so-called *American car* may be manufactured in foreign countries, while a *foreign car* may be largely built in the United States.

"Is your Sony born in Japan? Probably not—Japanese electronic firms now make far more color TV's in other parts of Asia,"[7] reports the *Far Eastern Economic Review*. A brand name can no longer be identified by the country of origin because it might be manufactured anywhere in the world.

I was shocked recently to discover that a shipment of Franklin Electronic Bibles had been "Made in China"!

The board of directors of Mercedes Benz was challenged to change the standard procedure of imprinting its products with "Made in Germany" to "Made by Mercedes" on the argument that the company is global. Its products are no longer limited to Germany but are being built in many parts of the world.

Thus we see that global corporations and financial institutions are the number one driving force toward world unity.

While America has progressed tremendously since World War II, Europe has progressed faster, and for all practical purposes has overtaken the U.S.A. in leadership. This was made painfully clear several years ago when the German car manufacturer BMW began its search for a "cheap labor nation." The manufacturer found that whereas one manufacturing hour in Germany costs BMW 30 dollars, one manufacturing hour in South Carolina, U.S.A., costs the company only 12 to 15 dollars per hour! South Carolina became the home of the company's new plant.

Our Position Toward a Global World

How are we to respond to the globalization of the world? As Christians, we must remember that we are *in* the world but not *of* the world. This means we must take full advantage of these developments for one purpose only: the proclamation of the gospel of Jesus Christ to all people everywhere. Never must we debase ourselves to be actively involved in opposing or supporting the one-world global community. Scripture has clearly told us that this will come about whether we like it or not.

Any attempt to oppose the progressive evolution of a one-world government is doomed to fail. God installs governments, whether they be Communist, dictatorship, socialist, or democracy. Never must we forget that the entire Gentile government system has been placed under the temporary jurisdiction of the devil. He is the god of this world, the prince of darkness.

How much power the devil has is evident from Matthew 4, which describes the temptation of Jesus by the devil. The weapon our Lord used against the devil's temptation was the Word–"It is written." The aim of the devil in this temptation was to receive worship from the Lord. Here we are reminded of the Scripture prophesying that all knees shall bow to Jesus and all tongues shall confess that Jesus is Lord. The devil wants to get that glory for himself, so he offered Jesus "all the kingdoms of the world and the glory of them" (verse 8) "if thou wilt fall down and worship me" (verse 9). It is quite obvious that the devil cannot give anything away that does not belong to him. He rules this world, for he is the god of this world!

When we begin to realize the seriousness of this message and the commandment our Lord has given to us to preach the gospel to the uttermost parts of the world, we will never find the time, energy, or finances to pursue any other activity except preaching the gospel.

Europe, the Final Kingdom

Having examined Europe's superiority and the integration of the entire world, let us now take a closer look at the unity of Europe.

Since the founding of the United States of America in 1776, Europeans have looked toward America with envy. America's European immigrant forefathers did not continually war with one another (except in the Civil War), but all became one: Americans! Instead of diversity came unity. Instead of segregation of the European immigrants came integration. Between the 1800s and the beginning of the 1900s, the success became evident. A diverse group of peoples had surrendered its heritage, customs, traditions, and language to become one.

Most U.S. government figures indicate that the approximately 37 million immigrants arriving between 1820 and 1940 originated from the following countries: 6 million Germans; 4.7 million Italians; 4.5 million Irish; 4.2 million British; 3.5 million Russians; 2.5 million Austrians; 1.5 million Swedish, and smaller numbers of other nations. But they all became *one.*

In Europe the people were divided by customs, language, tradition, and religion, but in America they became one nation, using one language, one currency, one government, one military, and one economy under one flag!

Another reason behind the success story of America is hardly recognized in our day: "freedom of religion." The old Roman system, which Europe had apparently forgotten, was implemented in the New World, just as during the original Roman world empire. Each and every group of people was free to practice its religion—but under the jurisdiction of Caesar. This spirit of unity of America created the material success story of the twentieth century.

Europe: Center of World Religion

Religion, therefore, must become a minor issue if Europe is to be united. The progress toward religious unity has been a long one. Today religion is an insignificant factor in the minds of most Europeans. The conflict between Catholics and Protestants is of no significance except for occasional skirmishes in Northern Ireland. Jews are welcomed and Islam has become the fastest-growing religion in Europe. Europeans no longer oppose Far Eastern religions; they learn from them.

An article in *Voice,* a publication of the Diocese of Newark, dated January 1989, described the progress of the ecumenical spirit even in America:

> "In the fall of 1988," wrote Newark Episcopalian Bishop John D. Spong, "I worshipped God in a Bhuddist temple. As the smell of incense filled the air, I knelt before three images of Buddha, feeling that the smoke could carry my prayers heavenward. It was for me a holy moment; beyond the creeds that each [religion] uses, there is a divine power that united us; I will not make any further attempt to convert the Buddhist, the Jew, the Hindu or the Moslem. I am content to learn from them and to walk with them side by side toward the God who lives, I believe, beyond the images that bind and blind us."[8]

L'Observatore Romano wrote in the February 10, 1986, issue:

> Speaking to Hindu audiences at the University of Calcutta, Pope John Paul II noted, "India's mission is crucial, because of her intuition of the spiritual nature of man. Indeed, India's greatest contribution to the world can be to offer it a spiritual vision of man. And the world does well to attend willingly to this ancient wisdom and in it to find enrichment for human living."[9]

Need we say more about the religious unity the world is striving for under the leadership of Rome?

The Last Empire

Let me reemphasize that only Europe qualifies for end-time world rulership. The unique new system now being established corresponds precisely to the prophetic Word as found in the book of Daniel, which describes for us the world rulership of the Gentile empires. Notice that Daniel takes great pains to explain the fourth and last world empire. In chapter 2 he addresses King Nebuchadnezzar of Babylon:

> Thou art this head of gold. And after thee shall arise another kingdom inferior to thee, and another third kingdom of brass, which shall bear rule over all the earth. And the fourth kingdom shall be strong as iron: forasmuch as iron breaketh in pieces and subdueth all things, and as iron that breaketh all these, shall it break in pieces and bruise (verses 38-40).

The uniqueness of this fourth empire consists of the fact that the last part is made up of a mixture of iron and clay. No doubt iron represents the Roman government, for she is the last Gentile empire. No place better qualifies for the title "Mystery Babylon" than the European city of Rome. In Revelation 17 we notice that this evil woman, the mother of harlots, an abomination of the earth, is identified with this city: "The woman which thou sawest is that great city which reigneth over the kings of the earth" (Revelation 17:18). According to verse 9, this city is built on seven hills, the hills for which Rome is famous. And according to verse 6, in the city was shed "the blood of the martyrs of Jesus." Furthermore, in Revelation 18:3 we see the political-religious activity of this woman called Mystery Babylon. We may search globally, but we will not find another city on earth in which the blood of the martyrs of Jesus was shed, a city that is built on seven hills, and a city that is the world center of religion mixed with politics.

Regarding the clay, we read the following in Jeremiah 18:6: "O house of Israel, cannot I do with you as this potter?

saith the Lord. Behold, as the clay is in the potter's hand, so are ye in mine hand, O house of Israel." No other group or race of people has been integrated into the nations of the world more than the Jews. Today, however, for the first time in 2500 years, the Jews have their own nation, their own land, and their own identity. Based on the prophetic Word, they will be integrated into the family of Gentile nations and become united with the global one-world empire. This fulfills their own prophetic utterance "We have no king but Caesar" on the one hand, and Daniel's prophecy, "Whereas thou sawest iron mixed with miry clay, they shall mingle themselves with the seed of men; but they shall not cleave one to another, even as iron is not mixed with clay" (Daniel 2:43) on the other hand.

In Daniel 7 Daniel sees these world empires pictured by animals—first, a lion; second, a bear; and third, a leopard. But when he comes to the fourth beast, he finds no animal with which to compare it. He writes, "Dreadful and terrible, and strong exceedingly; and it had great iron teeth: it devoured and broke in pieces, and stamped the residue with the feet of it, and it was diverse from all the beasts that were before it; and it had ten horns" (verse 7). The last and final Gentile empire, under the auspices of democracy, is being established today. It is headquartered in Europe and will be worldwide. "The fourth beast shall be the fourth kingdom upon earth, which shall be diverse from all kingdoms, and shall devour the whole earth, and shall tread it down and break it in pieces" (verse 23).

The Hindering Elements

For the final implementation of this last empire, two hindering elements must be overcome. The church of Jesus Christ, which is the light of the world, is one. As long as this light is on earth, darkness cannot fully develop and complete its work of deception. Therefore, we know that the rapture of the church of Jesus Christ must be at hand.

The other hindering element is Israel. It is God's special chosen people and is incomparable to any other nation. Israel must become one with the Gentiles. They will be fully incorporated in the new Roman world empire, the European Union. While at this moment Israel has no chance of being accepted into the Union, the day will come when that door will be opened. Then Israel will finally realize what her forefathers shouted almost 2000 years ago: *"We have no king but Caesar!"* That will be the moment of Israel's greatest deception. Fortunately, it will be of temporary endurance. The Bible says, "Alas! for that day is great, so that none is like it; it is even the time of Jacob's trouble; but he shall be saved out of it" (Jeremiah 30:7). Europe's power play is leading to world unity, even incorporating Israel, and will be successful in establishing the greatest world empire in history. But the end thereof will be the greatest destruction humanity has ever known.

PART THREE

At the Brink of Apocalypse

❖ ❖ ❖

12

Man Targeted for Extinction

David Benoit

We live in a very confused world today. We are saving the whales and killing our babies. We are protecting eagles' eggs while disposing of fertilized human eggs.

We hear the cry of environmentalists who claim that the animal kingdom is vastly underpopulated and the human race is vastly overpopulated. They hold a conference to protect wildlife one week, then stage a conference to control human population the next.

This observation might cause some to think of me as a radical extremist, but before you draw that conclusion you may want to read an interview with the French oceanographer Jacques Cousteau which appeared in the November 1991 edition of the *Unesco Courier*. He stated: "To stabilize world population we must eliminate 350,000 people per day. It is a horrible thing to say, but it's just as bad not to say it." This is a man who has dedicated his whole life to preserving wildlife!

The Georgia guidestone is an erected monument in
Elberton, Georgia. Dedicated to the New Age movement, it
features the Ten Commandments of the New Age Movement. The first commandment declares that the world's population should be depleted to 500,000,000 in perpetual
balance with nature. On September 13, 1994, delegations
from more than 180 countries converged on Cairo, Egypt,
to rally a mission to stabilize the world's population. This
U.N.-led community drew up a 20-year plan for controlling
the world's population.

Politicians use high-sounding phraseology such as *a
woman's right to choose* and champion supposedly noble causes
such as defending against overpopulation in order to justify
killing babies in the womb through legalized abortion.
Planned Parenthood has as one of its major objectives the
determination to convince people that they should not
become parents. Do you think for one minute that when a
young woman walks into an abortion clinic she is going to
be told that she ought to be a mother? Abortion clinics do
not get paid to counsel young women to keep their babies;
they get paid for every baby they extract. Abortion is big
business, and I don't know of one big business that got to be
big by turning business away.

The Overpopulation Theory

The question must be asked of the people involved with
the United Nations population control, "Was Hitler a friend
or foe of this committee?" According to Jacques Cousteau,
we need to eliminate 350,000 people every day. It took Hitler
years to exterminate 6 million Jews. Cousteau's program
would take less than 18 days.

Let's examine this overpopulation theory. The belief that
"this town is not big enough for the two of us" has threaded

its way throughout history. In fact, the earliest attempt to control population was found in the original family—Adam and Eve. Cain felt that the only way to rid himself of the guilt he acquired as a result of his disobedience to God was to kill his brother Abel.

Today we see man's futile attempt to reject God's ability to supply the world's population. Those who reject God's ability as a provider of food would laugh at those of us who believe that God fed 5000 men with five barley loaves and two small fish (see John 6:5-13). Humanists believe there is no God to provide for us, so we must work only with our own limited resources. I too would be fearful if I had to provide for billions of people with my resources. But the lack of resources serves as yet another storefront for a license to kill. If we truly do have a food shortage, why does our government pay farmers for not producing crops? Why do we hear of government waste? The answer is easy: *There is no actual shortage.*

Fearmongers have made projections of gloom and doom. In 1948 Fairfield Osborn wrote a book entitled *Our Plundered Planet*, in which he predicted that the world could not feed the 2 billion or so people living at that time. He was wrong. In 1968 Paul Ehrlich had *The Population Bomb* published. This Stanford University biologist predicted that the U.S. would be rationing food by the end of the 1970s. He was wrong. Again in 1984 he predicted, "The United States will quite literally be dying of thirst." He was wrong. Instead of millions of people dying of starvation in America, millions of people are on diets to control overeating!

Yes, famine is on the horizon, but not because of overpopulation. It is because God will cut off His resources to men. Are people starving today? Yes. People are starving in India because they will not eat beef (cows are considered to be gods). In Ethiopia, governments make laws to restrict people from producing other necessary food. In some parts of the world, war has not only destroyed the crops but has turned farmers into fighters. The environmentalists are daily turning farmland into unusable wetlands. To deny that people are starving would be ludicrous, but to say that God has not provided the knowledge and resources to provide for man is even more ludicrous.

The problem is not that our earth is unable to feed the billions, but that man cannot control the behavior of the billions. One of the oldest tricks in political strategy is *crisis management*. In other words, a government creates a crisis so that people will accept the government's solution to the crisis, no matter how horrible the solution may seem. If the real conflict were truly population versus resources, the United Nations could spend billions of dollars to teach people how to grow food and harvest crops. But the U.N. solution is not the harvesting of crops, but rather the harvesting of souls. Its silos are stockpiled with the souls of men, women, and children, and its assembly lines are working full-time and at peak production in order to maximize its lethal destruction. Here are four ways that population is being controlled today.

1. Infanticide

Politicians today say they are for the family. They claim they must ensure a better life for children while they legally exterminate them. Doesn't it seem strange that women from around the world traveled to China for a women's rights convention, when women in China don't have the right to bear more than one child? Countless millions of babies die there every year because of legalized abortion.

Sadly, even many Christians in good churches have fallen for the humanist view of abortion. One key issue that keeps cropping up is "What about cases of rape, incest, or the child that is not wanted?" These may be legitimate questions for those who do not believe that God is the Author of life. If you believe that man plus woman plus no God equals a child, then abortion seems right. But if you believe that man plus woman plus God equals a child, then rape, incest, and unwanted children are no excuse for abortion.

Rape and incest

We believe that God is the Creator of life. Genesis 1:27,28 says that God made man in His image and after His likeness, and He told Adam and Eve to be fruitful and multiply, and to populate the earth. God gave the man and the woman the ability to reproduce. But with that ability comes responsibility; He intended conception to take place within God's holy institution of marriage. God does hate rape and incest, but I believe that if conception should occur through these violent acts, He doesn't want that baby aborted. At the moment of conception God's heart is toward that child and He has a plan for its life, regardless of why it was conceived.

Unwanted children

The Bible tells us about children who were killed because they were not wanted. Chapters 1 and 2 of Exodus tell us how the king of Egypt was into selective births. Unlike today, when we have sophisticated equipment to determine the gender, the people in those days had to wait until birth to see whether the child was a boy or a girl. If the baby was a male, the midwives were to drown him because he was unwanted. Had all of the midwives carried out that process of elimination, we would never have heard of a man named Moses. Herod, after hearing about the birth of Jesus, ordered all the male children under the age of two killed.

The Bible teaches that life begins by God, not by chance.

Sarah and Abraham

> [The angel of the Lord] said, I will certainly re-
> turn unto thee according to the time of life; and,
> lo, Sarah thy wife shall have a son. And Sarah
> heard it in the tent door, which was behind him.
> Now Abraham and Sarah were old and well
> stricken in age; and it ceased to be with Sarah
> after the manner of women (Genesis 18:10,11).

Sarah, beyond the childbearing age, was thinking in the human realm and not in the supernatural realm when she laughed at God's promise that she would bear a son. Genesis 21:2 tells us, "For Sarah conceived, and bore Abraham a son in his old age, at the set time of which God had spoken to him." Life in the womb is no accident. God did not let Abraham and Sarah have Isaac until Abraham was 100 years old and Sarah was 90 years old. Many Christian couples have prayed for years for a baby and at the set time God answered their prayer.

Noah and his family

If the miracle of Isaac's birth to 100-year-old Abraham and 90-year-old Sarah seems incredible, consider Noah and his family. God told Noah to build an ark. He had three sons–Shem, Ham, and Japheth–and they each had a wife. Genesis 7:13 says, "In the selfsame day entered Noah, and Shem, and Ham, and Japheth, the sons of Noah, and Noah's wife, and the three wives of his sons with them, into the ark."

Simple math tells us that eight people entered the ark and 1 Peter 3:20 confirms that math: "Which sometime were disobedient, when once the longsuffering of God waited in the days of Noah, while the ark was preparing, wherein few, that is, eight souls were saved by water." This means that out of the entire human race only eight people went into the ark.

As Paul Harvey would put it, here's the rest of the story. According to Genesis 6 and 7, it took 120 years to build this ark. During that span, God did not allow Noah's wife or the wives of Noah's three sons to conceive. Under normal circumstances, a 120-year span of the lives of four families would have found the ark filled with people! Yet only eight entered the ark. Some might say maybe they were sterile, but after the flood these four couples replenished the entire world's population. Here is another fantastic thought: The animals were on board a ship for a year and not even the rabbits multiplied! God is the giver of life for animals as well as humans.

Please don't misunderstand me—abortion has affected millions of lives, even in the Christian community. It is not the intent of this chapter to point a finger of condemnation at the victims, but to warn the innocent so they will not become victims. Many Christian men and women face the guilt associated with abortion today. Yes, God is the giver of life, but He is also the author of forgiveness. We no longer need to rationalize our sins. We need God to forgive us of our sins and to reconcile us unto Himself.

2. Euthanasia.

According to media reports, Dr. Jack Kevorkian, also called "Dr. Death," has assisted in more than 30 so-called suicides. The most recent Kevorkian-assisted suicide involved a woman who, according to the coroner's report, was only depressed, not fatally ill. Dr. Kevorkian has escaped several attempts to convict him of murder, or homicide. So far the doctor has been acquitted of any wrongdoing. If he escapes prosecution in the latest incident, the comprehensive euthanasia could become legally acceptable and perhaps even covered by health insurance. If Dr. Kevorkian can do it, then anyone can do it. The precedent will have been established.

According to Noah Hutchings in *Bible in the News:*[1]

> Those involved with population control again hide their true motive behind compassion. Read what The *New York Times* has ... to say about euthanasia: "The memorandum ... proposed that it shall be possible for physicians to end the tortures of incurable patients, upon request, in the interests of true humanity. This proposed legal recognition of euthanasia—the act of providing a painless and peaceful death. ... "

I failed to tell you the title of the *New York Times* article and the date of its release. The title is "Nazi Plan to Kill Incurables to End Pain; German Religious Groups Oppose Move." The date was October 10, 1933. For some reason the media today want us to believe that this idea of helping hurting people out of their misery is the unique idea of Dr. Death. But here it is 63 years later and the headlines are the same: "Compassionate Dr. Kevorkian Meets with Opposition from Right Wing, Wacko Christians."

Hutchings concludes his *Bible in the News* piece with this observation:

> The *New York Times,* in an article titled "1933, Hitler's Amazing Year," brought out that in that year Hitler was made Chancellor of Germany, replaced all political offices with Nazis, suspended all constitutional rights, eliminated undesirables, established prison camps like Dachau, and confiscated the wealth of all political opponents. Thousands were killed under the deception of humane euthanasia. In putting Hitler's program of euthanasia in its proper perspective, we wonder if history will repeat itself here in the United States. Will euthanasia, as in Germany, be a sign

of the end of our republic and the rise of a totalitarian state?[2]

Yes, the crimes are the same—declare war on the help-
less unborn, then implement mercy killing of those who can't
defend themselves, then destroy those who disagree with
you. The travesty of the whole thing is that they do it in the
name of benevolence. We should all check the mouth of this
gift horse lest we one day wake up to find it was a Trojan
horse.

3. Teenage Deaths.

The killing of the teen population is on the rise. For years
I have spoken against the destructive lyrics in rock music.
Many rock musicians promote death in their music, and
many young people die on the "Highway to Hell" (rock song
by AC/DC). According to testimony given at a Parent Music
Resource Center hearing before the Senate Commerce Committee on September 19, 1985, "teenage suicides have gone
up a whopping 300 percent in the last thirty years, while the
adult rate has stayed the same."[3]

This hike in the suicide rate is not by accident but by
design. Thirty years ago, rock bands were not singing songs
like:

1. *99 Ways to Die,* performed by Megadeth

2. *Suicide Solution,* performed by Ozzy Osborne

3. *Die Young, Stay Pretty,* performed by Debra
   Harry

4. *Looking Down the Barrel of a Gun,* performed by
   Anthrax

5. *I Hate Myself and I Want to Die,* performed by Nir-
   vana. (These were not idle words for the lead

singer Kurt Cobain. He ended his own life by
shooting himself in the head.)

Rock musicians hide behind the first-amendment rights.
Rock musicians like Ozzy Osborne have been taken to court,
but the cases always get thrown out.

Then we have what I call "death education" right in our
public schools. Classes take field trips to funeral homes. Students learn how to write their own epitaphs, and even suicide notes. Social engineers believe that if teenagers are so
weak-minded that they will commit suicide while listening
to music, then they should not be taking up space on planet
Earth anyway. The theory is that we all live on this big ship
that is overcrowded, so why should we discourage anyone
who wants to jump overboard?

Troubled teens face suicide, gang violence, drug abuse,
deadly sexually transmitted diseases, and domestic violence.
Many of these very real tragedies in the lives of teens conclude with suicide. Teens are not as defenseless as babies,
and they are not as feeble as the elderly, so they must be
encouraged to self-destruct.

4. Homosexuality.

This is the final way to curb the world's population. If
the world's entire population were homosexual, the population growth would be zero. That's right—homosexuality
promotes zero population growth. Homosexuals today are
fighting for their rights to same-sex marriages.

> Walt Disney Co. will extend health benefits to
> domestic partners and children of homosexual
> workers next year, becoming one of the last major
> entertainment groups to do so. Disney spokesman
> John Dryer said the change does not apply to

heterosexuals. He wouldn't comment on the
policy's impact on Disney's image.[4]

If you think homosexuals are not powerful in the political arena, think again.

When Republicans met in San Diego, their
openly gay delegates (all four of them) didn't or-
ganize a caucus. But the 150 openly gay Democratic delegates, the Gay and Lesbian Caucus,
have engaged in some of the livelier unrehearsed
and unscripted sessions here.

Tuesday, gay delegates gave a rousing reception
to Tipper Gore, who said, "Al and I are proud to
call Barney and Herb (Representative Barney
Frank, D-Mass. and his partner, Herb Moses) our
friends." They cheered when she thanked them
for their "crucial support in 1992" and mentioned
"more than 100 openly gay persons serving in the
Clinton administration."[5]

This is the same administration which claims to stand for
family values, while promoting those who cannot produce
a family. The Bible clearly describes homosexuality as sin
(see Genesis 19). (By the way, I believe the Antichrist will be
a homosexual, as implied in Daniel 11:37: "Neither shall he
regard the God of his fathers, nor the desire of women, nor
regard any god; for he shall magnify himself above all." Why
wouldn't the Antichrist be a homosexual—he will stand for
everything God stands against!)

"Likewise also the men, leaving the natural use of the
woman, burned in their lust one toward another: men with
men working that which is unseemly, and receiving in themselves that recompense of their error which was meet"
(Romans 1:27).

God loves homosexuals but He hates the sin of homo-sexuality. For God so loved the world that He gave His only begotten Son.

The homosexual community will not totally stop population growth. Teen deaths will not stop population growth. Abortion will not stop the world's population growth. But these will all work together to *curb* the growth.

In conclusion, I must say that the reason murder is so natural to unregenerate people is they are only obeying their father: "Ye are of your father the devil, and the lusts of your father ye will do. He was a murderer from the beginning, and abode not in the truth, because there is no truth in him. When he speaketh a lie, he speaketh of his own, for he is a liar, and the father of it" (John 8:44).

One of these days the United Nations population control delegates will get their wish. During the tribulation period, one-half of the world's entire population will be destroyed in less than 3fi years. Then they will understand that God is not only the One who gives life, but He is also the One who takes life.

13

Riders of Revelation 6, Mount Up!

J.R. Church

John's vision of the horsemen of the Apocalypse is perhaps the most powerful vision presented by all the prophets. These four specters riding across the world scene will introduce the most terrifying time in the history of mankind.

The biblical tribulation period approaches as they make their appearance upon the world stage. They ride under the direction of Jesus Christ, who is shown releasing them as He breaks the seals of a scroll taken from the hand of God the Father. Through them God unleashes His judgment upon an unbelieving world.

The four horsemen represent more than mere men upon simple steeds. They symbolize things far greater. Not limited to a particular geographical area, they represent world-shattering events destined to decimate the nations. Under their command, a fourth of the earth's population will die.

316 ❖ J.R. Church

Hundreds of millions more will be injured or maimed. It will be a time more horrible than history has ever witnessed.

Exiled in his latter years to the island of Patmos, John was taken into heaven and shown visions of the future. In these visions, the horsemen are symbolic of an era of conflict. They represent what would otherwise be indescribable events, presented in the simple tongue of John's day. They allowed the prophet to use his limited language to explain a series of complex events which will come to pass just prior to the return of Christ.

As Christ breaks the first seal, John writes, "I saw, and behold a white horse; and he that sat on him had a bow; and a crown was given unto him, and he went forth conquering and to conquer" (Revelation 6:2).

We shall call the rider of this first horse the Deceiver. In John's earlier epistles he is called the Antichrist. Someday, perhaps soon, this infamous world leader will emerge. He will be honored by governments as the apparent savior of mankind—Mr. Wonderful. He will become the leader of a one-world political and economic system. I believe this world government is presently under development and am convinced that we live in those momentous days just prior to the onset of the tribulation period.

Messianic Fever

Jews are looking forward to the coming of their long-awaited Messiah. In recent years Jewish groups have become convinced that He is about to appear. Billboards throughout Israel announce the expectation of the Messiah's appearance. In their haste, these people just might accept the Antichrist. The highlight event of the tribulation concerns this false messiah and his dealings with Israel. I am inclined to believe that he will have family ties to one of the tribes of Israel, making him a pretender to the office of Messiah.

However, even though he may claim to be a descendant of Judah, I think he will be from the tribe of Dan, because in Genesis 49 the dying Jacob gave prophecies concerning the last days. Among his predictions were statements about the Messiah and His enemy: "Gather yourselves together, that I may tell you that which shall befall you in the last days" (Genesis 49:1). The dying Jacob looked into the far future—to the last days—and told each son what would befall his tribe. He indicated that the Messiah would descend from Judah:

> Judah, thou art he whom thy brethren shall praise: thy hand shall be in the neck of thine enemies; thy father's children shall bow down before thee. Judah is a lion's whelp: from the prey, my son, thou art gone up, he stooped down, he couched [lay down] as a lion, and as an old lion; who shall rouse him up? The scepter shall not depart from Judah, nor a lawgiver from between his feet, until Shiloh come; and unto him shall the gathering of the people be (Genesis 49:8-10).

History attests to the fulfillment of this prophecy: Judah has been the leading tribe throughout the centuries! In fact, every Israeli today bears the name of Judah; he is commonly called a "Jew." According to rabbinical commentaries, Shiloh refers to the Messiah. I think Jacob gives the definitive statement that He will be a member of the tribe of Judah. But concerning the enemy, Jacob had these words to say about Dan:

> Dan shall judge his people, as one of the tribes of Israel. Dan shall be a serpent by the way, an adder in the path, that biteth the horse heels,

so that his rider shall fall backward (Genesis 49:16,17).

In these two verses the dying Jacob prophesied that the tribe of Dan would bring judgment upon the tribes of Israel, that he would be a "serpent by the way, an adder in the path." It is here that we see the trail of the serpent–Satan. We learned this from the first chapters of Genesis, in which the serpent beguiled Eve. Ever since then the serpent has been symbolic of the devil. Satan is found working in the tribe of Dan. I guess we could call Dan the black sheep of the family. So wicked was the tribe of Dan that it was eliminated from the 12 tribes recorded in Revelation 7. Those 144,000 Jews are made up of the 12 tribes of Israel, 12,000 from each tribe. They are listed in Revelation 7:5-8 as Judah, Reuben, Gad, Asher, Naphtali, Manasseh, Simeon, Levi, Issachar, Zebulun, Joseph, and Benjamin. Dan is not listed. Why? Because through him will come the seed of the serpent. Therefore it is reasonable for us to consider that the Antichrist could be from the tribe of Dan. (My book *Guardians of the Grail*[1] devotes an entire chapter to Dan, which gives a great deal more information on the subject.)

Daniel also writes as if the Antichrist will arise out of one of the tribes of Israel:

> Neither shall he regard the God of his fathers, nor the desire of women, nor regard any god, for he shall magnify himself above all. But in his estate shall he honor the God of forces; and a god whom his fathers knew not shall he honor with gold and silver, and with precious stones and pleasant things (Daniel 11:37,38).

That statement leads me to believe that the Antichrist will be an Israelite. He has no regard for the God of his fathers–the God of the rabbis.

The Abomination of Desolation

According to Paul's second epistle to the Thessalonians, a future Jewish sanctuary will be desecrated by the Antichrist:

> Let no man deceive you by any means, for that day shall not come except there come a falling away first, and that man of sin be revealed, the son of perdition, who opposeth and exalteth himself above all that is called God or that is worshiped, so that he as God sitteth in the temple of God, showing himself that he is God (2 Thessalonians 2:3,4).

The Bible tells us that when the Holy Spirit, "He who now lets [hinders]" (verse 7), is taken out of the way, "the wicked [one] shall be revealed" (verse 8). When the Holy Spirit is taken away, you can be sure that all believers will go with Him. After that the Antichrist can be revealed. His policy of peace is described in 1 Thessalonians 5. In this verse we are told that the day of the Lord will come as a thief in the night: "For when they shall say, Peace and safety, then sudden destruction cometh upon them" (1 Thessalonians 5:3).

The message of the Antichrist may be peace, but war will be the result. Millions of people will die.

Today when Jewish couples recite their marriage vows, the groom places a glass on the floor and crushes the vessel with his heel. This reminds the wedding celebrants of the past destruction of the Jewish temple in 70 A.D. and the prophecy of its future restoration. When that temple is rebuilt in Jerusalem, the Antichrist can be revealed. His appearance was predicted by Daniel:

> And in his estate shall stand up a vile person, to whom they shall not give the honor of the

320 ❖ J.R. Church

> kingdom: but he shall come in peaceably, and
> obtain the kingdom by flatteries (Daniel 11:21).

According to this verse, the Antichrist will not be elected president of a world government; he will not be given "the honor of the kingdom." However, he will have control of it, perhaps from behind the scenes. As the tribulation period progresses, the Antichrist will attempt to control all communication and transportation. By the middle of the tribulation period he will introduce an image of this beastly New World Order in which he will control the world's monetary system. He will require a mark in the hand or forehead of every person in the world. It will be necessary for people to accept his mark to participate in the marketplace. He will take over the reins of world government and establish Jerusalem as his capital. When he arrives in the Holy City, he will proceed to the Temple Mount, enter the Jewish sanctuary, stop the sacrifices, and proclaim himself to be God.

The world confederation of nations may have other thoughts about that. Making himself deity may not go over too well with the rest of the world. This could be the reason for the resulting battle of Armageddon. By this time it will appear to the rest of the world that they have been enslaved by this dictator. They will likely blame him and Israel. Anti-Semitism will be at its worst. All nations will send their armies to converge upon Israel for a genocide of the Jews. The last 3½ years of the seven are referred to as the "great tribulation." This time will be filled with natural disasters— earthquakes, wild weather, floods, and drought. This is the story of the Deceiver, who is introduced in Revelation 6.

The Destroyer

As Christ breaks the second seal, John describes the next horseman:

> And there went out another horse that was red;
> and power was given to him that sat thereon to
> take peace from the earth, and that they should
> kill one another; and there was given unto him a
> great sword (Revelation 6:4).

The second horse of the apocalypse is red. I call its rider the Destroyer. Never before will mankind have experienced a more devastating and terrible conflict than this prophesied war. The horse's distinctive color could not be more fitting for the twentieth century. The rise of Soviet Communism in 1917 may well have set the stage for the fulfillment of this second seal. In the twentieth century mankind has witnessed more bloodshed than in any other generation in history. World War I recorded 8 million casualties. In World War II some 78 million people were killed. Additional multitudes have died in Korea, Vietnam, Bosnia, Kuwait, Somalia, and other countries around the world. Among all of the previous wars of history there were a total of 200 million casualties. The casualties in this century alone constitute over 60 percent of all deaths in all recorded wars. Politicians cry "Peace! Peace!" but there is no peace. That elusive Utopia can only be realized when the true Prince of Peace arrives.

Over the past 6000 years of record-keeping there have been less than 268 years of peace. History is littered with the bodies of the slain. However, during the conflict introduced by the red horse, a fourth of the world population will die. Over a billion people will be slaughtered. The coming war will be more devastating than all the wars in the annals of history combined. According to the descriptions of the prophets, the next world war could be a nuclear war.

Jesus spoke of "wars and rumors of wars . . . nation shall rise against nation, and kingdom against kingdom" (Matthew 24:6,7). His warning appears to coincide with the description

322 ✤ J.R. CHURCH

of this second horseman of the Apocalypse. We should notice that this horseman's purpose is to take peace from the
earth. What a picture of our world today! Until recently,
Russian Communism, whose symbolic color just happens
to be red, had attempted to take over the world. The states
of the former Soviet Union still continue to build armaments
and prepare for aggression. Communist leaders in China
have said they are willing to lose 700 million of their population in order to rule the world. These groups are still responsible for taking peace from the earth.

Coupled with Communism is militant Islam. Iran, Iraq,
Afghanistan, Pakistan, Libya, and Syria continue to train and
finance terrorism around the world. Once supported by the
Soviet Union, these regions are more militant than ever.

In view of the Islamic threat to world peace, we should
note that the symbol of Islam is a sword. Coincidentally, the
program of the rider on the red horse involves a sword.
Could this be the sword of Islam? The Bible says, "There
was given unto him a great sword" (Revelation 6:4). While
men are looking for peace, they are arming for war. The *Air
Force Journal of Logistics* (Winter 1991) describes an advanced
concept of ground support for the United States Air Force
operations based on the idea of "RED HORSE" units:

> RED HORSE units are self-sufficient and inde-
> pendent engineering organizations for large-scale
> heavy repair projects. These units gained promi-
> nence during the Vietnam War with the con-
> struction of Tuy Hoa and Phu Cat air bases.
>
> Base closures overseas have signaled a departure
> from a forward defense posture to one of rapid
> force projection. Accordingly, [Air Force head-
> quarters] is reviewing proposals to transition RED
> HORSE units to smaller, more deployable enti-

ties capable of executing war-fighting and nation-building missions of the future.[2]

Note from this description that the RED HORSE concept arises from a change of philosophy in the way our military power is deployed in foreign strategic areas. Since
World War II we have relied upon our forward air bases in
foreign countries for the control of such areas. Apparently
the old system is becoming impossible to support. For financial and political reasons, forward air bases are closing. Military planners are now faced with the necessity of speeding
military units to trouble areas. These compact, rapidly
moving units seem well-named. They remind us of the biblical picture of war in the latter days. Here is another candidate for the "red horse" of war, moving with great speed
across the earth. This horse may soon be ready to move.

Drought

On the heels of the Destroyer comes the third horseman
thundering across the world stage:

> And when he had opened the third seal, I heard
> the third beast say, Come and see. And I beheld,
> and lo, a black horse, and he that sat on him had
> a pair of balances in his hand. And I heard a voice
> in the midst of the four beasts say, A measure of
> wheat for a penny, and three measures of barley
> for a penny; and see thou hurt not the oil and the
> wine (Revelation 6:5,6).

I call the third horseman Drought—one of the major
causes of famine. In certain areas of the world many people
go to bed each night with very little to eat. They are starving
by the millions. The 28 countries that comprise the earth's
equatorial belt are turning into dust bowls. According to a

324 ◆ J.R. Church

special report in *Newsweek* magazine of November 11, 1974, during that year at least 460 million people were threatened with starvation. The article reported, "Ten million will probably die . . . most of them children under five years old."[3] In 1961 the United States had 170 million tons of grain reserves—enough to feed the entire world for 95 days. By 1974 the supply had fallen to a buffer of 22 days.[4]

In Asia and Africa, nearly one quarter of the 2.7 billion population subsisted on less than a thousand calories a day. It was estimated that by the year 2025 there will be a million child deaths a month from starvation. About 3.5 billion acres are currently under the plow, and the USDA estimated that about 6.6 billion acres could be tilled if governments were willing to pay massive development costs. American farmers, who form one-tenth of one percent of the world's population, have long been able to feed at least 25 percent of its people. However, all that will change as the population continues to grow.[5]

In 1976 the Club of Rome issued a report on the subject in a book entitled *Mankind at the Turning Point.* The book suggested:

> By the year 2000 the demand for food in southeast Asia will be about 30 percent more than the supply, an alarming but conceivably manageable gap. With advanced planning the gap could be reduced to as low as 10 percent. However, if the same projections are extended another 25 years, the deficit rises to over 100 percent, clearly a catastrophic disparity.[6]

With emphasis, the statement is made that the analysis in the book extends over a period of 50 years:

> If, during the coming half-century, a viable world system emerges, an organic growth pattern will

have been established for mankind to follow thereafter. If a viable system does not develop, projections for the decade thereafter may be academic.[7]

The most precious of all resources is food. According to a UNESCO report, it has been calculated that the availability of food per capita worldwide has not increased since 1936. Actually, it has decreased over the past decade.

Ten years ago world stockpiles of food for emergency relief amounted to an 80-day supply. Today those reserves are sufficient for only 30 days of consumption. Before World War II the world was about evenly divided into regions that imported food and regions capable of exporting food. Since the war some regions—most significantly Latin American and Eastern Europe—that were once exporters, have become importers. Present estimates consider only the United States and Australia as major potential sources of exported food supply.

According to the Club of Rome, America is the hope of the world, but what would happen if our food supply were curtailed, if the United States were not able to supply the world? The 1976 report predicts that a catastrophe would peak around the year 2010. The normal death rate would double due to food shortage. After that the deathrate would decline, but only because the earlier deaths reduced the birthrate for a later generation, or, to put it more simply but cruelly, the people who would be normally having babies died when they were still babies themselves. The number of people under 15 years of age who will die of starvation by the year 2025 is estimated to be 500 million. In John's generation a penny was considered a day's wages, and a measure of wheat was considered one day's food supply for one person. What an incredible picture of our world in the years ahead! Someday it will take a full day's wages to buy food for that day.

The prophecy of famine first came from the lips of our Savior Himself. During His Olivet Discourse He mentioned famine as one of the major signs of the end time: "Nation shall rise against nation, and kingdom against kingdom; and there shall be famines and pestilences and earthquakes in diverse places" (Matthew 24:7).

Population Growth

Another cause of famine has been the astounding increase in population. More people are alive today than have died throughout all of history. There is not enough food to feed the starving millions. A report on population growth in the May 16, 1993, *Oklahoman*, entitled "World's Population Booming," should give us cause for alarm. It deals with certain demographic features published as part of an annual survey by the Washington-based World Population Reference Bureau. The survey predicted that the world population would reach "5.5 billion by mid-1993, 40 percent of it in China and India. The bureau said population is growing each year by 90 million."[8] The fastest-growing areas of population are those that can least afford growth. As stated in the report, "We are at a point where, except for the United States, population growth is essentially a Third World phenomenon."[9] One of those who worked on the study said, "The world population took 15 years to increase by one billion to its four billion total in 1975, 12 years to increase to five billion in 1987 and is expected to take only 10 years to rise to six billion in 1997."[10]

The U.S. population growth continues relatively high because so many people from the Third World are clamoring to enter our country. Our net immigration totals about

900,000 per year. Europe, on the other hand, is currently showing a stagnation in population growth, and may actually show a population decline by the end of the century. The poorest area on the globe has the fastest-growing population: sub-Saharan Africa, with a population growth rate of 3 percent per year. At that rate, the region's population will double in only 20 years. It is here that we see many people dying of starvation.

Latin America runs a close second at 1.9 percent each year. This compares with the U.S. rate of 0.8 percent and Europe's at 0.2 percent.[11]

With billions of new mouths to feed, it is only a matter of time until starvation spreads. The famine that is now seen only in India, Africa, and Latin America will creep inexorably across the globe, finally reaching virtually every spot on earth. Hunger always gives rise to social unrest—even revolution. By the time of the great tribulation, famine will be fully manifested. At the opening of the "third seal," in Revelation 6:6, basic food staples will be meted out in small amounts and sold at rates that make possible only a bare subsistence. This is the fate of the common man. Note that the wealthy will still have access to their "oil and . . . wine." As always, during hard times, the division between rich and poor grows wider. Not only the Bible, but the population figures themselves point to a future global famine.

Death

As the earth reels from the first three horsemen, John describes the rider on the fourth horse:

> I looked, and behold, a pale horse; and his name that sat on him was Death, and Hell followed with him. And power was given unto them over the fourth part of the earth, to kill with sword, and

with hunger, and with death, and with the beasts
of the earth (Revelation 6:8).

The fourth horseman of the Apocalypse is Death. The word "pale" refers to a green, ghoulish color, the color of a corpse or of leprosy. This horseman tells a gruesome story: A fourth of the population of earth will die. Over one billion people! As stated previously, in all of the wars of history some 200 million have died, but five times that many will die in the introductory years of the horsemen of the Apocalypse. The Matthew account of our Savior's Olivet Discourse reminds us that accompanying war will be famine, pestilences (diseases), and earthquakes. Given enough time, any one of these could completely rid the planet of all life. Jesus emphasized this fact:

> For then shall be great tribulation, such as was
> not since the beginning of the world to this time,
> no, nor ever shall be. And except those days
> should be shortened, there should no flesh be
> saved; but for the elect's sake those days shall be
> shortened (Matthew 24:21,22).

Diseases

Diseases have always been the enemy of man, and the most deadly disease—Acquired Immunodeficiency Syndrome (AIDS)—happens to be the most recent as well. Originally, AIDS was called Gay Related Immunodeficiency Disease (GRID), but an embarrassed homosexual community successfully lobbied to change its name. Many in the news media were quick to warn fundamentalist Christians not to blame the gay movement for bringing about some kind of "judgment from God." Nevertheless, according to one New York resident, "Everywhere one goes in Harlem you hear about the wrath of God!" New York and San Francisco are noted for 44 percent of all AIDS cases in the United States. It must be considered as a venting of God's anger upon the sin of sodomy. No nation can violate God's laws and get away with it.

Most news media outlets blast morality and Christianity while at the same time praising Rock Hudson and Liberace as heroes in their own time. Evidently God is not impressed. The playboy lifestyle has fallen under the judgment of an offended God. There is no other way to explain it. Some say by the end of the decade, or shortly thereafter, every spare hospital bed in America will be filled with an AIDS patient. According to Gene Antonio, author of *The Aids Cover-Up*, there are 6915 hospitals in the United States. Of these, 5863 are short-term facilities. There are a total of 1,360,000 beds available in these hospitals. On the average, 76 percent of these beds stay occupied. This leaves 326,000 beds empty at any given time.[12] Eventually those beds will be filled with AIDS patients. Most hospitals are short-term facilities, but AIDS patients need prolonged care, often several months at a time. In addition, many hospitals are not equipped to handle heavy demands on a long-term basis. Their staff and resources will be taxed to the limit. It is not difficult to understand why some hospital officials see the whole hospital system collapsing under the load.

The disease is presently growing on an exponential curve, doubling in some areas every six months, in Europe every nine months, and in other areas once a year. Even at the most conservative estimates, the next decade will be bleak for hospitals. According to U.N. projections, "Some forty million people will become infected with HIV, which causes AIDS, by 2000."[13]

For every AIDS victim reported, there are a hundred more not counted. Present estimates are staggering. In the

United States there are more than 3 million people infected, and across the world an additional 20 million. Some researchers estimate that within 50 years the entire population of the planet could be dead from AIDS. It has become the most feared of all diseases. Antonio warned that AIDS is destined to be a worse epidemic than the bubonic plague of medieval Europe.[14]

In the 1970s, heart disease was the number one killer of Americans. Cancer was second on the list. Other major causes of death included stroke, accidents, influenza, pneumonia, diabetes, and cirrhosis of the liver. However, all that is rapidly changing. In New York City, men between the ages of 25 and 44 are more likely to die of AIDS than any other disease. Diagnosed for the first time in 1981, the disease has become the number one killer of men in New York City.

Newsweek Magazine reported on April 29, 1985:

> AIDS has become one of the most sinister infectious diseases of this or any other century, threatening the world's general population and assuming the proportions of what epidemiologists call a "pandemic."[15]

Dr. James Curran of the Centers for Disease Control in Atlanta said, "AIDS is now recognized as a worldwide problem, with cases diagnosed on almost every continent."[16]

Dr. John Seale of London has been studying the outbreak of AIDS in tropical areas, particularly Africa, "where it is reported tens of millions have been infected by AIDS and large numbers have already died of the disease."[17] Dr. Seale said, "If my hypothesis is correct, and we wait perhaps 20 years before we take drastic preventive action, half the population of the Western world will be wiped out."[18]

According to Dr. Harold Jaffee at the Centers for Disease Control in Atlanta, 73 percent of those who have AIDS are homosexuals and 17 percent are drug users.[19] AIDS can only be correctly perceived as judgment meted out by an offended Deity. At this point the Centers for Disease Control has cautioned Americans not to panic. Yet the epidemic continues to spread at a fantastic rate. In some parts of Africa more than half of the population is infected. It is feared that this contagious disease could be propagated by mosquitoes, thus endangering every person on earth. Insurance companies are now asking for blood test results before accepting new policyholders. The United States armed forces are testing all military personnel for the disease. The average medical cost for a person with AIDS has soared to nearly 150,000 dollars. Somehow every citizen in the United States will have to bear that cost, either through increased insurance premiums or through tax-supported medical care.

The virus grows a thousand times faster than any other disease known to mankind, and is virtually always fatal. The number of victims is doubling every six months. The Atlanta Centers for Disease Control has isolated the virus in both tears and saliva. It is a highly contagious disease. Eventually AIDS victims will have to be quarantined—isolated from others. In the next few years everyone will know someone with AIDS. No one is safe from the fatal disease. A doctor once told me that if an AIDS victim coughed in your presence, the virus could enter your body through the membranes in the mouth or eyes. He said that the virus could live in a dry state for up to seven hours, awaiting its next victim.

The biblical injunctions against sodomy and homosexuality can no longer be scoffed at, and we are reminded that Jesus described the last days as being like the judgment of Sodom and Gomorrah:

> Likewise also as it was in the days of Lot: they
> did eat, they drank, they bought, they sold, they

planted, they builded; but the same day that Lot went out of Sodom it rained fire and brimstone from heaven and destroyed them all. Even thus shall it be in the day when the Son of man is revealed (Luke 17:28-30).

The sins of Sodom are rampant today. Let it be known that God will not allow the world to get away with it. His judgment has already begun and will continue to increase at an exponential curve throughout the coming years. If unchecked, AIDS could annihilate life on earth during the next century. The epidemic increases with the passing of every month. Of this one thing we can be certain: The Bible predicts a raging epidemic during the days before the second coming of Christ.

Earthquakes

Jesus also reminded us of earthquakes in various places. We are specifically told about an earthquake as Jesus opens the sixth seal of the scroll:

And I beheld when he had opened the sixth seal, and, lo, there was a great earthquake; and the sun became black as sackcloth of hair, and the moon became as blood (Revelation 6:12).

Of some 68 major earthquakes recorded in history, 46 have occurred in this century. Our generation is experiencing more earthquake activity than in any other time in history. Let us think back for a moment to the beginning of this millennium and take a look at the increase in the number of earthquakes:

The 10th century – 32 earthquakes
The 11th century – 53 earthquakes
The 12th century – 84 earthquakes

The 13th century –   115 earthquakes
The 14th century –   137 earthquakes
The 15th century –   174 earthquakes
The 16th century – 253 earthquakes
The 17th century –   378 earthquakes
The 18th century – 640 earthquakes
The 19th century – 2119 earthquakes[20]

The twentieth century is proving to be the century for more earthquakes than ever before. Obviously, we have arrived at that climactic season in God's calendar with "earthquakes in diverse places" (Matthew 24:7). The crust of the earth actually floats like islands upon a molten sea. The interior of the earth is liquid. These islands, or tectonic plates, join together in various places around the world. Such a place is called a fault. When those plates are dislodged along a fault line they create an earthquake. There have been many devastating earthquakes in the past. Hundreds of thousands of lives have been lost in the recorded earthquakes of history.

Out of the 13 most devastating earthquakes, ten have occurred in this century. The first significant quake occurred in 1902 at Martinique, where 40,000 people died. In 1906 700 people died during an earthquake in San Francisco, California. In 1920 an earthquake in Kansu, China, killed 180,000 people. In 1923 an earthquake in Tokyo killed 143,000 people. In Morocco, in 1960, 12,000 people lost their lives in an earthquake. In 1964 Alaska recorded one of the greatest earthquakes in history. It was reported at 8.6 on the Richter scale; however, because it occurred in a remote region, only 114 people died.[21]

The 1970s began with a devastating earthquake in Peru, where 67,000 people died. In 1972, in Managua, Nicaragua, an earthquake killed 10,000 people. In 1973 an earthquake shook Hawaii. This quake, though not as severe as the others, was very interesting. Scientists recorded that about an hour before the earthquake hit the island, the ionosphere above the island disappeared. No explanation can be given for that unusual event.[22]

An earthquake in Murkden, China, in 1975, was said to have leveled several villages and killed a great many people. The Chinese government refused to publish the number of casualties. However, it was said to be very high.[23] Then came 1976, with more devastating earthquakes than any other year in history. On February 4 of that year an earthquake hit Guatemala, killing more than 22,000 people. On May 6 an earthquake shook northeastern Italy, taking the lives of 946 people. On June 26 an earthquake devastated New Guinea. Some 443 lives were lost. On July 14 an earthquake rocked Indonesia, killing 500 people. On July 28 a massive earthquake, perhaps the most destructive in history, hit Tangshan, China. Nearly a million people died. No other earthquake in history has destroyed so many lives (other than perhaps the earthquake in China during the fifteenth century). On August 17 an earthquake rocked the Philippines, killing 8000 people. On November 24 an earthquake devastated eastern Turkey, killing 4000 people. On March 4, 1977, an earthquake devastated a large area of Romania. A reported 1541 people were killed. Another earthquake hit the Persian Gulf, where 60 lives were lost.[24]

It is difficult for us to comprehend the terrible destruction wrought by earthquakes around the world. America has enjoyed the blessings of God for so many years. Yet in other parts of the world, death and despair are becoming commonplace. In addition to the lives lost in earthquakes, more people are injured, and some are crippled for life. Thousands of people are left homeless. Newspapers are filled with stories of earthquake catastrophe:

- Armenia, December 7, 1988 (Richter 6.9)
- Northwest California, October 17, 1989 (7.1)
- Northwest Iran, June 21, 1990 (7.7)
- Yucca Valley, California, June 28, 1992 (7.4)
- Flores, Indonesia, December 12, 1992 (7.5)
- Northern Japan (Kobe), July 12, 1993 (7.8)
- Los Angeles, California, June 17, 1994 (6.6)[25]

Five of the above seven earthquakes were magnitude 7.0 or greater. Just these few quakes took over 100,000 lives! And there is an even greater frequency of tremors in the 6.0 to 7.0 range.[26]

The world's longest rift valley runs from Syria southward along the Jordan River, through the Dead Sea and the Gulf of Eilat and on into Eastern Africa. It is geologically unstable, and has produced major earthquakes down through the centuries. Some have said that if this fault line becomes active, it could produce a truly "world-class" earthquake, registering above 8.0 on the Richter scale.

In 1993 this region was hit by a series of tremors that began on July 31 and peaked on August 2. On the latter date a tremor in the Gulf of Eilat measured 5.8 on the Richter scale. According to the August 14, 1993, *Jerusalem Post,* "The epicenters extended from the Dead Sea to a spot in the Red Sea about 130 km [80 miles] south of Sharm el-Sheikh."[27]

The majority of the quakes were centered in the Gulf of Eilat. Gadi Shamir of the Energy Ministry's Seismological Institute reported that it was probably just a coincidence that quakes emanating from both the Dead Sea and the Gulf of Eilat had taken place at the same time. The Institute's routine statement about the event stated, "This is normal for Israel."[28] In general, geologists regard earthquake activity as falling into a "normal pattern," as defined by comparing today's rates with historical observations.

Some say modern rates of earthquakes are higher. However, when geologists are asked if they believe earthquakes are increasing over previous generations, they usually answer that the rate has not changed over the millennia since man has been keeping records. They contend that the observed increase is simply due to better instrumentation and more complete record-keeping. Nevertheless, when one looks at modern records, one invariably sees a steady increase in earthquake activity, ranging across the spectrum from large events to small tremors.

A good example of this phenomenon came to us through a friend who forwarded us a copy of the March 1993 "Survey Notes–Utah Geological Survey." This survey published findings taken from two three-month periods of earthquake activity in the State of Utah. The second period displayed a 15 percent increase in activity over the first. The report states:

> During the three-month period of October 1 through December 31, 1991, the University of Utah Seismograph Stations located 169 earthquakes within the Utah region. The total includes four earthquakes in the magnitude 3 range . . . and 66 in the magnitude 2 range.[29]

The following period, January 1 through March 31, 1992, exhibited more and larger earthquakes. During this period the same group reported "180 earthquakes within the Utah region. The total includes one earthquake in the magnitude 4 range . . . and 64 in the magnitude 2 range."[30]

Not all earthquake reports indicate an advance in frequency and intensity, but this general trend may be noticed all over the world. All told, there are literally thousands of miniquakes around the world each year. There seems to be a steady increase in their numbers. While geologists, schooled with the uniformitarian secular viewpoint, see no significant change, Christians see an emerging pattern.

It is at this point that the Bible describes a companion traveling with death—one who conquers. The Bible says, "Hell followed with him." Unbelievers who die during the tribulation period will be cast into hell without hope for eternity. In fact, Isaiah 5:14 reports that hell will enlarge itself because of the millions who will die.

The Deliverer

We can readily see that the four horsemen of the Apocalypse are ready to ride. They will introduce the predicted seven-year tribulation period. However, that is not the end of the story. There are actually *five* horsemen in Revelation! In chapter 6 we are shown the Deceiver, the Destroyer, Drought, and Death. This is a terrible picture of events introducing the tribulation period, but there is a fifth horseman of the Apocalypse—the Deliverer. Revelation 19 describes Him for us:

> And I saw heaven opened, and behold a white horse; and he that sat upon him was called Faithful and True, and in righteousness he doth judge and make war. His eyes were as a flame of fire, and on his head were many crowns; and he had a name written that no man knew but he himself. And he was clothed with a vesture dipped in blood; and his name is called The Word of God (Revelation 19:11-13).

The Lord Jesus Christ is coming back to this earth. This is not just the sweet Baby in the manger. This is not the kind Lord Jesus Christ who lifted children into His lap. Oh, this is the same Jesus, but this time He comes not in peace, but in war. He will come not as the Giver of eternal life to mankind but as its Judge.

The first time He came, He hung upon a cross and wore a crown of thorns; the second time He comes, He will sit upon a throne and wear a golden crown–a royal diadem. The first time He came, He stood before Pilate; the second time He comes, Pilate will stand before Him.

Christ is described here as the great Deliverer, for He will conquer the armies of this world. He will put down Satan and his followers. He will lay hold of the Antichrist and throw him into hell. The Lord Jesus Christ will establish the kingdom of heaven on earth and reign as King of Kings and Lord of Lords!

14

Royal Ambassadors' Endtime Diplomacy

David Benoit

Kerri Strug was on her last event of the evening. She stood 82 feet away from her dream. The vault was to be one of Kerri's strongest events in the Olympics. All she had to do was to complete one vault. On her first try she missed her landing, injuring her leg. Every American watching knew that Kerri seemed to be our last hope. Without her vault, America's Women's Gymnastic Team apparently had no chance of winning a gold medal. We watched as she gingerly walked back to her starting position. The pain in her face was clearly visible. The question in the minds of millions of people was, Could Kerri do on one good leg what she had failed to do on two legs: land and hold her stand?

We who watched by television could hear her coach screaming above the crowd, "You can do it, you can do it!" In a moment her face, once filled with pain, was suddenly filled with determination. She looked at her coach, took a few deep breaths, and ran down the runway. Kerri was launched high into the air by the takeoff board. Her hands hit the vault, causing her body to twist and torque. Now for the test: Would her legs have the strength to hold her? Her landing was good and she helped win the gold medal for America.

It didn't seem that there was a dry eye in the place. The Russians were crying because they came up short of the gold medal, and Americans were crying because Kerri represented America. As the women's gymnastic team stood on the platform, no one knew whether Kerri was crying because of the pain or because she had won the gold. When the national anthem was played, I could not hold back the tears, but I wasn't crying because of her pain. I was crying because I was proud to be American. I counted it a great honor to have someone like Kerri representing our country. She was an outstanding ambassador for the U.S.A.!

Am I an Ambassador?

The thought that goes through my mind is, Am I an outstanding ambassador of my heavenly country? As a Christian, I represent heaven. Paul said, "For which I am an ambassador in bonds, that therein I may speak boldly, as I ought to speak" (Ephesians 6:20). The word "ambassador" means "one who represents." Do you realize that you represent heaven? Do you realize that your testimony is important? Yes, you are an ambassador, or representative, of heaven. As never before, it is vital for Christians to maintain a testimony. Without a testimony we have no witness.

Most fundamental Bible students see Lot as an example of God removing His people before He rained down His wrath. Genesis 19:22 says, "Haste thee, escape thither; for I cannot do anything till thou be come thither." If you do not remember the story, Lot separated himself from Abraham and found himself a citizen of a wicked society. According to the Bible, God could not find even ten righteous people in these twin cities. Sodom and Gomorrah didn't have churches on every corner like we have today. Lot had no Christian radio station to listen to. He had no Christian television to watch. He could not find one Christian bookstore in the Yellow Pages. Lot didn't have Bible studies with his neighbors for fellowship. Basically, sin was abundant. Lot compromised his testimony, and it ultimately cost him his family: "Lot went out and spoke unto his sons in law, which married his daughters, and said, Up, get you out of this place, for the Lord will destroy this city. But he seemed as one that mocked unto his sons in law"(Genesis 19:14).

The devil may purchase your testimony cheaply, but he will not sell it back without making a substantial profit. Lot had bartered his testimony for a financial position.

Jesus, asked by His disciples to describe the events that would lead up to His coming, responded: "Likewise also as it was in the days of Lot, they did eat, they drank, they bought, they sold, they planted, they builded; but the same day that Lot went out of Sodom it rained fire and brimstone from heaven and destroyed them all" (Luke 17:28,29).

Notice that Lot and Noah were both removed before God's judgment. If God is consistent, which I believe Him to be, I believe that we too will be taken out before the tribulation period. This is the pretribulation view. Many people in the last few years have changed their view from pretribulation to other views that place Christians here on earth during the tribulation period.

Why should we, as American Christians, believe that we will miss the coming persecution? There is a difference between persecution and tribulation. Christians have always been persecuted by wicked people. The tribulation period will not be primarily a time when evil people will lash out at God's people. It will be a time when *God Himself* will unleash His judgment on the ungodly. The plague that God sent on the Egyptians in Exodus gives a great biblical example of this. God also prepared a secure place for His people in the land of Goshen (Exodus 8–12).

Dr. Harold Willmington, one of my professors in college and a good friend, explained the rapture as the calling home of God's ambassadors. "The first thing a nation would do before declaring war on another nation was to remove the ambassadors," he would say. I believe that everything is set for us to depart this world. I also believe that most of you reading this book now also believe this doctrine. So the question is not "When is Jesus coming?" but "What should we do until He comes?"

It was no accident that I started this chapter with the Olympics. The Bible offers several examples which compare the Christian life to athletic competition. These examples may help to shed light on the goals we want to achieve for Jesus. A very important thing to keep in mind while preparing to meet those goals is the conditions under which you will compete. Athletes must perform in extreme heat and cold. They take into consideration such elements as the elevation of the land and the time zone in which they will be competing. Consideration of these things gives prepared athletes the advantage.

Know the Playing Field

Paul tells Timothy the conditions under which believers will live right before Christ's coming: "This know also, that in the last days perilous times shall come" (2 Timothy 3:1). We must understand that the field is treacherous.

"For men shall be lovers of their own selves. . ." (2 Timothy 3:2a). Probably one of the most dangerous philosophies today is the one that says to love yourself. It seems that every problem in modern psychology stems from a bad self-image. The Bible tells us to love others as we love ourselves. It is natural for a man or woman to love himself or herself. But it's more difficult to love others. Self-love leads to humanism, and humanism opposes the love of God. Antichrist will be a self-lover: "The king shall do according to his will, and he shall exalt himself, and magnify himself above every god . . . " (Daniel 11:36).

It is very easy for a person to turn self-love into self-worship. The devil knows that self-worship is as much idolatry as worshiping pagan gods. In Isaiah 14:12-14 we read:

> How art thou fallen from heaven, O Lucifer, son of the morning! How art thou cut down to the ground, which did weaken the nations! For thou hast said in thine heart, I will ascend into heaven, I will exalt my throne above the stars of God; I will sit also upon the mount of the congregation, in the sides of the north; I will ascend above the heights of the clouds, I will be like the Most High.

This tells us that Lucifer had a problem with self-love and self-determination.

The world tells us that the only way to succeed is to exalt yourself. But the Bible tells us that we must decrease and Christ must increase. That is totally opposite of the world's philosophy.

In 2 Timothy 3:2b-3, we find this description: . . .*covetous* (desiring the things of others), *boasters* (those who boast about things they really don't have), *proud* (pride goes before a fall), *blasphemers* (they hate God), *disobedient to parents* (they hate parents because parents represent authority and the devil will always break the chain of command, causing confusion), *unthankful* (if a person praises himself for all his accomplishments, why does he need to be thankful to God?), *unholy* (self-reliance always means the elimination of God, which always leads to the elimination of holiness), *without natural affection* (having no love for their family), *truce-breakers* (they are not trustworthy), *false accusers* (those who try to take the place of God must always blame someone else for their failures), *incontinent* (without self-control), *fierce* (no mercy), *despisers of those that are good.*

Today Christianity is looked upon by many as bad. Because we are against abortion, it is said that we have no compassion on women. Because we stand against homosexuals, we are called homophobic. Because we are not pantheists, we are accused of hating nature. Witchcraft is being accepted as a normal religion, and Christianity is being labeled a cult.

"Traitors, heady, high-minded, lovers of pleasure more than lovers of God" (2 Timothy 3:4). The description Paul gave Timothy nearly 2000 years ago is like reading today's newspapers.

Know the Rules

Can you imagine the chaos of having a sport without rules? Years ago I sat in front of a woman at a football game who became irate when one of the players was tackled. She screamed, "He's pulling his jersey, ref! He's pulling his jersey, ref!" I turned and assured her that tackling was legal. She seemed quite embarrassed by her lack of knowledge of the rules of football.

Rule 1: The contestants are not bound by age. "Let no man despise thy youth, but be thou an example of the believers in word, in conversation, in charity, in spirit, in faith, in purity" (1 Timothy 4:12).

I am amazed at the age at which children begin training to become Olympians. Some gymnasts start when they are four or five years old so they can compete when they are 14. Many times Christians underestimate the power of training children to serve God at an early age. If you do not train your children to serve God, the devil's crowd will take it upon themselves to recruit them for his service.

Rule 2: The Bible is our rulebook. "Till I come, give attendance to reading, to exhortation, to doctrine" (1 Timothy 4:13).

The Word of God must be the ultimate authority. The other evening I appeared on a Christian television talk show. My opening remarks were as follows: "There is absolutely nothing wrong with homosexuality. There is nothing wrong with abortion." Needless to say, the mouths of the host and cohost fell open. I finished this statement by saying, "There is nothing wrong with homosexuality and abortion outside of the Word of God."

One debate today concerns whether or not the Southern Baptist Convention should boycott Disney because of its alignment with the homosexual movement. There is no debate if both sides believe the Bible. You cannot debate philosophies with the devil. He has a master's degree in philosophy. He talked one-third of the angels out of heaven. How can we debate philosophy with the master? We need to stay close to the rulebook, the Bible, or we will be swept away by all kinds of philosophies in the last day.

Paul knew that if he didn't obey the rules he would be disqualified. "But I keep under my body and bring it into subjection, lest that by any means, when I have preached to others I myself should be a castaway" (1 Corinthians 9:27).

Rule 3: Christians in the latter day must know the course. Paul said, *"I have fought a good fight, I have finished my course, I have kept the faith"* (2 Timothy 4:7).

Paul did three things:

1. He fought a good fight. Paul didn't shadowbox. He fought for keeps: "So fight I, not as one that beateth the air" (1 Corinthians 9:26b). Most Christians today are not fighters. They have been told by the devil's crowd that they are intolerant, so now they tolerate everything.

2. He finished his course. "I therefore so run, not as uncertainly" (1 Corinthians 9:26). The writer of Hebrews tells us in chapter 12 to run with patience the race that is set before us. This means that the race is not a sprint but a marathon. There is a totally different method of training for a marathon runner. It takes endurance, strength, and courage. Christians who look at this race as a sprint come out of the blocks with fury, only to fall short of the finish line.

3. He kept the faith. Paul was accused of a lot of things, but never of compromise.

   > Of the Jews five times received I forty stripes save one. Thrice was I beaten with rods, once was I stoned, thrice I suffered shipwreck, a night and a day I have been in the deep; in journeyings often, in perils of waters, in perils of robbers, in perils by mine own countrymen, in perils by the heathen, in perils in the city, in perils in the wilderness, in perils in the sea, in perils among false brethren; in weariness and painfulness, in watchings often, in hunger and thirst, in fastings often, in cold and nakedness. Besides those things that are without, that which cometh upon me daily,

the care of all the churches (2 Corinthians 11:24-28).

Rule 4: Christians must look toward the long term rewards and not the temporal benefits. We cannot do anything of eternal value unless we do it with eternity in mind. An old saying goes like this: "He is so heavenly minded that he is no earthly good." But I do not see that today. What I see is that Christians have become so earthly minded that they are no heavenly good. It is very easy for Christians to take their eyes off the Lord and put them on the world. As a matter of fact, the Bible tells us to keep our eyes on the Lord: "Looking unto Jesus, the author and finisher of our faith" (Hebrews 12:2a). *Even Hymn gone*

Thousands of distractions could cause Christians to quit. How ironic that this morning as I came downstairs to write this chapter, my wife called to me and said someone had exploded a pipe bomb at the Olympic Games. The reporters all asked the athletes the same question: "Do you feel the games should go on?" The reply was always the same: "Yes, they should!" One athlete said that when the athletes reach the level of the Olympics, they must be able to put away all distractions. We as Christians could learn something from this statement. We must be able to perform even in a hostile environment.

We need to understand that even while the Olympic Games are going on, the fighting continues. The Olympic athletes are not excluded from terrorism. Every precautionary measure is taken to ensure their safety because these athletes are so focused that they don't consider the danger all around them. They see only the games at hand. For many of these athletes, while they prepare for the games, the battles at home seem a million miles away. They must stay focused on the games even though they know that the battle still rages.

Likewise, we as Christians need to be protected from the spiritual danger that is all around us. We need to put on the whole armor of God, found in Ephesians 6, which has been provided for us, because even though we are in the game to win crowns, we are also in a very real battle—a spiritual battle for the souls of men and women.

God has given me many opportunities to speak to professional athletes. The text I generally use is Hebrews 12:1,2: "Wherefore, seeing we also are compassed about with so great a cloud of witnesses...." Professionals understand that having the home court advantage is important. Something about the cheering crowds inspires the home team to dig a little deeper when they are at home.

After reading the Scripture that tells us we have a great cloud of witnesses, I always ask the athletes, "When are the greatest number of people cheering for you: when you are at home, or when you are away?" Their answer is always the same: "When we are at home." Technically, that is not always the right answer. Let me give you an example. I live in Charlotte, North Carolina, where the Charlotte Hornets play. When the team is in town, games are usually blocked out to local viewers. So the only people in the area who can see them are the 26,000 or so fans present at the coliseum. This excludes millions of possible viewers. Yet when the players are on the road, there are potentially millions of fans via television who are cheering for them. The problem is the players cannot see or hear the cheers from the fans at home. Our cheers are drowned out by the crowds that are in the opponent's coliseum.

This is true in the spiritual realm also. Many times the only voices we can hear are those that surround us. We listen to the secular media telling us we are a minority, and that we are outnumbered by the ungodly. You might say that we are playing on the devil's home court. If athletes could only understand that there are millions of fans back home cheering for them, they too could dig a little deeper. In the very same way, if we as Christians could grasp Hebrews 12:1, which tells us that there are those we cannot see who are cheering for us, then we would be able to understand that our home court advantage is in heaven.

"Let us lay aside every weight, and the sin which doth so easily beset us." I was speaking one night to the Atlanta Hawks, and a player named Spud Web attended my chapel service. Now Spud is quite a ballplayer, yet to look at his stature you would never believe that he was an NBA player, since Spud stands only 5 foot 6 inches tall. I asked him, "Spud, how would you like to play basketball with ankle weights on? Just one pound on each leg. Surely one pound on each leg is not a lot." He replied that he could never keep up with the other players on the court with ankle weights on. To that I responded, "The Bible tells us to lay aside every weight that hinders us from running the good race." The weight might be ungodly music for teenagers. Sex, drugs, alcohol, lying, stealing, hatred, and an unforgiving spirit are just a few of the sins that hinder our performance for God.

"Let us run with patience the race that is set before us, looking unto Jesus, the author and finisher of our faith" (Hebrews 12:1b,2a). Let me illustrate: Peewee coaches work hard at teaching their children to run toward the first base coach because it's only natural for children to pay more attention to where the ball is going than to where they should be going. Many times, we watch our own accomplishments, which takes our eyes off Jesus. We can't look at the stands to see if our mother is looking, to wave at our father, or any-thing else. We must run with all our energy toward our

Coach, who is Jesus Christ, the Author and Finisher of our faith.

Rule 5: Christians must understand the award system. It is amazing to see how the Olympic judges keep score. They are so well-trained that they can score a gymnastic routine or a diver's performance with near-perfect accuracy. To the untrained person the performance of all these athletes is great. Yet the judges are trained to spot the minute subtleties of movement and action, things that you and I cannot see.

The awards for the Olympics athletes are gold, silver, and bronze. The awards for Christians will be gold, silver, precious stones, wood, hay, and stubble.

> For other foundation can no man lay than that is laid, which is Jesus Christ. Now if any man build upon this foundation gold, silver, precious stones, wood, hay, stubble, every man's work shall be made manifest; for the day shall declare it, because it shall be revealed by fire; and the fire shall try every man's work of what sort it is. . . . If any man's work shall be burned, he shall suffer loss; but he himself shall be saved, yet so as by fire (1 Corinthians 3:11-15).

Christians will not lose their souls at this judgment seat, but they will lose their temporal rewards of wood, hay, and stubble that could not withstand the fire.

Lehman Strauss explains it this way:

> In the large Olympic arenas there was an elevated seat on which the judge of the contest sat. After the contests were over, the successful competitors would assemble before the bema to receive their rewards or crowns. The bema was not a judicial bench where someone was condemned;

it was a reward seat. Likewise, the Judgment Seat of Christ is not a judicial bench. The Christian life is a race, and the divine umpire is watching every contestant. After the church has run her course, He will gather every member before the bema seat for the purpose of examining each one and giving the proper reward to each.[1]

The Five Events

In the modern-day Olympics, athletes can participate in hundreds of events. Yet in the Christian faith there are only five events whereby Christians can receive awards. These awards are called crowns. Sad to say, most Christians could not even name the events for which they are capable of receiving awards. Here are the events:

1. The incorruptible crown. This is given to those who overcome the old nature and finish the course. "Every man that striveth for the mastery is temperate in all things. Now they do it to obtain a corruptible crown, but we an incorruptible. I therefore so run, not as uncertainly; so fight I, not as one that beateth the air; but I keep under my body and bring it into subjection, lest that by any means when I have preached to others I myself should be a castaway" (1 Corinthians 9:25-27).

2. The soul-winner's crown. "The fruit of the righteous is a tree of life, and he that winneth souls is wise" (Proverbs 11:30).

"Many of them that sleep in the dust of the earth shall awake, some to everlasting life and some to shame and everlasting contempt. And they that be wise shall shine as the brightness of the firmament, and they that turn many to righteousness as the stars for ever and ever" (Daniel 12:2,3).

"For what is our hope, or joy, or crown of rejoicing? Are not even ye in the presence of our Lord Jesus Christ at his coming? For ye are our glory and joy" (1 Thessalonians 2:19,20).

3. The crown of life. This crown is given to those who die for the cause of Christ. This is called the martyr's crown. "Fear none of those things which thou shalt suffer; behold, the devil shall cast some of you into prison, that ye may be tried; and ye shall have tribulation ten days; be thou faithful unto death, and I will give thee a crown of life" (Revelation 2:10).

4. The expectancy crown, or the crown of righteousness. This crown is given to those who look forward to Christ's coming by living righteously. "Henceforth there is laid up for me a crown of righteousness, which the Lord, the righteous judge, shall give me at that day; and not to me only, but unto all them also that love his appearing" (2 Timothy 4:8).

This is one of the reasons I hold to the pretribulation view. I believe Jesus could come back at any minute, so I want to live in expectancy.

5. The crown of glory: the shepherd's crown. This is the crown given to faithful ministers called of God to instruct His people. "Feed the flock of God which is among you, taking the oversight thereof, not by constraint, but willingly; not for filthy lucre, but of a ready mind; neither as being lords over God's heritage, but being examples to the flock. And when the chief Shepherd shall appear, ye shall receive a crown of glory that fadeth not away" (1 Peter 5:2-4).

Paul shows us that he wanted this crown as much as any athlete could desire a gold medal: "Wherefore I take you to record this day that I am pure from the blood of all men. For I have not shunned to declare unto you all the counsel of God. Take heed therefore unto yourselves, and to all the flock, over which the Holy Ghost hath made you overseers, to feed the church of God, which he hath purchased with his own blood" (Acts 20:26-28).

The Power of Your Testimony

Don't ever underestimate the power of your testimony. The Bible tells us just how powerful the Christian testimony will be in the latter days: "They overcame him [Satan] by the blood of the Lamb, and by the word of their testimony; and they loved not their lives unto death" (Revelation 12:11).

The faithfulness of God's people is the one defense that Satan's army cannot penetrate. Corrie ten Boom was a tremendous testimony of God's grace. When she was young she feared that she wouldn't have the strength to die for Jesus. This concerned her so much that she asked her father if it was wrong of her to think that she couldn't die for Jesus. Her father looked at her and said, "Corrie, when your father puts you on the train, when does he give you your ticket—before you get on the train, or when he puts you on the train?" She said, "You always give me the ticket when I get on the train." He said, "That's the way it is with Jesus. Jesus will not give you the strength to die for Him until He puts you in that position." Corrie ultimately had to live her life on the edge of death because of her commitment to the Lord Jesus Christ.

The Bible says, "For God hath not given us the spirit of fear, but of power and of love and of a sound mind" (2 Timothy 1:7). +Ps 56:3

The greatest enemy of faith is fear. As I speak at prophecy conferences around the country, people come up to me and ask what I think they should do to prepare for whatever the future might hold for them. Sometimes their voices reflect their anxiety, but feeling anxious about the future is totally contrary to what Scripture tells us. The same God who

354 ❖ David Benoit

perfect
casts out
fear

warned us what would happen in the latter days is the same God who said, "Let your conversation be without covetousness, and be content with such things as ye have, for he hath said, I will never leave thee nor forsake thee. So that we may boldly say, The Lord is my helper, and I will not fear what man shall do unto me" (Hebrews 13:5,6).

This same thought is reiterated when Jesus talked with His disciples, and His counsel to them is still applicable to us today: "Fear not them which kill the body but are not able to kill the soul, but rather fear him who is able to destroy both soul and body in hell" (Matthew 10:28).

All that man can do is destroy the body. One time a young man asked me what I thought about someone who wanted to kill someone. I knew the name of that someone he was talking about. It was me! I looked at the young man and said, "You can't touch me unless God gives you permission." The late John R. Rice once told a man who threatened to kill him, "Don't threaten me with eternal life." This is the kind of courage, love, and compassion that will touch the hearts of the cold and cruel when the time of Jesus is at hand. May the Lord find us faithful till He comes.

15

Escape from Planet Earth

John F. Walvoord

Our modern world in the twentieth century has provided an amazing combination of events and situations that compare to the end times predicted in the Bible. Major events of the future begin with the rapture of the church, referring to the catching up of the church from earth to heaven. But significantly, the Bible never mentions a specific sign for the rapture itself, because it is always presented as an imminent event that could take place at any moment.

What can be the meaning, then, of talking about signs of the rapture? Being enacted before our eyes in this twentieth century is a preparation of the world's stage for events which will follow the rapture. These are detailed in both the Old and New Testaments, providing a panoramic view of the tremendous climax of human history leading up to the second coming of Christ. But the rapture comes first, and this event has no specific signs preceding it. What the world is seeing today is the preparation for events that will *follow* the rapture. Logically, this means that the rapture itself could be very near. This is the point of all the discussion concerning current events which are viewed as prophecy being fulfilled today.

Paramount, however, in all the evidence for the coming of the Lord is the fact that the Scriptures themselves provide the details for what is necessary to support the conclusion that Christ is coming for His own. Fulfillment could be any day. A study of the prophecies concerning the coming of Christ is still our best proof for the imminence of these earth-shaking events.

Principles of Interpreting Prophecy

In the exercise of interpreting prophecies of the Bible, there has been a woeful neglect of basic rules of interpretation. This has resulted in prophecies being wrongly claimed as currently being fulfilled, as well as other important prophecies being ignored. It is amazing to see books on the end times that just skip, for example, the rapture and proceed as if we are already in the great tribulation. To avoid this interpretive error, we must understand clearly the rules of interpretation of prophecy.

First of all, the context of any prophecy needs to be thoroughly explored and understood. Second, it is most important to examine the details of the prophecy and carefully go over each aspect of the prophetic interpretation. Third, it is necessary to understand that prophecy is usually literal and given in plain statements of Scripture. To be sure, symbolic and apocalyptic presentations of prophecy appear in many passages, but even here the Bible itself interprets these symbols as prophetic predictions. It simply is not true that prophecy is a hopeless puzzle that no one can understand.

The main points of prophecy are clearly written in the scriptural record.

Once the facts of prophecy are determined, then the practical application of the prophecy can be attempted. In the case of prophetic interpretation, this emphasizes the importance of being ready for the coming of the Lord. If His coming is truly imminent, it is of utmost importance to have assurance of salvation, commitment of life and property to the Lord, and a life of purity and devotion to the Lord. As given in Scripture, prophecy always has a practical context. In other words, it is intended not only to teach but also to exhort.

In carrying out these basic rules of interpreting prophecy, it is necessary first of all to examine carefully the Old Testament to see what it reveals and what it does not reveal and then to continue in the new revelation given in the New Testament as well. A careful search of all prophecies reveal that there are at least a thousand basic passages on prophecy in the Bible, some single verses and some whole chapters; of these thousand passages, 500 have already been literally fulfilled. This provides a reasonable and intelligent basis for assuming that prophecies yet to be fulfilled will likewise be literal in their fulfillment. With these facts in mind, it is very important then to ask: *What was intended by the prophecy? To whom was it given? And what would be the normal comprehension of it?*

The Coming of Christ in the Old Testament

In the Old Testament, not only are there hundreds of prophecies, but many of these are of major impact upon the history of the period. Beginning in the Garden of Eden, God told Adam and Eve that they would surely die if they partook of the forbidden fruit. When they sinned against God and partook of the fruit, they died spiritually immediately and ultimately physically.

The major predictions of the flood were literally fulfilled. Abram received extensive prophetic revelation, much of which has already been precisely fulfilled. Abram became a great man in history and in the Bible. He was the progenitor not only of the nation of Israel but of many other ancient nations as well. Through him came the line that led to Jesus Christ and provided blessing to all the world. This is summarized in three very important verses in Genesis 12:1-3.

To Abraham also was given the important promise that his descendants would inherit and possess the Promised Land (Genesis 12:7). One of the major mistakes of prophecy is to refuse to take this literally and instead try to equate this land with heaven. Throughout the Old Testament, every use and reference to the word "land" refers to real estate: what is commonly known as the Holy Land, extending from the River of Egypt to the River Euphrates, as detailed in Genesis 15:18-21.

The departure of the children of Israel to Egypt was predicted in Genesis 15:13,14, and their return was literally fulfilled. Though they wandered for 40 years in the wilderness, they eventually conquered at least a major portion of the land.

As long as Israel obeyed the law, God blessed them in the land. But it was freely predicted by Moses that if they disobeyed the law, they would be scattered and driven out of the land (Deuteronomy 28:58-68). This was tragically fulfilled, first by the Assyrian invasion of the land in 722 B.C. (2 Kings 17:5-8), when the ten tribes were carried off captive. Later, in 605 B.C., Jerusalem was conquered by Nebuchadnezzar, and subsequently captives from Judah were carried to Babylon (2 Kings 24:8-16).

In the midst of Israel's apostasy, Jeremiah the prophet, who had predicted the Babylonian conquest of Judah, predicted that after 70 years God would bring the captives back from Babylon to Israel (Jeremiah 29:10). This was literally fulfilled after the Medes and Persians conquered Babylon. Though their history was troubled, the Jewish people eventually built the temple. In the time of Nehemiah they built the wall, and then in the years following Nehemiah they rebuilt the city of Jerusalem, replacing its ancient ruins. In all of these predictions there was literal fulfillment of the many prophecies that dealt with the nation of Israel as well as the nations that surrounded them.

Throughout the Old Testament, however, there also was prediction of the coming of the Messiah. The prophecies of the coming of the Lord as the Jewish Messiah and King of the line of David are interwoven with the major prophetic revelations of the Old Testament. As early as Genesis 3:15 it was predicted that the coming Son of the woman would destroy Satan. In the promise to Abraham, the Coming One was not only indicated to be the son of Abraham but it was also predicted that He would be a blessing to the entire world. This was fulfilled in Christ's death, as mentioned previously in Genesis 3:15. Intimately related to all of this was the fulfillment of the promise of the land as Israel's everlasting inheritance.

Later in the Old Testament, in the covenant with David (2 Samuel 7:12-16), God promised to perpetuate the kingdom of David, which ultimately would be fulfilled by the coming of the Messiah. Psalm 89 repeats and reiterates the unconditional nature of this promise that is related to the second coming of Christ. In connection with Israel's restoration, there is a time of terrible trouble spoken of as the great tribulation (Daniel 12:1), which would be ended, however, by the restoration of Israel (Jeremiah 30:5-11). The fact that

Israel would be restored to her land in connection with the fulfillment of the Davidic covenant is the major theme of Jeremiah 31. In Ezekiel 39:21-29 the promise is given that all Israelites would be regathered to their Promised Land at the time of the coming of the Messiah except for those who are purged out. In Ezekiel 20:33-38 it is clear that the rebels are unbelievers who will be purged out in that regathering. Only those who have come to trust in their Messiah will enter the Promised Land. Ezekiel 48 pictures the 12 tribes of Israel, each with its own inheritance in the Promised Land following the coming of the Messiah.

The prophecy of a Messiah who would suffer and die, as predicted in Isaiah 53 and Psalm 22, alongside these promises of glorious restoration, puzzled the rabbis as they attempted to interpret the Old Testament. This is mentioned in 1 Peter 1:10,11.

It is most important to realize that the Old Testament in its prediction spoke of both the first and second comings of Christ, but no one understood that they were two separate events. The first coming would involve His sufferings and death and resurrection, while in the second coming He would conquer the world and reign gloriously on earth. Interpreters of the Old Testament, however, never understood that there were two comings, and they attempted to merge these two conflicting predictions into one major prophecy. Though they gave various explanations, probably the most popular one identified the sufferings of Messiah with the sufferings of the nation of Israel but predicted the glorious reign of Christ as being brought about by His first coming. As far as Scripture reveals, nobody in the Old Testament or in the gospel period, except for Christ Himself, understood that there were two separate comings of Christ. This is most significant in considering the problem of separating the rapture from the second coming, except that this time thousands of people can see the difference.

It is most important to understand that the Old Testament, in its presentation of the coming of the Messiah, was universally misunderstood. The result was that the disciples came to follow Christ anticipating the fact that He would be a glorious reigning Messiah but ignoring the fact that He had to die first. And Christ did not immediately correct the disciples' anticipation. It is doubtful whether they would have followed Christ if they thought He was going to die and not fulfill His role of leadership. However, in the events leading up to His death, He predicted on several occasions that He would be crucified and die and then be resurrected (Matthew 12:38-42; 16:21-23; 17:22,23; 20:17-19; Mark 10:32-34; Luke 18:31-34).

The disciples immediately rejected this concept and so thoroughly erased it from their minds that when Christ actually died they did not recall His predictions of His death and resurrection. By contrast, the enemies of Christ remembered; they appointed soldiers to watch the tomb and seal it to make it impossible for anyone to steal the body. Their attempts only added to the certainty of the fact that Christ actually rose from the dead in spite of the efforts to prevent removal of the body. The disciples were not credulous and eager to believe the fact of His resurrection; instead, they required solid proof—as given in the tomb and the appearances of Christ—that He was actually raised before they would accept this important miracle in fulfillment of prophecy.

In view of the many attempts to interpret Scripture as not teaching an imminent return of Christ in the rapture, it is a common interpretation by posttribulationists (who put the rapture at the end of the tribulation) and amillennarians (who ignore the rapture) also to insist that the disciples knew all about the rapture and therefore understood the predictions of the second coming as referring to the rapture. Actually there is not a scrap of evidence anywhere that indicates the disciples understood anything about this. How could the disciples understand the doctrine of the rapture as distinct from the second coming when they had not even comprehended the difference between the first and second comings of Christ?

In interpretation of prophecy, it is most important not only to observe in great detail what is said but also to carefully examine what is not said, and there is no mention of a rapture anywhere in the Gospels until the prediction in John 14. The fact that the disciples could not distinguish the first and second comings of Christ explains how some today have difficulty in distinguishing the rapture and the second coming. The reason these two events are properly distinguished, however, is based upon the biblical facts concerning them as two events that are totally different in what they accomplish. Also, the context of what precedes the rapture and the events that follow are in sharp contrast.

The First Prophecy of the Rapture

As the public ministry of Christ had moved on to more than three years, the disciples were beginning to despair whether His promises of a glorious reign were going to be fulfilled as they had anticipated. They saw instead a weakening of His followers, with many disciples turning away, and they were aware of the activities of the leaders of Israel to capture Christ and put Him to death. All these problems did not indicate any progress toward their goal of a glorious reign of Christ on earth. This was the reason they came to Christ in Matthew 24 and asked the questions concerning the signs of His coming and the end of the age.

As the disciples gathered in the upper room on the night before His crucifixion, Christ seized the opportunity to give them what hope He could. Their problem was that Christ told them He was to leave them and they could not follow Him. Also, one of their number was going to betray Him. They could not understand any of these predictions because they did not fit into their scheme of Christ gloriously reigning on earth. In the context, John 14 records the first revelation of Christ's coming to take His own out of the earth.

The entire fourteenth chapter of John is directed at the anxiety of the disciples. It gives them assurance that God is on the throne and will certainly fulfill His plan and purpose for the world and for His own. Christ exhorts them not to be troubled. The first thing He mentions is the fact that He would be going to heaven to prepare a place for them, and then come back to receive them to Himself: "In My Father's house are many mansions; if it were not so, I would have told you. I go to prepare a place for you. And if I go and prepare a place for you, I will come again and receive you to Myself; that where I am, there you may be also" (John 14:2,3 NKJV).*

It should be quite clear that the disciples did not have the slightest idea as to what Christ was talking about. There was nothing in their understanding of endtime prophecy that involved Christ coming to take His own out of the world. What they were anticipating was the kingdom on earth, in keeping with the Old Testament prophecies of Christ gloriously reigning on earth. Had not the Lord also assured them that they would sit on thrones judging the 12 tribes of Israel (Matthew 19:27-30)?

---

* All Scripture quotations in this chapter are taken from the New King James Version. Used by permission. See credit line on copyright page.

Christ made no attempt to explain the doctrine of the rapture to them or even to correct their misunderstanding of His future kingdom. The dark days that followed as they watched Him die on the cross were left without relief until He rose from the dead and the disciples were assured of His resurrection. It is doubtful that even then they understood the difference between the first and second comings of Christ.

Later, when they saw Christ ascend into heaven, it apparently gradually dawned on the disciples that His sufferings and death had to do with His first coming, and that His second coming was to be fulfilled in a future event when He would return. They probably had no idea how long this period would be (which has now stretched to almost 2000 years). They anticipated the possibility that He might come back to establish His kingdom while they were still living.

The doctrine of the rapture was given by revelation to Paul. While undoubtedly the other disciples heard about it, it is not clear from the New Testament whether all the apostles understood that Christ would come for them first before He came to establish His kingdom.

The Revelation of the Rapture to Paul

When the apostle Paul was arrested in his mad course of persecuting Christians on the road to Damascus, he ultimately went through an experience of being taught by the Lord in special revelation the great truths that characterized his later writings. He was indoctrinated into the truth of grace, which apparently he had not completely understood in his life as a Pharisee, and in addition he was given the great revelation of Christ's next coming to take His own out of the world.

In his missionary journey, Paul incorporated these two main doctrines into his preaching, teaching first that Christ had come, died for our sins, and rose again, and is now able to save all those who put their trust in Him. This was coupled immediately with the truth that Christ might come at any time to take His own out of the world.

This truth is detailed for us in Scripture in connection with Paul's ministry to the Thessalonian church. Acting on divine instruction, he had left Asia Minor and gone over to Greece to preach at Philippi and then later at Thessalonica (Acts 16:8-10).

Paul's painful experience at Philippi, where he was beaten and placed in prison, did not deter him from preaching the gospel boldly at Thessalonica. As was his custom, he had gone to the synagogue there and preached the gospel to both Jews and Gentile converts for three Sabbath days (Acts 17:1-4). However, because of threats on his life on the part of those who rejected his message, he thought it best to leave.

Later, while in Athens, Paul had sent Timothy, his young disciple, to the Thessalonian church to see how they were getting along. Timothy found them standing true to the faith in spite of terrible persecution, and he did what he could to reassure them and encourage them. However, they had some important doctrinal questions which Timothy could not completely answer. So Timothy took those questions back to Paul for his consideration. One of the questions concerned some of the Thessalonians who had already died: *If the Lord came for those living in the rapture, would they have to wait for some future time before their loved ones would be resurrected?* In his first epistle to the Thessalonians, Paul expressed his joy at their standing true to the faith, but he also answered their theological questions and gave them more detail than anywhere else in the Scriptures concerning what would happen at the rapture of the church.

As stated earlier, it is most important to pay close attention to what is said and what is not said. So many wrong interpretations of the rapture come from neglect of the details or refusal to accept the revelation itself. As stated in 1 Thessalonians 4:13, Paul said, "I do not want you to be ignorant, brethren, concerning those who have fallen asleep, lest you sorrow as others who have no hope." God has a purpose in giving prophecy. If one-fourth of the Bible was prophetic when it was written, it certainly is evident that God does not want us to neglect this important truth, as many do today. It is also essential to listen carefully to what God says because there are no inaccuracies in His Word and nothing is omitted that is important to us. God does not want us to be ignorant or uninformed.

In Paul's letter to the Thessalonians, he addressed them as "brethren." Belief in the rapture is not essential to salvation, as there are thousands of Christians today who are ignorant of this great truth. Salvation relates to the first coming of Christ and what Christ did for us on the cross. There is an important reason, however, for understanding this truth of the rapture: *Paul does not want us to have hope without content.* While many Christians believe they are going to heaven, they are practically at a loss to state anything about this event or what their state would be or when this would occur. Paul makes it clear that it is God's purpose not to keep us ignorant or uninformed but to give us a wonderful hope, in contrast to a world with no hope at all.

This wonderful hope is particularly brought out in a Christian funeral. On one occasion I attended the memorial service of an 11-year old girl who had died of leukemia. Her parents were prominent Christian workers. The church was packed with well-wishers and sympathizers. It was a glorious occasion, however, as the girl's family and friends recounted the wonderful hope that they would see their loved one again. When Christ comes, the family will be reunited. What a difference if the little girl had not been a Christian and the parents had not been Christians! What could extend any hope or comfort to those left behind? In proportion as our future with the Lord is real and our personal love for the Lord and desire to see him is real, so will prophecy become real for us as we attempt to understand what God has predicted in His Word.

In 1 Thessalonians 4:14 the absolute certainty of the rapture is revealed: "For if we believe that Jesus died and rose again, even so God will bring with Him those who sleep in Jesus." The death and resurrection of Christ was a major subject of Old Testament prophecy. Implied in all the passages of His glorious reign is that after His death He would need to be raised from the dead. Now that Christ has come, however, and has died and been resurrected, it is prophecy fulfilled. There is absolutely no uncertainty about the prophecy having a literal fulfillment.

From the divine point of view, prophecy is just as certain as history. From the human point of view, however, it is reassuring to see that predictions are literally fulfilled. Today we can believe with certainty that Christ died and rose again. Paul's argument is that, just as the death and resurrection of Christ, a central doctrine of the Christian gospel, is true, so the rapture is also absolutely certain and absolutely true. In describing this event he is predicting what actually will happen.

When the rapture occurs, Christ will take the souls of Christians in heaven and bring them with Him as He comes back to the earthly sphere. When a Christian dies, a medical doctor can declare a person dead because the signs of life are absent. Theologically, a Christian who dies experiences death when the soul leaves the body and goes immediately to heaven, as indicated in 2 Corinthians 5:8. It is customary, however, to put the body of Christians who have died in the grave. When the rapture occurs, Christ will bring the souls of these from heaven back to the earthly sphere with the obvious purpose of causing them to be raised from the dead, and the soul will reenter the resurrection body.

Paul follows this with a detailed description of exactly what is going to happen on the occasion of the rapture. As stated in 1 Thessalonians 4:15-18:

> For this we say to you by the word of the Lord, that we who are alive and remain until the coming of the Lord will by no means precede those who are asleep. For the Lord Himself will descend from heaven with a shout, with the voice of an archangel, and with the trumpet of God. And the dead in Christ will rise first. Then we who are alive and remain shall be caught up together with them in the clouds to meet the Lord in the air. And thus we shall always be with the Lord. Therefore comfort one another with these words.

First of all, Paul points out that this is not a revelation of the Old Testament, and he does not quote Old Testament passages dealing with the second coming; rather, it is a new truth given by direct revelation. He then describes the scene: Christians who are alive at the time of the rapture will not precede those who have died. One of the problems of the Thessalonian church was that they were concerned that, when those who were living were raptured, their dead brethren would not be raised. But Paul replied that there was no need to worry about this issue because their resurrection would precede by a moment the translation and rapture of the living Christians. He then described how the Lord would bodily descend from heaven to the air above the earth.

Though Christ is everywhere, omnipresent in His divine deity, in His resurrected human body He can be in only one place at a time because this is the nature of a body. At the rapture He will come bodily from heaven as a token of the importance of this event. He will issue a shout which is also a command of resurrection to Christians all over the world who have died. Their souls will reenter their bodies. He will command living Christians to be caught up and meet Him in the air. Living Christians will experience what Paul later described in his first letter to the Corinthians indicating that our present bodies, which are subject to death and corruption and sin, will be exchanged for bodies that are suited for heaven. Paul writes in 1 Corinthians 15:51-53:

> Behold, I tell you a mystery: We shall not all sleep, but we shall all be changed—in a moment, in the twinkling of an eye, at the last trumpet. For the trumpet will sound, and the dead will be raised incorruptible, and we shall be changed. For this corruptible must put on incorruption, and this mortal must put on immortality.

Taken with 1 Thessalonians 4, the 1 Corinthians passage gives a complete picture of what will happen on the occasion of the rapture.

When the trumpet sounds, not only will the dead be raised with new bodies that will be suited to be in the presence of the Lord forever, but the living Christians who now have sinful bodies and experience mortality and age will be instantly changed into bodies which will last forever without sin and without corruption.

Three basic problems of the human body will be settled instantly. First, our present bodies have a sin nature, as indicated in Ephesians 2:1, and they are not suitable for the presence of the Lord. Second, our bodies grow old, and we need a body that does not deteriorate. Third, our bodies are subject to death, and we need bodies that are immortal. All these changes will take place instantly when the trumpet of the rapture sounds.

Christians who died would be resurrected a moment before Christians who are living are translated. According to 1 Thessalonians 4:17, we will be caught up or raptured with those resurrected. There is no record that Christ's feet will ever touch the earth at the time of the rapture. Instead, Scripture predicts that we will be forever with the Lord.

John 14:1-3 indicates that when Christ comes for us He will take us to the Father's house, which is heaven. In other words, we will not be floating around in space right after the rapture, but will go immediately into the presence of the Lord. This is anticipated, for example, in 1 Thessalonians 3:13, which teaches that we will be presented before God our heavenly Father.

The reference to the clouds could refer to atmospheric clouds, which would also characterize the second coming. Some believe that the reference is to the multitude or "clouds" of those who are resurrected or translated, similar to Hebrews 12:1, which speaks of a cloud of witnesses. From then on we will be wherever the Lord is, whether in heaven in the Father's presence during the terrible time of tribulation, on earth during the millennial earth, or in the new heaven and new earth (and the new Jerusalem) for all eternity. The assurance of this plan of God is a comfort to us because these promises are given as something that could occur at any time. It is a reminder of how our present time of suffering and bereavement may be suddenly cut off by that trumpet sound from the blue.

It is most important to realize that the scriptural rapture is totally different from the picture of the second coming as given in Revelation 19:11-16. Here Christ comes back to the earth with the purpose of judging the world and bringing His kingdom to bear upon the earth. He is accompanied by the armies of heaven, including the angels and the saints, and the church, which had previously been raptured. They all come to be with Christ during His thousand-year reign on earth. While many questions are left unanswered, the main facts are perfectly clear for anyone who will accept what the Scriptures say. At the time of the rapture there is no judgment on earth and there is no heavenly host accompanying Christ, for His purpose in this event is to take the church to heaven. In contrast, His purpose in Revelation 19, where He comes from heaven to earth, is to bring His judgment and power to bear upon a wicked earth. The fact that no intervening events are ever mentioned between the present moment and the rapture gives assurance to believers, even if they differ on many other points of prophecy, that Christ could come very soon.

The Rapture and the Day of the Lord

After the rapture is described as an imminent event, it is only natural to ask: *When will it occur?* First Thessalonians 5 deals with this issue. In this connection a new term is introduced: "the day of the Lord." Most expositors hold that the reason the day of the Lord is introduced is that it begins at the time of the rapture. This is commonly held not only by pretribulationists but also by posttribulationists.

The problem then becomes the question, *What is the day of the Lord?* An examination of the Old Testament reveals that *the day of the Lord* refers to any period of God's intervention in the affairs of man in judgment. *The day of the Lord* sharply contrasts the present time, which is *the day of grace*. Frequently God brought upon Israel invaders, failure of crops, drought, pestilence, and other difficulties referred to in the Scriptures as a "day of the Lord." Typical is the passage found in Joel 1:14-20:

> Consecrate a fast, call a sacred assembly; gather the elders and all the inhabitants of the land into the house of the Lord your God, and cry out to the Lord.
>
> Alas for the day! For the day of the Lord is at hand; it shall come as destruction from the Almighty. Is not the food cut off before our eyes, joy and gladness from the house of our God? The seed grain shrivels under the clods, storehouses are in shambles; barns are broken down, for the grain has withered. How the beasts groan! The herds of cattle are restless, because they have no pasture; even the flocks of sheep suffer your punishment.
>
> O Lord, to You I cry out; for fire has devoured the open pastures, and a flame has burned all the trees of the field. The beasts of the field also cry out to You, for the water brooks are dried up, and fire has devoured the open pastures.

Joel goes on to speak of the day of judgment as the day of the Lord. Frequently in the Old Testament, the prophecy goes beyond the immediate judgment of God to the ultimate day of the Lord which precedes the second coming. This is the content of Joel 2:1-11. Also in the same chapter is the dramatic passage of 2:30-32:

> I will show wonders in the heavens and in the earth: Blood and fire and pillars of smoke. The

sun shall be turned into darkness, and the moon into blood, before the coming of the great and terrible day of the Lord. And it shall come to pass that whoever calls on the name of the Lord shall be saved. For in Mount Zion and in Jerusalem there shall be deliverance, as the Lord has said, among the remnant whom the Lord calls.

Here are the promises that a day of divine deliverance will come at the second coming of Christ. Most of the book of Joel is occupied with not only the theme of judgment but also the theme of deliverance, as in chapter 3. Some of the historic applications to Israel are also found in Amos (see 5:16-20). The theme is also picked up in Isaiah 13:6-16. All of this forms a dramatic background for the declaration that the future day of the Lord will begin at the rapture.

Some of the particulars of the period of judgment following the rapture are itemized in 1 Thessalonians 5. The day of the Lord is declared to come as a thief in the night, just as the rapture occurs. That is, there are no warnings and it can be expected at any time. In 1 Thessalonians 5:3, the proclamation of peace and safety which follows the covenant of Daniel 9:27 at the beginning of the seven years is interrupted as the great tribulation begins when the covenant is broken and sudden destruction comes upon the people. Christians are described as those who live in the light, not in the darkness, whereas those who live in that future period are described as living in darkness.

An important fact is presented in 1 Thessalonians 5:9: "For God did not appoint us to wrath, but to obtain salvation through our Lord Jesus Christ." In contrast to the day of the Lord, the time of divine wrath, Christians are not appointed to that day. In other words, we are appointed to a different time frame, namely, the period *before* the day of

the Lord. If the day of the Lord is fulfilled in the period preceding the second coming of Christ, then it should be
obvious that the rapture of the church also precedes this time
of judgment when the day of the Lord will begin.

The Rapture and the Man of Sin

An important and additional predictive revelation is
found in 2 Thessalonians 2. Here the context is very important. It is clear from 2 Thessalonians 2 that between the two
epistles false teachers had come in who were legalizers and
who had told the Thessalonian church that the sufferings
which they were going through in their persecution were
those of the day of the Lord. In other words, the day of the
Lord had already begun. They claimed that this was the
teaching of Paul and that they had manuscripts and special
messages from him to this effect.

When Paul heard of this, he was of course indignant that
the Thessalonian church was alarmed. Were they going to
go through the day of the Lord, or had they missed the rapture and therefore were already in the day of the Lord? In
either case, they had reason for alarm.

In chapter 2 of 2 Thessalonians, Paul addressed this
problem directly. He began by reminding them of his
teaching which they had heard when he was there. In 2 Thessalonians 2:1 he wrote, "Now, brethren, concerning the
coming of our Lord Jesus Christ and our gathering together
to Him, we ask you." He was specifically speaking about the
coming of Christ and our gathering or rapture on that occasion. He followed in verse 2 by observing that they are not
to be disturbed, as if there had been a message from God by
a spirit or by word or by letter from Paul. He stated that they
should "not . . . be soon shaken in mind or troubled, either
by spirit or by word or by letter, as if from us, as though the

day of Christ had come." (In many texts the word "Lord" is
used instead of Christ.") Paul stated in verses 3 and 4:

> Let no one deceive you by any means; for that
> Day will not come unless the falling away comes
> first, and the man of sin is revealed, the son of
> perdition, who opposes and exalts himself above
> all that is called God or that is worshiped, so that
> he sits as God in the temple of God, showing him-
> self that he is God.

The expression "that Day will not come" is of course
added to the text. It is not in the original, but it brings out
the point of what is being discussed in the sentence. Two
things in particular are mentioned as having to occur before
the day of the Lord can come: a falling away, referring to
doctrinal apostasy, and a revelation of the man of sin, who
is the future Antichrist and world ruler and who is described
in verse 4 as the one who in the great tribulation occupies
the temple and is worshiped as God. Paul reminded the
Thessalonians that he had taught them about this when he
was with them.

What does it mean when the day of the Lord comes?
This point is often obscure in current exegeses of this passage. Note that the passage does not say when the day of the
Lord *begins.* As a time period, it *begins* at the rapture but *comes*
when the major events take place. To illustrate this concept,
consider the statement "When the Fourth of July comes we
will have a parade." This does not refer to 12:01 A.M. on July
4; it refer to 10 A.M., the time of the parade. The day *begins*
at 12:01 but it *comes* at 10 A.M. In other words, he is referring
to the first major event after the day of the Lord begins, and
this is the revelation of the man of sin.

Prophecy here requires reconstructing the major
events of the end times in their chronological order. This

is commonly neglected in most works on prophecy but is essential to understanding the period.

When the rapture occurs, several Scriptures indicate that either immediately before the rapture or immediately afterward there will be a revival of the ancient Roman Empire in the form of ten countries, as predicted in Daniel 7:7. As pointed out in previous chapters in this book, Europe is ripe for just such an arrangement because the countries of Europe for the first time in centuries are on a friendly basis in which they can easily get together politically, as they are currently attempting to do in the common economic market.

When they are formed as a ten-nation group, a dictator will rise, described as the little horn of Daniel 7:8, and he will apparently conquer three of the ten countries. From then on Scriptures regard him as the ruler of all ten, though no explanation is ever given as to why the other seven capitulate. It is obvious that when he conquers the three countries, he will already be identified as the man of sin and the future dictator and Antichrist, and when he conquers all ten, this will be further confirmed.

From his position of power, the man of sin will bring about the covenant of Daniel 9:27, which describes the last seven years leading up to the second coming of Christ. It is the final seven years of Israel's prophesied prophetic program, 483 years of which were completed before the crucifixion of Christ. The present age has intervened. The last seven years will be resumed when this covenant is signed. According to Daniel 9:27, the first 3fi years will be a period of relative peace, though it may include the invasion of Israel and the sneak attack by six nations as described in Ezekiel 38 and 39. In the middle of the seven years, however, the covenant will be broken and the leader of the ten countries will assume control over the entire world by proclamation.

This will begin the world government of the end times, of which the Antichrist will be the head.

Scripture describes him as being aligned with Satan (Revelation 13:1-4). His supernatural powers apparently come from Satan himself. He will demand that everyone worship him at the pain of death. Those who do not worship the world ruler as well as Satan will be put to death (Revelation 13:15). The full revelation of his character and evil attributes will appear when he breaks the covenant with Israel at the beginning of the last 3½ years. It should be obvious, however, that this is the final climax rather than the beginning of the revelation of who he is. Actually he is identifiable as soon as he has control of the three countries of the Roman Empire, and then the ten countries later. When he makes the covenant with Israel for seven years, he is certainly the same person who at the middle of the seven years becomes the world ruler aligned with Satan.

What Paul is teaching in 2 Thessalonians 2 is that the man of sin cannot be revealed until after the rapture. If he is revealed more than seven years before the second coming of Christ, then the rapture has to occur before the seven years, and this wipes out all the contenders for posttribulationism, partial rapturism, or midtribulationism, leaving only the pretribulational view as that which is in harmony with the Scriptures.

Paul further supports this idea of a pretribulational rapture by calling attention to the fact that the day of the Lord cannot begin until the restrainer of sin is taken out of the way (2 Thessalonians 2:7). While there is debate as to who this person is, obviously the suggested powers for good such as human government do not exist in the endtimes because the government is wholly evil. It certainly is not Satan himself, and the historic answer based on Genesis 6:3 is that the ultimate One who restrains sin is the Holy Spirit. As He is indwelling the church prior to the rapture, the Holy Spirit is not free to be "removed." But if He is removed, the church would have to be removed with Him. This does not mean that He is entirely taken out of the earthly sphere, but that He is removed in the same sense as when He came on the day of Pentecost. He will still be in the world; people will still be able to be saved by Him, but He will lift the restraint of evil that now exists because the church indwelt by the Holy Spirit influences the world with its moral principles. It may fairly be concluded that it will be impossible to remove the Holy Spirit in the sense given in 2 Thessalonians 2:7 unless the church is also raptured.

Accordingly, Paul offers two major arguments here. One, they are not in the day of the Lord because the man of sin has not been revealed; and two, the restrainer has not been removed. This effectively presents a scriptural basis for the pretribulational rapture which is no longer just an inference but the result of biblical exegesis.

The Practical Value of the Rapture

The fact that Christ could come any day and remove His church from the world is a dramatic fact of our current civilization. If there are many evidences in the world that the world scene is set up for precisely what the Bible predicts for the days after the rapture then it is also clear that the rapture itself is not only imminent but that it could be very soon. This has tremendous practical implications.

First of all, it raises the question for everyone concerning personal salvation. Only those who are born again and who have the life of Christ in them will be raptured. They are the ones who are in Christ by the baptism of the Holy Spirit. It may be debated whether the Old Testament saints are raised at the same time or later at the second coming, but it is clear that the rapture of the church is imminent. If it is true that our lives may suddenly be cut short, it makes time very precious. The challenges of full commitment to Christ, proper use of our opportunities for witness, and proper investment of our substance in the Lord's work all become very acute and important.

The Bible does not suggest radical means of approaching this commitment, such as giving away all our property or making no plans for the future. Even Paul, who believed in the rapture of the church, made plans for the future until he knew for sure that he was going to be executed before the rapture. Instead, Scripture calls for a "far view" as well as a "near view" of the future. In other words, we should be living in such a way that we will have no regrets if the Lord should come any day; on the other hand, we must have a reasonable plan for the extension of our lives to their normal limits in case the Lord's coming does not occur in our lifetime.

Few doctrines of the Scriptures are more dramatic, more practical, and more applicable to the challenges of our present life before the Lord. John recorded all the dramatic prophecies that deal with the second coming, including the millennium and the eternal state, but ended his treatment of it with a prayer: "Even so, come, Lord Jesus!" (Revelation 22:20). This sentiment could also be applied to the whole scenario of Christ's second coming, but John, like other Christians, anticipated that before these events would take place he would have the joy of being caught up to heaven if the Lord came in his lifetime. We too can be looking up to the blue, waiting for that joyous event of the coming of the Lord and the trumpet sound that will signal the end of our earthly pilgrimage and the beginning of our glorious experience in the eternal presence of our Savior.

Bridge over the Abyss

William T. James

You and I are privileged to be living at the most exciting time in the history of the human race. Why is this the most exciting time? Is it because people of this generation are witnessing the formation of governmental power spheres precisely configured like those prophesied for the end of the age?

Is this the most exciting time to be alive because socio-economic, technological, and religious conditions seem to be rearranging in the exact order that God's Word predicts they will be as the climax of history approaches? Or are these the most exciting times because the geophysical and astrophysical worlds around us more and more display dynamic upheaval like those prophesied for the apocalypse (awesome displays such as great earthquakes, violent storms, environment-changing volcanoes, devastating floods, and spectacular stellar cataclysms—for example, comets slamming into planets)?

Fear can be a powerful stimulus upon the process of generating excitement. Since the indicators strongly suggest that we stand at the very precipice of that horrific period that Jesus called the great tribulation, these are fearful signals indeed. Certainly, however, it would be inaccurate to say that it is a *privilege* to live in times that are exciting based solely on the fearful events we see occurring all around us. To be *privileged* implies living in conditions that are enjoyable. Fear-engendered excitement produces no enjoyment for rational-thinking people.

Steps Leading into the Abyss

News accounts coming at us in barrage after barrage from the many media outlets around the world report in large measure the most tragic aspects of the human condition. None are more tragic than instances of violence against children. Nothing that man perpetrates against his fellowman tears at our hearts more than the beastly activities engaged in by child pornographers.

A recent account involving child pornography sheds light on this sin-putrefied symptom of our times.

The report detailed the indictment of 16 men "... on charges they participated in an international Internet pedophilia ring in which members once chatted on-line while a 10-year-old girl was being molested...." According to the report, the men belonged to a club, a "... chat room in which users swapped stories about child sex and conspired to produce and exchange sexually explicit images of girls as young as 5....[1]

Although we can be thankful that this particular abominable operation was crushed, it was, statistics tell us, only the proverbial tip of the iceberg. The knowledge that even one child is at this very moment being subjected to such horrendous activity is heart-shattering. Yet thousands, perhaps millions, around the world endure this vileness which must regurgitate directly from the mind of Satan himself.

Child pornographers exhibit the fact that they are "*without natural affection*"–one of the major characteristics that Paul the apostle said would mark the end of the age (2 Timothy 3:3). For who with God-given *natural* affection can look into the beautiful, bright-eyed faces of little ones and conjure up the absolute abomination of child pornography?

The Homosexuality-Abortion-Euthanasia Connection

How Satan hates God's creation called man! The creature God loved so much that He sent His Son Jesus Christ to die for continues to follow in the devil's footprints, which lead to the abyss.

Homosexuality is now termed "gay." The act that God indicts as being an *abomination* the Satan-controlled minds of men now call bright, happy, and *alternate lifestyle.* Despite the reality that AIDS and other deadly diseases such as hepatitis are directly attributable to their "gay lifestyle"–thus making it in fact a death-dealing existence–they refuse to cease their life-ending activity. God's Word says that they receive in themselves the recompense of their error which is fitting (Romans 1:27). God, in other words, says that they get what they deserve when they refuse to repent of their abominable activity.

Homosexuality cannot procreate, which further attests that Luciferian hatred is behind it. How better to kill off the human creation?

Abortion in the United States is a highly profitable business that delivers death on demand. Congress, as of this writing, is considering making legal the French-produced RU486 abortion pill.

Reprobate thinking dominates our culture today—thinking that calls good evil and evil good, thinking that condones killing for the sake of expediency. As proof that ours is a generation steeped in reprobate thinking—that is, thinking that is convoluted, irrational, and even demented—consider the following.

Rational, loving parents would never for a moment think about giving their child a cyanide capsule. Many of these same parents, however, would support legalizing the abortion pill and would themselves take the pills, effectively poisoning their children in the womb. Death on demand is made attractive when it is legitimized and comes nicely merchandized and packaged. Expedience and convenience declare to the reprobate mindset that the unwanted pregnancy equates merely to an upset stomach or a headache that must have a quick fix.

Euthanasia raises its Luciferian head during the last days of societal collapse. Whether considering the ancient Babylonians, Greeks, Romans, Mayans, Incas, or Aztecs—or the more recent atrocities inflicted upon those under the Nazi regime, the systematic murdering of sick, disabled, and elderly people marked those cultures in the last stages of their decline and fall. Unwanted people were and continue to be discarded through genocide, such as that currently taking place in China, where girl babies reportedly are drowned by the millions.

Satan's hatred for God's creation called man is easily observable in our own time. "Dr. Death" is the nickname given a medical doctor who routinely involves himself in so-called "assisted suicides." The doctor's own words obviously betray his feelings about the sanctity of life and the Creator who gives it:

During a luncheon before the National Press Club, [Dr. Jack] Kevorkian defended himself and attacked the religious community, boasting: "Had Christ died in my van, with people around him who loved him, [it] would have been far more dignified."[2]

Attempts made to convict him of murder have thus far failed. With each failure of justice comes the desensitizing effects. Ours is a generation quickly becoming anesthetized to the fact that euthanasia is murder. How near we must be to the time when God says, "*Enough is enough!*"

Homosexuality-abortion-euthanasia are inalterably linked to Satan's ravenous desire to destroy human beings. God's Word says that Satan "as a roaring lion walketh about, seeking whom he may devour" (1 Peter 5:8).

These rampant anti-God activities increasingly find acceptance, even among those who call themselves Christians. But homosexuality, abortion, and euthanasia represent a satanically inspired death wish for all people. Individually and collectively, these hellish practices oppose the one and only Lifegiver.

The Drug Abyss

God's prophetic Word tells us in unequivocal terms about the rebellious, blasphemous generation that will populate planet Earth during the time of the apocalypse, the closing years of this earth age, which Jesus referred to as a period of great tribulation.

"Neither repented they of their murders, nor of their sorceries, nor of their fornication, nor of their thefts" (Revelation 9:21).

The word "sorcery" is translated from the Greek word *pharmakeia.* The approximate equivalent is the English word "pharmacy," which means the art of preparing and dispensing drugs.

Drugs will flow through the veins of that endtime generation while those people blaspheme God even though they know His judgment is upon them. The people of apocalypse will refuse to repent and turn from their total immersion in drug addiction and every other imaginable sin even though their very souls hang in the balance.

Our evening newscasts are all we need to validate that we are already waist-deep in a cesspool of illicit drugs. Every crime on the books, it seems, can in one way or another be linked to the mind-altering poisons routinely distributed on the streets of every city in America. We have only to recall our last local news broadcast to remember a reporter saying something like ". . .police believe this [shooting, murder, robbery, etc.] was probably drug-related."

Gangs with members as young as seven years old willingly become slaves to drugs and the dealers who live luxuriantly on the billions of dollars generated. Governments are demonstrably inadequate to the task of stopping or even curbing drug trafficking. Politicians promise wars on drugs but inevitably prove impotent in fulfilling those promises once the electioneering is over.

A recent news item testifies that politicians and their mouthpieces view the drug problem as nothing to be concerned about, even if their own staff members are alleged to be heavily involved in illicit drug usage.

> Barry McCaffrey, national drug control policy director, asked in Washington that all politicians stop trying to make an issue of whether an opponent has used drugs because "no good can come from it," adding, "Drug use was a generational thing, and we should just accept that and move on."[3]

Drug infection gushes through the nation's and the world's bloodstream, not only degenerating thought processes, but feeding lust and greed as well. Paul's words ring true today: "The love of money is the root of all evil" (1 Timothy 6:10).

People of the great tribulation era will not repent of their sorceries because, like the addicts and dealers of this present hour, they will be willing to pay any price to continue feeding their insatiable appetites. The tremendous growth we are witnessing in illicit drug trade is a foreshock of the coming Antichrist and his system—a system which will, no doubt, at the outset of Antichrist's reign, promise seemingly brilliant solutions to all problems, including those involving illicit drugs.

The Economic Abyss

Governmental and business institutions grow increasingly concerned about instability within world money markets. Stock market record highs, followed by wild fluctuations, cause worry and sometimes panic for global financial analysts. Despite the chaos, international banking conglomerates continue to merge and meld and network into what surely will soon become a one-world economic order.

The exponential growth in computer technology is without question moving our generation toward the time prophesied in Revelation 13.

Again, Antichrist will offer solutions to unbelievably complex fiscal problems produced when the four horsemen of the Apocalypse ride across the world, bringing war, famine, pestilence, and death. "It's the economy, stupid" might have been a catchy—if somewhat deceptive—political slogan during the 1992 U.S. presidential campaign. Such a slogan will not be necessary during that future time of tremendous economic turmoil. Everyone will be agonizingly aware of the abyss in which they will be mired. They will beg the beast and his totalitarian system of computer control to institute world order.

Gods of the Abyss

New Age thought runs throughout government, business, and religion at all levels. Sadly, even evangelical Christianity suffers with New Age infection.

The same serpent who seduced Adam and Eve with the lie promising that they would be as God when they ate from the forbidden tree now whispers in the desensitized ears of this generation the same lie: "*You will become gods when you follow the New Age pathways laid out for you by the ascended masters.*" But they are pathways leading to the endtime abyss of apocalypse.

Lucifer's soothing lie that proposes many ways to God's salvation salves the guilt-ridden conscience of fallen man. It appeals to the supremely arrogant pride that mankind inherited from father Adam when that first man determined to disobey his Creator and instead accept Satan's offer of godhood.

People today by and large think of salvation, of going to heaven when they die, as obtainable through self-effort. If one lives a good life, God will weigh this against the bad and the person will be found worthy based upon his or her personal accomplishments on the side of good. They need no atoning sacrifice by Jesus Christ to save them. Such is a narrow-minded concept they reject, even though the still, small voice convicts them of the *truth* during those lonely, empty times when their souls yearn for something, for someone to fill the void.

Doug Groothuis, assistant professor at Denver Seminary, and noted researcher and author on the New Age movement, recently pointed out who Jesus Christ is—rather, *was*—according to New Age thinking. He addressed the fact that New Age thought proclaims that there is no need for a Redeemer. Groothuis said:

> The emphasis on Christ is not Christ as the unique and final liberator, the saviour of the human race because of what He's done through His [crucifixion and resurrection], but that He is kind of an example, the model for what we can do. Jesus was a man who [tapped into] the *Christ energy* for the *Christ potential....* It's not biblical Christianity at all....[4]

Groothuis, in further explaining the insidious influence the New Age movement inflicts on this generation, talked about Jean Houston, the New Age guru who spent considerable time with America's First Lady in the White House during the summer of 1996 as part of the now-famous Eleanor Roosevelt contact incident.

Groothuis said:

> [Jean Houston] is very influential. She leads seminars all over the country and in fact all over the world basically on how to release the divine potential within us all. She has referred to herself as a global midwife. She means by that ... we all have god within us. We all have the fullness of [deity] within us. But that somehow this god within us is stuck and we don't realize it, we don't actualize it so it's up to people like her to tell us we are divine and how to put that energy out into the world.[5]

Groothuis went on to say that New Age theosophy purports that there is a latent, divine energy that makes up the universe. God is that energy. But there is no distinction

390 ❖ William T. James

between the Creator and the creation. Everything is one and we are all part of that *great cosmic unity.*

Groothuis said that according to Jean Houston and other New Age thinkers:

> . . . the problem of the human race, the reason we have ecological problems, military crises, economic crises, etc., is not because of human sin against a holy God that has affected us all. It's because somehow we are suffering from a kind of *divine amnesia.* We have forgotten the divinity within ourselves. So her role is to be a catalyst or midwife to bring out the latent divinity inside of all of us. . . .[6]

Groothuis said that consulting channelers, mediums, and indulging in other occultic techniques to achieve one's goals instead of going to God in prayer is dangerous. He said, " . . . in fact, doing this sort of thing can lead to some kind of encounter with the demonic. We have to remember that Paul said Satan himself masquerades as an *angel of light.* . . . If [anything] is leading away from Christ and His gospel, then it's not of God."[7]

Despite such warnings, mankind strives pridefully closer to the abyss and eternal separation from God. One of the New Age movement's most reknowned contemporary leaders sums up the audacious claim that man does not need God because he *is* God!

> The great and growing interest in Eastern philosophy and religion, in reincarnation or the law of rebirth and the power of mind over matter, this is part of a great shift in consciousness which is everywhere taking place and a direct result of our sense that the old molds of thought and feeling are no longer adequate to express our

growing awareness of reality, thus revealing a readiness for a new revelation.

There is no doubt of a spiritual awakening which is everywhere taking place, which must eventually lead to an era of world brotherhood. The keynote of the coming **Age of Aquarius.**

What is happening now is the outcome of inner forces which are affecting great changes in human thinking and consciousness. This will result in the complete reorganization of the world's institutions and social structures which no longer answer man's true need.

This will entail the reorganization of our political, economic, and financial systems along more rational and just lines.[8]

New Agers will achieve their paradigm shift to a society that is the antithesis of what God intended for man. The most vicious dictator ever known will then rule over that darkest period in human history, the black abyss of apocalypse.

The Bridge over the Abyss

People do not need to discover, then nurture, the *Christ-consciousness* within themselves. No such entity exists. People need Jesus Christ to fulfill the God-shaped void that exists within every man, woman, and child born since Adam brought sin into the world, thus separating himself and his progeny from God.

The Carpenter of Nazareth rebuilt the bridge over the abyss of eternal separation with timber constructed in the shape of the old rugged cross upon which He willingly bled and died for you and me. Christ's atoning sacrifice is God's chosen way to reconcile us to Himself. There is none other.

Foreshocks of the coming Antichrist are everywhere. Those fearful signals that the beast of Revelation 13 could very soon make his appearance upon the world stage should produce for the Christian not excitement based upon fear, but excitement based upon joyful anticipation. We are promised not Antichrist but Jesus Christ! (Read Revelation 3:10 and John 14.)

No prophecy stands between this generation and the rapture. Christ's return for His church in the air above planet Earth is imminent. You too can be part of those who excitedly anticipate that unimaginably exhilarating microsecond when Jesus shouts "*COME UP HITHER!*"

Accept Him today and receive God's inward peace which assures that in life or in death, you are His own. So shall we ever be with the Lord.

Even so, come, Lord Jesus.

Biographies of
Contributing Authors

❖ ❖ ❖

William T. James

William T. James ("Terry," as he is addressed by those who know him) prefers to be thought of as an intensely interested observer of historical and contemporary human affairs, always attempting to analyze that conduct and those issues and events in light of God's Holy Word, the Bible. He is frequently interviewed in broadcasts throughout the nation.

James has authored, compiled, and extensively edited four previous books: *Storming Toward Armageddon: Essays in Apocalypse; The Triumphant Return of Christ: Essays in Apocalypse II; Earth's Final Days: Essays in Apocalypse III; and Raging into Apocalypse: Essays in Apocalypse IV.* Each book presents a series of insightful essays by well-known prophecy scholars, writers, and broadcasters.

As public-relations director for several companies, James has written and edited all forms of business communications, both in print and electronic media. Prior to that he worked as creative director for advertising agencies and did extensive political and corporate speech writing as well as formulated position papers on various issues for clients he served. In addition to writing, he worked closely with clients and broadcast media in putting together and conducting press conferences and other forums.

As with all his books, Terry James' overriding desire for this book is that Jesus Christ be magnified before the world so that all people might be drawn to the Savior, that the lost might be redeemed, and that the child of God might be persuaded to faithfully work to sow the gospel message while expectantly watching for the soon return of the Lord.

Bob Anderson

Bob Anderson, former radio and TV sports broadcaster and TV executive, heads Take Heed Ministries, a Christian apologetics ministry dedicated to bringing people involved in cults out of bondage and into relationship with Jesus Christ. His sensitive and scripturally sound presentations on the pitfalls of modern-day cults, including the New Age movement, have edified and informed more than 350 churches around the world. His teachings explore various theological and sociological problems found in cults, and provide information that equips his listeners and viewers with the answers they need for effective ministries.

Anderson is a graduate of Youngstown State University with a B.S. in telecommunications. He has attended Elim Bible College in Lima, New York, and East Coast Bible College in Charlotte, North Carolina. He also taught apologetics and served as guest lecturer and workshop leader at several Bible schools and seminaries.

Anderson hosts a television broadcast, "Exposing the Lie," which deals with a wide range of religious topics. It can be received via satellite throughout North America.

Take Heed Ministries publishes the *THM Journal,* a quarterly newsletter exposing cults and the occult. For a free one-year subscription, a resource catalog, or information on how to have Bob Anderson speak at your church, contact:

Take Heed Ministries
P.O. Box 350
Murraysville, PA 15668
phone/fax: 1-412-327-2948
email: takeheed@nb.net
Website: www.nb.net/~takeheed

David Benoit

David Benoit (Ben-wah´), a native of Louisiana who was born March 14, 1955, accepted Christ as his Savior in 1972 after a rebellious teenage life had led him to reform school. He graduated from Liberty University in 1978, and in June of 1984 he was led of the Lord to establish Glory Ministries in an effort to expose the damaging effects of rock music on society—the only solution being regeneration by Jesus Christ.

In the past several years, David has used his vast knowledge of the occult and the New Age movement to show how Satan is subtly gaining entrance into our families and our churches through seemingly harmless children's toys, movies, and cartoons. He has written two books on this subject: *Fourteen Things Witches Hope Parents Never Find Out* and *Who's Watching the Playpen?*

David has appeared on hundreds of local radio and television talk shows across the country, including Inspirational Network, Family Broadcasting, Trinity Broadcasting Network (TBN), Moody Broadcasting Network, KGO radio (San Francisco), WGST radio (Atlanta), WWWE radio (Cleveland), Point of View (Dallas), D. James Kennedy's nationally televised program, and Bob Larson Live (Denver).

With a rare ability to communicate his message to young people as well as parents, David is a regular speaker in churches as well as at Christian school conventions and family seminars. The goal of his ministry is to assist the fundamental, Bible-believing churches of America and overseas in evangelism outreach and subsequent church growth.

Dave Breese

Dave Breese is an internationally known author, lecturer, radio broadcaster, and Christian minister. He ministers in church and area-wide evangelistic crusades, leadership conferences, student gatherings, and related preaching missions.

Dr. Breese is President of Christian Destiny Inc. of Hillsboro, Kansas, a national organization committed to the advancement of Christianity through evangelistic crusades, literature distribution, university gatherings, and the use of radio and television.

Breese is active in ministry to college and university students, speaking to them from a background of theology and philosophy. He graduated from Judson College and Northern Seminary and has taught philosophy, apologetics, and church history. He is frequently involved in lectures, debates, and rap sessions on university campuses.

Breese travels more than 100,000 miles a year and has spoken to crowds across North America, Europe, Asia, the Caribbean, and Latin America. His lectures and debates at universities in the United States and overseas center on the confrontation of Christianity and modern thought.

Breese is also the author of a number of books, including *Discover Your Destiny, His Infernal Majesty, Know the Marks of Cults, Living for Eternity,* and *Seven Men Who Rule from the Grave.* His books, booklets, and magazine articles have enjoyed worldwide readership. He also publishes *Destiny Newsletter,* a widely distributed periodical presenting the Christian view of current events, and *The Collegiate Newsletter,* a monthly publication dedicated to reaching college students with biblical truth and stimulating interest in the prophetic Word.

J.R. Church

J.R. Church, a man with a pastor's heart, has been preaching the gospel since childhood. Converted at age seven, he set out with one main goal in life–to win others to Jesus Christ. His love for history gave him insight into God's great Plan of the Ages and has prompted him to pursue his present field of prophetic research.

He and his wife, Linda, have been married 35 years. They have two children–a daughter, Terri, and a son, Jerry Jr. In 1964 he organized a church in Lubbock, Texas, where he pastored for 17 years, building a large bus ministry and a Christian school. During the 1970s his interest turned toward prophetic research and television as a means of sharing his studies with others.

In 1979 he moved his family to Oklahoma City, and over the years he has developed the ministry Prophecy in the News. He has traveled across America many times lecturing on the subject of prophecy. He has hosted several tour groups to Israel and the Middle East. His presentations have been a delight to thousands.

J.R. has authored several books on prophetic subjects. His latest book, *The Mystery of the Menorah*, has challenged thousands of Christians with a newly discovered divine design to the Bible. Another book, *They Pierced the Veil and Saw the Future,* provides insight into the 12 Minor Prophets and their messages.

His book *Hidden Prophecies in the Song of Moses* discusses the 1990s–this last decade of the sixth millennium–from a study of the life and writings of Moses. It is a sequel to his bestseller, *Hidden Prophecies in the Psalms,* which has warmed the hearts of thousands who look for the blessed hope of the second coming of Christ. Over 130,000 copies of his Psalms commentary have been distributed, not only in the United States but in other countries as well. It has been translated into the Korean, Dutch, and Finnish languages.

Another book, *Guardians of the Grail,* has also become a bestseller in the United States. It tells of European political intrigue and the move toward a New World Order. It has also been published in Korea and Norway.

The ministry publishes a monthly newspaper on prophetic research entitled *Prophecy in the News* as well as a syndicated television broadcast by the same name which airs on stations across the country and by satellite network to the entire Western Hemisphere.

J.R. Church is convinced that Jesus Christ will return soon, perhaps in his lifetime. Though he does not subscribe to date-setting, he feels that the return of the Jews to their Promised Land is the great fulfillment which has ushered in a series of events predicted to lead to Armageddon.

He is convinced that the only hope for this sin-cursed world lies in salvation through faith in Jesus Christ. The return of the Son of God will bring true peace and prosperity to a warring humankind. There really is a Utopia in the future—not through governments, but through God!

Christopher Corbett

Christopher Corbett is managing editor and senior writer for International Christian Media, which produces the nationwide Point of View Radio Talk Show. A graduate of the University of Chicago with a degree in political science, he is coauthor, with Marlin Maddoux, of *A Christian Agenda* and *Answers to the Gay Deception,* as well as the author of numerous articles and booklets on Christian worldview topics. He lives near Dallas, Texas, with his wife and two children.

Paul D. Feinberg

❖ ❖ ❖

Paul D. Feinberg, noted for his expertise in Christian ethics, the philosophy of religion, apologetics, bioethics, and theology, is Professor of Biblical and Systematic Theology at Trinity Evangelical Divinity School in Deerfield, Illinois. He has been at Trinity since 1974.

Prior to teaching at Trinity Evangelical Divinity School, Feinberg taught courses at the Trinity College and Moody Bible Institute. He also taught at the Japanese Bible Seminary in Japan, the Asia Theological Seminary in Manila, Tyndale Theological Seminary in Amsterdam, the Italian Bible Institute, Central American Theological Seminary in Guatemala City, and Theological Seminary of Haiti.

Feinberg received the Bachelor of Arts degree from the University of California at Los Angeles, the Bachelor of Divinity and Master of Theology from Talbot Theological Seminary, and the Master of Arts from Roosevelt University. He is currently a candidate for the Doctor of Philosophy from the University of Chicago.

Feinberg is a member of the American Academy of Religion, the American Philosophical Society, the Evangelical Theological Society, and the Evangelical Philosophical Society.

Among his published works are *Ethics for a Brave New World,* (Crossway, 1993) and *Continuity and Discontinuity* (Crossway, 1988), both of which he coauthored with his brother and faculty colleague, John Feinberg.

Feinberg and his wife, Iris, reside in Mundelein, Illinois. They have three children. In his spare time, Feinberg enjoys travel.

Arno Froese

Arno Froese, born in Windenberg, East Prussia (today's Russia) was the sixth child in a family of ten. After the Second World War, the Froese family settled in Grefrath, West Germany. In 1959, Arno emigrated to Australia, where he was involved in several successful business ventures. In 1965 he emigrated to the United States.

After becoming a Christian in 1967, he married his wife, Ruth, the following year. Together they raised three sons, Joel, Micah, and Simon, all of whom occupy key positions with them in ministry at Midnight Call.

An effort that began with a manual typewriter on a picnic table in a humid basement in Hamilton, Ohio, in 1968, the ministry has experienced amazing growth. Today, busy computer terminals, the rumble of modern presses, the hot lights of a television studio, and the whir of audio-cassette duplicators are the signs of a large publishing operation that is shipping millions of Bible-centered magazines, tracts, videos, and cassettes into virtually every corner of the world.

In addition to serving as executive editor of *Midnight Call* and *News from Israel* magazines, two of the world's leading Bible prophecy monthlies, Froese is also the writer and speaker for the monthly Message of the Month Club and is the host of a unique semimonthly Video Club. He is the author of hundreds of magazine features and has sponsored more than 45 national and international prophecy conferences.

The *Midnight Call* appears 12 times a year and is also published in German, French, Italian, Dutch, Spanish, Portuguese, Korean, Bengali, Romanian, and Hungarian languages and is distributed to over 148 countries.

Extensive global travel and a rare international outlook have equipped Mr. Froese with valuable insight that helps people understand Bible prophecy in a fundamental way as never before. His ability to picture Bible prophecy from an international point of view has earned him a place among the leading Bible scholars in the field of eschatology.

Grant Jeffrey

Internationally recognized prophecy researcher Grant R. Jeffrey and his wife, Kaye, have been serving the Lord in full-time ministry since the 1988 publication of Grant's first book, *Armageddon*. That book became an instant bestseller, as did his five successive books: *Heaven, Messiah, Apocalypse, Prince of Darkness,* and *Final Warning* (released in May 1995). Since 1988, Grant has reached readers with the message of Christ's soon return through the worldwide sales of more than a million copies. Sales of the books support the Jeffrey's ministry activities, which include conferences in North America, Europe, Kenya, Barbados, and Singapore.

Grant, who resides in Toronto, Ontario, was a professional in the pension and insurance brokerage field for 18 years prior to entering the ministry. During the 1970s and 1980s he taught eschatology part-time at L.I.F.E. Bible College and Christianview Bible College in Canada. Bible prophecy has fascinated him since he was 14; that keen interest has led him to acquire more than 5000 volumes on eschatology, theology, and archaeology.

In 1994 Grant received an honorary Doctor of Literature degree from Louisiana Baptist Theological Seminary for his research in eschatology.

The material in Chapter 4 is reprinted from Grant Jeffrey's excellent book, *Final Warning: Economic Collapse and the Coming World Government*.

Grant Jeffrey's most recent book is *The Signature of God: Astonishing Biblical Discoveries of Inspiration*.

To order any of Grant Jeffrey's books, call 1-800-883-1812 or write Frontier Research Publications Inc., Box 129, Station U, Toronto, Ontario, M8Z 5M4.

Berit Kjos

Berit Kjos is a widely respected researcher, the author of books and magazine articles, and a popular conference speaker.

Kjos first became aware of New Age and occult influences in society at a 1974 conference on holistic health. As a registered nurse, she was interested in methods of healing, but soon discovered that the occult powers found in New Age methods brought bondage instead of true healing. As a parent, Kjos became aware of similar New Age influences in education. She began to monitor the schools for classroom programs that taught occultism and New Age spirituality, then began to share what she learned with other parents and teachers.

Kjos has given workshops and seminars at conferences such as the Association for Christian Schools International. She has spoken at conferences for the Constitutional Coalition, Education Policy, Child Evangelism Fellowship, Concerned Women for America, and Citizens for Excellence in Education.

Kjos' book, *Brave New Schools,* surveys the scene in today's public schools and provides guidelines for parents who are concerned about their children's education. Kjos shows how myth, feeling, imagination, and politically correct stories are replacing truth, facts, logic, and history in the classroom. She also explains what programs such as Goals 2000 are all about, and why students—even homeschoolers—eventually will be required to demonstrate competence in the new social and thinking skills before they can move on to higher education or jobs.

Kjos is also the author of *Your Child and the New Age, Under the Spell of Mother Earth,* and *A Wardrobe from the King.*

Zola Levitt

Zola Levitt is a Jewish believer thoroughly educated in the synagogues and brought to the Messiah in 1971. He is best known as the host of the weekly national television program *Zola Levitt Presents*, and was formerly the host of two top-rated radio talk shows, *The Heart of the Matter* in Dallas and the nationally syndicated *Zola Levitt Live*. Zola is also a widely published author, with some 40 books in several languages, and the composer of some 150 spiritual songs. His two musicals, *Beloved Thief* and *Mine Eyes Have Seen*, have been televised nationally.

A specialist in biblical sites, Zola leads several tours each year to Israel, Greece, and Turkey. He holds music degrees from Duquesne University and Indiana University, and an honorary Th.D. from Faith Bible College.

Zola Levitt Ministries, a teaching and evangelistic association, is guided by the standards of Romans 1:16: "To the Jew first and also to the Gentile." Like the apostle Paul, Zola Levitt Ministries works through the Gentiles to reach the Jews by informing Gentile viewers and listeners of those principles of the faith which will be most helpful to them in understanding and witnessing to their Jewish friends.

By the way of doctrinal statement, Zola Levitt Ministries holds to a strictly literal and inerrant Bible interpretation, salvation through Christ alone, an imminent pretribulational rapture of all believers, and the establishment of a thousand-year kingdom on earth. The evangelism of unbelievers and the exhortation of believers take precedence over all other activities of the ministry.

Chuck Missler

An expert on Russia, Israel, Europe, and the Middle East, Chuck Missler gives intriguing behind-the-scenes insights to his audiences. He has spent more than 30 years in the corporate world as CEO of four public corporations contracting with the U.S. Department of Defense and has an extensive network of overseas contacts. With affiliates and associates in nine countries, Missler is a major contributor to several international intelligence newsletters. He has also negotiated joint ventures in Russia, Israel, Malaysia Japan, Algeria, and Europe. In addition, Missler is an authority on advanced weapons and strategic resources and has participated in projects with SAMCOM-USSR, DSL, JCS, USACADA, DOJ, CCIA, and SDI. A member of the International Press Association, he is an honors graduate from the U.S. Naval Academy.

For 20 years Chuck Missler taught a Bible study in Southern California that grew to more than 2000 attendees. In 1992 he moved to Coeur d'Alene, Idaho, where he founded Koinonia House to distribute his books, lectures, and tapes. His dynamic style, conservative values, and adherence to biblical principles have made him a highly acclaimed speaker and critic.

His newsletter, *Personal UPDATE*, a 32-page Christian prophecy and intelligence newsletter, has grown to reach more than 50,000 monthly subscribers. He also has more than 8 million tapes in circulation worldwide.

If you wish to receive a 12-month complimentary subscription to *Personal UPDATE,* contact:

Koinonia House
P.O. Box D
Coeur d'Alene, ID 83816-0347
1-800-546-8731

John Walvoord

John Walvoord, theologian, pastor, and author, is described in the *Twentieth Century Dictionary of Christian Biography* as "one of the most influential dispensational theologians of the twentieth century."

Walvoord, who has been "prominent in prophetic conferences advocating a pretribulational rapture, a literal thousand-year millennium, and distinction between Israel and the church," has written 30 books, including *The Rapture Question* (1957), *The Millennial Kingdom* (1959), and *The Prophecy Knowledge Handbook* (1990), as well as commentaries on Daniel (1971), Philippians (1971), and the Thessalonian epistles (1976). With R.B. Zuck, he edited the two-volume *Bible Knowledge Commentary* (1983, 1985).

Born in Sheboygan, Wisconsin, Walvoord graduated from Wheaton College, Texas Christian University, and Dallas Theological Seminary, where he later earned his Th.D. and joined the faculty (1936–1986). He became President in 1953 and Chancellor upon retirement in 1986. He pastored Rosen Heights Presbyterian Church in Fort Worth from 1934 to 1950 and edited *Bibliotheca Sacra*, the seminary's theological journal, from 1952 to 1985.

David Webber

David F. Webber, a speaker for more than 35 years on Southwest Radio Church (a long-running radio broadcast ministry founded by his father, E.F. Webber, in the 1930s) is a well-known author of significant books on prophecy. He has conducted tours to Israel and to other regions of interest to Christians. He is an internationally known conference speaker and publishes a monthly newsletter, *David Webber Reports*. David Webber Ministries produces a daily radio broadcast and a weekly shortwave radio program heard worldwide.

During his many years of Christian broadcast work, Dr. Webber has interviewed almost every prophetic scholar of note from around the world. Additionally, he himself is often sought out for interviews on biblically prophetic matters as they relate to current events and issues.

Dr. Webber attended Oklahoma City University, where he obtained a B.A. in theology, and Belen Memorial University in Chillicothe, Missouri, where he received an honorary doctorate.

His published books include *The Image of the Ages* and *The Mark is Ready*.

Notes

Foreshock After Foreshock

1. Benjamin Netanyahu, address to joint session of U.S. Congress, Washington D.C., May 29, 1996.

2. Bill Kurtis, "Wired for Sex," in *Investigative Reports*, A&E (Arts & Entertainment), May 1996.

Chapter 1–Globalism's Siren Song

1. Batnog-Whittaker, "I Am But a Small Voice," (New York: BMG Music, 1994).

2. Ibid.

3. Ralph Epperson, *The Unseen Hand* (Westlake Village, CA: American Media, 1985), p. 370.

4. Kirby Anderson with Chris Corbett, Joan Veon, and Berit Kjos, *Point of View Radio Program*, USA Radio Network, Dallas, June 18-19, 1996.

5. J.R. Church, William T. James, et al., "How Near Is the Mark of the Beast?" in *Earth's Final Days* (Green Forest, AR: New Leaf Press, 1994), pp 288-289.

6. John Lennon.

7. John Gizzy, *Hal Lindsey's Week in Review*, December 3, 1994.

8. David Allen Lewis, "State of the World Forum: Looming World Government," in *Prophecy Watch International Insider's Report*, October 1995, p. 1.

9. Ibid., pp. 3-4.

10. Ibid., p. 4.

Chapter 2–Classroom Earth: Educating for One World Order

1. Naomi R. Goldenberg, *Changing of the Gods: Feminism and the End of Traditional Religions* (Boston: Beacon Press, 1979), p. 3.

2. Al Gore, *Earth in the Balance* (Boston: Houghton Mifflin Co., 1992), p. 260.

3. Ibid, p. 306.

4. Ibid, p. 274.

5. To change public opinion and win support for Goals 2000, the U.S. Department of Education sent the *Community Action Toolkit* to school districts from coast to coast in 1995. The next year, the U.N. introduced its detailed plan for local transformation: The *Local Agenda 21 Planning Guide;* and the President's (Clinton) Council on *Sustainable Development* published *Sustainable American: A New Consensus*. The striking similarities between the three action plans suggest an alarming collaboration as well as common goals and strategies for choosing leaders, winning supporters, manipulating "information," and monitoring change. All three share the following buzzwords or concepts: partnerships, consensus, lifelong learning, baselines or benchmarks, monitoring, assessment, data gathering, systemic change, system thinking, social development, etc. All stress the need to measure, assess, and monitor progress. All are designed to bypass traditional government and control people through a form of "citizens" or "grassroots participation" which the Encyclopaedia Britannica refers to as "totalitarian democracy" and Communist leaders have

called "people's government." As in Lenin's Soviets, neither U.N. forums nor the U.S. community meetings on education will acknowledge dissenting voices. Resisters are silenced by trained facilitators who only record voices that echo the "right" ideology.

6. Cynthia Weatherly, "The Second Annual Model School Conference," in *The Christian Conscience,* January 1995, p. 36.

7. The Declaration of Principles on Tolerance, adopted and signed by the Member States of UNESCO on November 16, 1995.

8. Alexander King and Bertrand Schneider, *The First Global Revolution* (New York: Pantheon Books, 1991), p. 115.

9. "Scan: Whale-song in the Rainforest," in *The American Enterprise,* November/December 1995, p. 9.

10. First John 5:19.

11. *The Whole People of God* (Grover Heights, MN: Logos Productions, 1993), p. 15.

12. Ibid., p. 16.

13. Ibid., p. 9.

14. Re-Imagining Conference Tape 2-1, Side A.

15. Re-Imagining Conference Tape 3-2, Side A.

16. Ibid., Tape 2-2, Side A.

17. Ibid.

18. Ibid.

19. "Anointing With Red Dot Ritual," Friday plenary, Tape 2-1, Side A. "Rainsticks" are mentioned in Re-Imagining Conference Program Book, p. 30.

20. Susan Cyre, "Women's conference re-imagines new god," in *Rutherford,* August 1994, p. 19.

21. Re-Imagining Conference, Tape 11-2, Side A.

22. *Women Who Run with Wolves,* the title of a top-selling book by Clarissa Pinkola Estes, gives many names to a woman who has unleashed her wildness and lives with abandon: The Light from the Abyss, the Wolverine, the Spider Woman, the Wolf Woman, Death Goddess, and Woman Who Lives at the Edge of the World. Cited by Clark Morphew in *Religion and Ethics (Saint Paul Pioneer Press),* October 29, 1994.

23. Clark Wissler, *Indians* (New York: Anchor Books, Doubleday), pp. 131-32.

24. Thomas Sowell, "The Right to Infiltrate," in *Forbes,* March 13, 1995, p. 74.

25. Ibid.

26. The World Commission on Environment and Development, 1987.

27. *Encyclopaedia Britannica* (Chicago: William Benton, 1968), Vol. 5, p. 163.

28. Paige Comstock Cunningham, "United Nations Agenda for Women Falls Short," in *Christianity Today,* October 23, 1995, p. 91.

29. Diane Knippers, "The Beijing Conference," in *Paradigm 2000,* Summer 1995, p. 17.

30. Nancy Smith and Donna Maxfield, "Spiritual Quest in Beijing," in RENEW Women's Network, *Good News,* November/December 1995, p. 35.

31. Thomas Sowell, "A Road to Hell Paved with Good Intentions," in *Forbes,* January 17, 1994, p. 62.

32. Ibid.

33. John 7:7 NKJV.

34. Jeremiah 8:9-9:1.

35. God's protection: Numbers 14:9; Micah 1:11; Isaiah 22:8,9; Deuteronomy 8:6-20; 31:17; Ezra 8:22.

36. Psalm 119:11.

37. Matthew 5:45.

38. Philippians 1:29; 2 Corinthians 1:4, 9-12; 1 Peter 4:12,13; 5:8-10.

39. Dietrich Bonhoeffer, *The Cost of Discipleship* (New York: The MacMillan Company, 1963), p. 26.

40. Ibid., pp. 97-99, 101.

41. 2 Corinthians 6:14-18.

42. Philippians 4:17-19.

Chapter 3—The Psychic Guide Dogs

1. Dave Hunt and T.A. McMahon, *The New Spirituality* (Eugene, OR: Harvest House, 1988).

2. George Barna, *What Americans Believe* (Ventura, CA: Regal Books, 1991), p. 175.

3. Colin Chapman, "The Riddle of Religions," in *Christianity Today*, May 14, 1990, p. 17.

4. Ron Rhodes, *The Culting of America* (Eugene, OR: Harvest House, 1994), p. 84.

5. Ibid., p. 109.

6. Ibid., p. 110.

7. *Nelson's Illustrated Bible Dictionary* (Thomas Nelson, 1986), p. 435.

8. John Ankerberg and John Weldon, *The Facts on Abortion* (Eugene, OR: Harvest House, 1995), p. 4.

9. John Ankerberg and John Weldon, *The Facts on Astrology* (Eugene, OR: Harvest House, 1988), p. 9.

10. "Just Say No to Astrology," in *Expression*, June 1988.

11. Hillary Rodham Clinton, "Keynote Address at the Dedication of Eleanor Roosevelt College," San Diego, CA, January 26, 1995.

12. "Methodist bishop defends Mrs. Clinton's talks with deceased leaders," in *Expression*, August 1996, p. 8.

13. Ibid., p. 6.

14. Jeane Dixon, *Yesterday, Today and Forever: How Astrology Can Help You Find Your Place in God's Plan* (New York: Bantam, 1977), p. 6.

15. Ruth Montgomery, *A Gift of Prophecy* (New York: William Morrow, 1965), p. viii.

16. Kurtz and Fraknoi, "The Tests of Astrology Do Not Support Its Claims," in *The Skeptical Inquirer*, Vol. 9, no. 3, p. 211.

17. John McGervey, "A Statistical Test of Sun-Sign Astrology," in *The Zetetic*, Vol.1, no. 2, p. 53.

18. *Gods of the New Age*, videotape, Johanna Michaelsen, Jeremiah Films.

19. John Ankerberg and John Weldon, *Cult Watch* (Eugene, OR: Harvest House, 1991), p. 248.

20. "Sure, Blame the Caveman," in *People*, October 12, 1992, p. 126.

21. John Ankerberg and John Weldon, *The Facts on Rock Music* (Eugene, OR: Harvest House, 1992), p. 43.

22. Ibid.

23. Ibid.

Chapter 5—Cyberspace: The Beast's Worldwide Spiderweb

1. "TCI Dishes Up a Satellite Spin-off Plan," in *USA Today,* June 1996.

2. Ibid.

3. Ibid.

4. Ibid.

5. Ibid.

6. Ibid.

7. "Tough Choices for Internet Icon at Crossroads," in *USA Today,* June 20, 1996.

8. Ibid.

9. "America Facing Cyberspace Pearl Harbor, CIA Warns," in *The Daily Oklahoman,* June 26, 1996.

10. Ibid.

11. Ibid.

12. "Big Brother wants to borrow your on-line keys," in *Family Issues Alert,* June 26, 1996.

13. "The Birth of the Internet," in *Newsweek,* August 8, 1994.

14. "The Strange New World of the Internet. Battles on the frontier of Cyberspace," in *Time,* July 25, 1994.

15. Ibid.

16. Ibid.

17. Ibid.

18. Ibid.

19. "The Wizard of ID," in *Time,* May 13, 1996, p. 62.

20. Ibid.

21. Ibid.

22. "Year 2000: Small Oversight Is Big Problem," in *USA Today,* March 15, 1996.

23. Ibid.

24. "Privacy: Do You Have Any Left?" in *USA Today,* December 19, 1995.

25. Ibid.

26. Ibid.

27. Ibid.

28. Ibid.

29. Ibid.

30. "No Escaping the Net," in *USA Today,* June 11, 1996.

31. Ibid.

32. Ibid.

33. Ibid.

34. Ibid.

35. "Political Race Has Its Place in Cyberspace," in *The Daily Oklahoman*, July 21, 1996.

36. "Low-Cost Internet Unit Arrives," in *The Daily Oklahoman*, July 11, 1996.

Chapter 7–Kings of the East Lust Westward

1. The biblical prophecies in Daniel chapters 2 and 7 summarize the succession of world empires until the final one. See *Iron Mixed with Clay*, a briefing by Koinonia House, Coeur d'Alene, ID, (800) KHOUSE1.

2. *Wall Street Journal*, February 7, 1996.

3. "Human Cost of Communism in China," in *Senate Internal Security Subcommittee Study*, 1970, as quoted in *McAlvany Intelligence Advisor*, April 1996. (See this issue for a detailing of the human-rights abuses in China.)

4. Alexei Voskressenski, senior research fellow, Russia-China Center, member of the Academic Council at the Institute of Far Eastern Studies, Russian Academy of Sciences, as published in the *Far Eastern Economic Review*.

5. Genesis 10:17. This tribe also appears in 1 Chronicles 1:15.

6. Although dictionaries of over 40,000 characters have been compiled, the number of absolutely necessary characters today is estimated at fewer than 4,000.

7. The Communist government has introduced a new phonetic system, *pinyin zimu*, for transliterating Chinese into the Latin alphabet. It is hoped that *Pinyin* will gradually replace the traditional characters altogether.

8. Kesses HaSofer, *Bereishis–Genesis, A New Translation with a Commentary Anthologised from Talmudic, Midrashic and Rabbinic Sources* (Mesorah Publications Ltd.).

9. Koran, 21:96.

10. A detailed study of the pertinent prophetic texts, as well as a summary of the little-known background of Central Asia and its role in Bible prophecy, may be found in the author's book *The Magog Invasion*.

Chapter 8–The U.S. and Other U.N. Serfdoms

1. William Jasper, *Global Tyranny . . . Step by Step* (Appleton, WI: Western Islands, 1992), pp. 254-55.

2. William Jasper, "Eco '92": Launching Pad for International Global Governance," in *New American*, July 13, 1992, p. 5.

3. Ibid., p. 4.

4. Ibid., p. 11.

5. William Norman Grigg, "Shaping the New World Order," in *The New American*, April 17, 1995, p. 4.

6. William Norman Grigg, "Interpretive Abortion Policy," in *The New American*, October 17, 1994, p. 8.

7. George Archibald, "Forum fights over free sex," in the *Washington Times*, September 1, 1995, p. 7.

8. John F. McManus, "Sovereignty Sellout," in *The New American,* July 11, 1994, p. 7.

9. Colum Lynch, "U.N. chief proposes fees and taxes to shield body from nonpayments," in the *Boston Globe,* January 16, 1996, p. 8.

10. David Felix, "The Tobin Tax Proposal," in *Futures,* March 1995.

11. See *Our Global Neighborhood,* published by the Commission on Global Governance (1995), "Financing an Effective United Nations" by the Ford Foundation, and Paul Kennedy and Bruce Russett, "Reforming the United Nations," in *Foreign Affairs,* September/October, 1995, pp. 68-71.

12. Grigg, "Shaping . . .", p. 6.

13. *Congressional Record,* January 22, 1996, regarding Senate Bill 1519.

14. Cable News Network report, *Our Planetary Police,* aired March 7, 1993.

15. James P. Snelling, "Eco Messiah or New Age Profit?" in *New York Guardian,* August, 1992, p. 1.

16. Ibid.

Chapter 10–The Mideast March to Megiddo

1. For a fuller treatment and defense of the understanding of this prophecy as espoused in this chapter, see Paul D. Feinberg, "An Exegetical and Theological Study of Daniel 9:24-27," in *Tradition and Testament: Essays in Honor of Charles Lee Feinberg,* by John S. and Paul D. Feinberg (Chicago: Moody, 1981), pp. 189-220.

2. For a defense of pretribulationalism, see my position and responses in Gleason L. Archer, et al., *The Rapture: Pre, Mid or Post?* (Grand Rapids: Zondervan, 1984).

3. What judgments and how many depends on how one structures the three sets of judgments, seals, trumpets, and bowls as revealed in these chapters.

4. G.M. Burge, "Armageddon," in *Evangelical Dictionary of Theology,* Walter A. Elwell, ed. (Grand Rapids: Baker, 1984), p. 830.

5. R.K. Harrison, ed., "Megiddo," in *The New Unger's Bible Dictionary* (Chicago: Moody, 1991), p. 15.

6. For a brief summary of the archaeological work done at Megiddo, see A.F. Rainey, "Megiddo," in *The International Standard Bible Encyclopedia,* Geoffrey W. Bromiley, gen. ed. (Grand Rapids: Eerdmans, 1986), vol. III, pp. 309-11.

7. Edgar C. James, *Arabs, Oil, and Armageddon* (Chicago: Moody, 1991), p. 15.

8. Karim Pakravan, *The Christian Science Monitor,* February 19, 1991.

9. Ibid.

10. William Dudley, ed., *The Middle East: Opposing Viewpoints* (San Diego: Greenhaven, 1992).

Chapter 11–United Europe's Power Play

1. Gary Belsky, "Escape from America," in *Money,* July 1994, p. 60.

2. Klaus-Dieter, "European Integration," in *Office for Official Publications of the European Communities,* L-2985, Luxembourg, pp. 9-10.

3. Ibid., p. 10.

4. Ibid., p. 11.

5. *Daily Mail,* April 2, 1994.

6. Wim Malgo, *Fifty Questions About the Second Coming* (Midnight Call, 1972, p. 66).

7. *Far Eastern Economic Review*, June 20, 1996, p. 64.

8. *Voice*, published by the Diocese of Newark, 1989.

9. *L'Observatore Romano,* February 10, 1986, p. 5.

Chapter 12–Man Targeted for Extinction

1. Southwest Radio Church program.

2. Ibid.

3. Jeff Godwin, *The Devil's Disciples* (Chick Publications, 1985), p. 8.

4. *USA Today*, October 9, 1995.

5. *USA Today*, August 28, 1996.

Chapter 13–Riders of Revelation 6, Mount Up!

1. J.R. Church, *Guardians of the Grail* (Oklahoma City: Prophecy Publications, 1989).

2. *Air Force Journal of Logistics*, Winter 1991.

3. *Newsweek*, November 11, 1974, p. 56.

4. Ibid., p. 58.

5. Ibid.

6. Mihajl Mesarovic and Eduard Pestel, *Mankind at the Turning Point* (New York: Signet Books, 1976), p. 17.

7. Ibid.

8. *Sunday Oklahoman*, May 16, 1993.

9. Ibid.

10. Ibid.

11. Ibid.

12. Gene Antonio, *The AIDS Cover-Up* (San Francisco: Ignatius Press, 1985), pp. 135-36.

13. *Daily Oklahoman,* August 3, 1996.

14. Antonio, *Cover-Up*, pp. 133-38.

15. *Newsweek*, April 29, 1995.

16. Ibid.

17. Ibid.

18. Ibid.

19. Ibid.

20. *Prophecy in the News,* January 1986.

21. Ibid.

22. Ibid.

23. Ibid.

24. Ibid.

25. Gary Stearman, *Prophecy in the News,* July 1996, p. 3.

26. Ibid.

27. *Jerusalem Post*, August 14, 1993.

28. Ibid.

29. Survey Notes, Utah Geological Survey, March 1993.

30. Ibid.

Chapter 14–Royal Ambassadors Endtime Diplomacy

1. Lehman Strauss, *God's Plan for the Future*, p. 111.

Bridge over the Abyss

1. Associated Press, "Members of alleged computer child porn ring indicted," *CNN Interactive*, www.cnn.com, July 17, 1996.

2. Carol J. Castaneda, "'Dr. Death' denounces his detractors," in *USA Today*, July 30, 1996.

3. "In the News," in the *Arkansas Democrat-Gazette*, August 9, 1996, Sec. A-1.

4. Doug Groothuis, *Point of View*, USA Network, July 14, 1996.

5. Ibid.

6. Ibid.

7. Ibid.

8. Benjamin Creme, *The Reappearance of the Christ in the Masters of Wisdom* (Los Angeles: Tara Press, 1980).

The William T. James monthly briefzing paper that presents analysis of current issues and events in the words of the world's best-known writers, speakers, and broadcasters

issues and events
from prophetic perspectives

For a free issue of "i.e." simply fill in, then clip the coupon below and send to:

James Informarketing
P.O. Box 1108
Benton, AR 72018-1108

Please include with the coupon a self-addressed, business-sized envelope stamped with first-class postage.

Please send me a free issue of "i.e." I have enclosed, along with this coupon, a business-sized envelope stamped with first-class postage.

Name _____

Address _____
        (Street)

_____
(City)   (State)   (Zip)

Thank you for your order!

If you are pleased with your order and would like to purchase additional products, here is an order form for your convenience. See next page for descriptions.

NAME:

ADDRESS:

CITY, STATE, ZIP:

PHONE:

Quantity	Publications	Check here to have book(s) signed by William T. James
	Book 1: Storming Toward Armageddon	
	Book 2: Triumphant Return of Christ	
	Book 3: Earth's Final Days	
	Book 4: Raging Into Apocalypse	
	i.e. newsletter: 1 year (8 issues) $16.50	

Low Book Prices

1 book – $14.95
2 books – $29.95
3 books – $42.00
Set of 4 – $48.00

Total Amount Enclosed:

$ _____

Please make your check or money order payable to:

James Informarketing
P.O. Box 1108
Benton, AR 72015

...ming Toward Armageddon: Essays in Apocalypse

335 pages
Texe Marrs, Tim LaHaye, Dave Breese, David A. Lewis, Robert Lindsted, and others

Triumphant Return of Christ: Essays in Apocalypse II

399 pages
Dave Breese, J.R. Church, John Wesley White, Phil Arms, Joseph Carr, and others

Earth's Final Days: Essays in Apocalypse III

367 pages
Don McAlvany, Dave Breese, Chuck Missler, Phil Arms, J.R. Church, D.A. Miller, David Webber, and others

Raging into Apocalypse: Essays in Apocalypse IV

312 pages
Grant Jeffrey, John Walvoord, Dave Breese, Chuck Missler, Henry Morris, and others

i.e. – issues and events from prophetic perspectives

newsletter presenting what foremost Bible and prophecy experts have to say about issues and events of our day.

The Collegiate Letter
A Dave Breese ministry

Help spark a college student's interest in prophecy and love for God's Holy Word. You can sponsor Dave Breese's Collegiate Letter, which will be mailed monthly to the young person of your choice, or to anyone.

A one-year subscription for only $20 includes free books, position papers, and many extras that will inform, fascinate, and inspire.

The Collegiate Letter is produced by

Christian Destiny Inc.
P.O. Box C
Hillsboro, KS 67063

Complete this form and mail it to us, or call 1-800-777-8806.

Your name _____
Address _____
City _____ State _____ ZIP _____

I wish to sponsor:

Name _____
Address _____
City _____State ____ZIP _____

Apostasy — Great falling away fr. God
Matt 24:24 False prophets + deceive

Globalism, New World Order, 1 World / Humanism

Earth Centered Educ., Religion, Mother Earth, No Cross
(Conformists) Dispute Bible, etc.

Occultism largely accepted (movies, music, etc.)

Pagan Apostate Church (1 world church)
Gospel Preached to all — Despite Matt 24. ?

Worldwide Spiderweb — Cyberspace

Peace Covenant — Nation of Israel — Antichrist

Israel — lightning rod (prophecy)

Kg, East will rise — $, power, military → wisg.

America ↓ (UN - Globalism) New World order + human race
(+ own Babel Bldg)

Russia regain power → march Israel

Middle East march — Armageddon

Final Kgdm. Europe
European Sys. Dominates World / 10 Power
World Commis, all Catholic church   Global Econ
                                        polit

Brink of Apocalypse
man — extinct — Homosexual, incest, abortion, suic
femine

Mt. 1st Horse apocalypse (Antichrist)
Behind scene — Deceiver (Satan?)

Be ambassadors Before Amt. Called Loo
p. 344 see all horrible words

Rapture 1st.   Christ is bridge over abyss   not he decen
Drug Trade   sex